KT-424-028

Language and Literacy in Social Context

Language and Literacy in Social Practice

A Reader edited by

Janet Maybin

at The Open University

MULTILINGUAL MATTERS LTD
Clevedon • Philadelphia • Adelaide
in association with
THE OPEN UNIVERSITY

Library of Congress Cataloging in Publication Data
Language and Literacy in Social Practice: A Reader/Edited by Janet Maybin.
p. cm.
Compiled as part of an Open University MA Course called E825: Language and
Literacy in Social Context.
Includes bibliographical references and index.
1. Literacy–Social aspects. 2. Sociolinguistics. 3. Language–Study and teaching–
Social aspects. 4. Functional literacy. 5. Educational anthropology.
I. Maybin, Janet. II. Open University.
LC149.L23   1993   93-29932
302.2′244–dc20   CIP

British Library Cataloguing in Publication Data
A catalogue entry for this book is available from the British Library.

ISBN 1-85359-216-1 (hbk)
ISBN 1-85359-215-3 (pbk)

Multilingual Matters Ltd
UK: Frankfurt Lodge, Clevedon Hall, Victoria Road, Clevedon BS21 7HH.
USA: UTP, 2250 Military Road, Tonawanda, NY 14150, USA.
Canada: UTP, 5201 Dufferin Street, North York, Ontario M3H 5T8, Canada.
Australia: Footprint Books, PO Box 418, Church Point, NSW 2103, Australia.

Index compiled by Meg Davies (Society of Indexers).
Printed and bound in Great Britain by Short Run Press Ltd.

Contents

Preface

This is one of four volumes of readings compiled as a part of an Open University MA course called *Language and Literacy in Social Context* (E825). The course draws on a variety of work in sociolinguistics, grammar, semiotics, media studies, anthropology, psychology and education and the interdisciplinary nature of the course is reflected in the articles collected together in this series. Each volume contains a mix of classic and newly published material which will be of interest to a wide audience.

Anyone who studies these papers will inevitably be drawn in to some of the most exciting intellectual debates of the closing years of the 20th century. The authors deal with many of the 'big issues' relating to life in the postmodern world — identity, social relations, social control, ideology, freedom, democracy, power, aesthetics, pleasure — but always with a concern for the way these very abstract notions manifest themselves in individual lives.

I would like to take the opportunity of thanking all those who, in various ways, supported, encouraged (and sometimes cautioned), the course team during the production process. In particular, I should mention Myra Barrs, Rebecca Bunting, Jane Cooper, Norman Fairclough, Gordon Gibson, Gunther Kress, Gemma Moss, Brian Street, Terry Threadgold, Gill Watson, many students and tutors of a predecessor course on language and literacy (E815), and colleagues in the School of Education at The Open University.

David Graddol
Course Chair

Sources

We would like to thank the authors and publishers concerned for kindly granting permission to reproduce copyright material in this reader. Every effort has been made to trace the correct copyright owners, both authors and publishers, as listed in the Contents and by chapter below.

1. Edited from the supplement to *The Meaning of Meaning* by C. K. Ogden and I. A. Richards. London: Rotledge & Kegan Paul, Trench, Trubner, 1923.
2. Edited from Chapters 1 and 2 of *Foundations in Sociolinguistics* by Dell Hymes. London: Tavistock, 1977.
3. Edited from Chapter 6 of *Language as Social Semiotic* by M.A.K. Halliday. London: Edward Arnold, 1978.
4. Excerpts from Part 1, Chapters 1 and 2, and Part 2, Chapter 4 of *Marxism and the Philosophy of Language* by V.N. Volosinov. Orlando: Academic Press Inc., 1973.
5. Edited from Chapter 2 of *Family Literacy: Young Children Learning to Read and Write* by Denny Taylor. Portsmouth, NH: Heinemann (A Division of Reed Publishing USA Inc.), 1983.
6. Edited from *Language in Society* 11, 49-76. Cambridge: Cambridge University Press, 1982.
7. Edited from *Worlds of Literacy* by M. Hamilton, D. Barton and R. Ivanic (eds). Clevedon: Multilingual Matters, 1993.
8. Edited from *Journal of Education* 167 (1), 88-110. Boston: Trustees of Boston University, 1985.
9. Edited from a chapter to appear in *Functional Literacy: Theoretical Issues and Educational Implications* by L. Verhowen (ed.). Amsterdam: John Benjamins, 1994.
10. From *Journal of Communication* 32 (1), 12-26. New York: Oxford University Press. 1982
11. From 'Orality and Literacy' by James Paul Gee. *TESOL Quarterly* 20, 719-46. Alexandria, VI: TESOL, 1986. © TESOL.
12. From *Language Policy for the European Community: Prospects and Quandries* by F. Coulmas (ed.). Berlin/ New York: Mouton de Gruyter, 1991.
13. Edited from *Oxford Literary Review* 9, 2-26. Oxford: Oxford Literary Review, 1987; and from 'Currying Favour: The Policy of British Educational and Cultural Policy in India, 1813-1854', in *Social Text*. New York: Coda Press, Fall 1988.
14. From *British Journal of Sociology of Education* 8 (2), 153-167. Abington: Carfax Publishing Co., 1987.
15. Edited from Part I of *Cultural Action for Freedom* by Paulo Freire. Harmondsworth: Penguin, 1972. © The Author.

Introduction

The contents of this volume reflect an important shift over recent years within the field of language and literacy studies. This has involved a move away from thinking about language and literacy in terms of skills and competences towards investigating their role as part of social practice. The key articles and accounts of recent research collected together in this volume introduce some major ideas and issues underlying this new approach.

There is a particular emphasis in the collection on anthropological studies, which have been a significant influence in the development of more socially and culturally sensitive theories and explanations. Articles written from linguistic, historical and sociological perspectives are also included.

Section One: Language, Culture and Meaning

This section includes four articles concerned primarily with theory building. The authors, writing at different times during this century and in very different cultural contexts, all argue that the study of language should be based on its actual use within everyday life. All are concerned to develop a language of description which can capture the interactive, culturally contextualised nature of language use, and to explore questions about how a theory of language might incorporate and account for the complex inter-relationships between culture, social structure, and the use and interpretation of language in specific settings.

1. Bronislaw Malinowski

Malinowski's 1923 essay which draws on his anthropological fieldwork among the Pacific Trobriand islanders is a seminal paper for both anthropologists and sociolinguists. He describes here the importance of the 'context of situation' to understanding the meaning of any piece of language in use. In addition to exploring how different aspects of the situation contribute to the meaning of specific words and phrases in his Trobriand data, Malinowski introduces the idea of 'language as action' (it makes things happen as well as facilitating reflection) and 'phatic communion', the important social function of apparently meaningless small talk.

2. Dell Hymes

Malinowski's emphasis on the social functions of language and the importance of context to its meaning is echoed in the article here by Hymes who has been an important influence on the development of American linguistic anthropology since the 1970s. Hymes proposed that there should be a new linguistic science rooted in the study of everyday communicative events, which would take into account the social and cultural values and beliefs shaping the function and meaning of individual 'speech acts'. Each community has its own ways of speaking associated with particular situations and events, and individual speech acts between speakers need to be analysed in the light of these different layers of context. Hymes criticises the traditional threefold distinction between speaker, hearer and message, suggesting that a far broader range of components needs to be taken into account in analysing speech.

3. Michael Halliday

This article, first published in 1975, gives an overview of Halliday's model of language as social semiotic — that is, as a vehicle for communicating both propositional meaning (relating to facts and experiences of the world) and social meanings (relating to a speaker's evaluation of facts, attitudes and beliefs, and social relationships with others). Halliday elaborates Malinowski's concept of 'context of situation'; in addition his particular concern with issues of social class and the role of language in social reproduction in early childhood and educational settings demonstrates the extent to which his work is informed by more recent European sociology. His association with the British sociologist and educationalist Basil Bernstein is visible here in his discussion of 'code'.

4. V. N. Volosinov

The increasing importance in the West which is now being attached to social aspects of language has recently led to a renewed interest in the Russian socio-historical writings from the nineteen twenties and thirties. Translated into English in the sixties and seventies, works by Vygotsky, Bakhtin and Volosinov amongst others provide a sophisticated exploration of the interdependence of language and context. Bakhtin and Volosinov were strongly influenced by early Marxism and see language as dynamic, contested and a site of ideological struggle. Their work adds a political and historical dimension to insights from the ethnographers' detailed descriptions of language practices in particular contexts, and to Halliday's systemic approach. The extracts from Volosinov's work reprinted here illustrate his influential ideas about the relation of language to social existence, the inherently evaluative nature of language, and what he calls the 'multi-accentuality' of words — that is, their potential to signify different values within different contexts.

Section Two: Studies of Language Practices

This section contains ethnographic accounts of language and literacy practices in families, schools and communities. These studies provide detailed evidence of the ways in which talk, reading and writing both reflect, and are constitutive of, social organization and cultural values. Children learning to read and write are also being inducted into specific kinds of social practice, and acquiring particular beliefs about relationships between people, communities and languages.

5. Denny Taylor

Taylor carried out a detailed ethnographic study over a three year period of six families, each of which included a child aged 6–7 judged by their parents to be successfully learning to read and write. Although the families were all white, middle class and living in suburban towns, one of her interesting findings is the wide range of individual reading and writing habits, and the diversity of parents' individual literacy histories. In her book *Family Literacy* Taylor provides evidence of the ways in which young children's reading and writing are part of their playing out and rehearsing of the social activities they observe around them, and she shows how school experience is mediated through individual family practices. In Chapter 2 of her book which is reprinted here she illustrates some of the dynamic relationships involved in the transmission and development of literacy practices in families.

6. Shirley Brice Heath

Heath's research has played an important part in the shifting of interest within the field of literacy from a focus on skills to the recognition that these are always embedded in social practice. She highlights the different social and cultural conceptions of literacy which children from different communities may bring with them to school, and demonstrates the social and cultural dimensions of all reading and writing practices. In 'What no bedtime story means: narrative skills at home and school' she contrasts the ways young children learn about narrative and reading in three different local communities, and suggests that these may have a profound effect on their educational experience and success.

7. Mukul Saxena

Saxena presents a case study of literacy practices in a Panjabi Sikh family in Southall, London. He sets this case study within the context of local economic, political and religious processes, and also within the historical context of changing cultural practices in the Punjab, Delhi and East Africa. He shows how within a multilingual context peoples' everyday literacy choices are influenced not only by their own personal history and experience, but also by the histories of the literacies themselves, and the differences in status and power between languages in different contexts. People, he suggests, have different identities; they 'operate in different worlds of literacies to achieve different goals'.

8. Michele Sola and Adrian Bennett

Sola and Bennett examine how the teaching of writing within three classes of Puerto Rican and Afro-American students in a school in East Harlem offers differing opportunities for the legitimation of students' own discourse which elicit quite different modes of classroom participation. Using ideas from Bakhtin and Volosinov, they describe the struggle in these classrooms between the official school instructional discourse with its fixed curriculum goals and knowledge and the more interactive, provisional and contemporaneous discourse of the local community. Only in one classroom does the teacher manage to legitimate community language practices while also accomplishing educational goals, and so achieve a genuinely dialogic discourse with her students.

Section Three: Literacy, Culture and History

The articles in this section move away from a local focus to review aspects of orality and literacy from a cross-cultural and historical perspective. The authors raise questions about personal agency, the role of social institutions, and the ways in which orality and literacy have been conceptualised in debates within the literature. They show how literacy is constructed and reconstructed through interactions between the state, institutions, local practices and individual experience.

9. Brian Street

Street uses evidence from anthropological studies to show how the collection of meanings around being a person varies across different cultures and he argues that 'what it is to be a person, to be moral and to be human in specific cultural contexts is frequently signified by the kind of literacy practices within which a person is engaged'. Studies of literacy practices in other cultures and of vernacular literacies within the US suggest that we need to clarify and refine our concepts of literacy and re-examine monolithic assumptions about what it means to acquire literacy. Street urges that we learn more about literacy practices in different cultural contexts and that programmes and compaigns should be built on people's own cultural meanings and uses of literacy.

10. Harvey Graff

Graff uses a historical review of the development of literacy in the West to refute what he calls the 'literacy myth', i.e. the belief that the acquisition of literacy has a generalised effect on socio-economic development, the social order and individuals' lives. The main problem for the historian is to reconstruct the actual practices of literacy, and its functions and meanings; statistics alone tell us little about how literacy was really used in people's lives, or whether it fulfilled their personal needs. Graff looks in particular at developments in the use of literacy by the state, the church and commerce which he sees as the continuing key institutions in determining its social functions.

11. James Gee

Gee draws together and synthesises the ideas and arguments which have marked the shift towards a more socially and culturally sensitive theory of literacy. He reviews what he sees as the key works on orality and literacy (including Heath, Street and Graff) within the debate about the significance and effects of literacy, and charts the general trend away from models of decontextualised skills towards a recognition of the plurality of practices and meanings. This shift, he suggests, has involved a deconstruction of traditional oppositions between the primitive and the civilised, between concrete and abstract thought, and indeed between orality and literacy.

Section Four: The Politics of Language and Literacy

The articles in this final section discuss political aspects of language planning and teaching within schools, the establishment of a literary canon and the and conduct of adult literacy classes. They show how the struggle between competing social groups and their different agendas is expressed through policy making, the constitution of what counts as literature, and discourse about adult literacy, learning and inequality.

12. Michael Stubbs

Stubbs reviews some major changes concerning language planning which have been taking place within the British education system. He suggests that in spite of the government rhetoric about increased opportunities for linguistic diversity, Britain remains a profoundly monolingual nation, and that in fact there have been recent major attempts to further strengthen the dominant position of Standard English. He analyses the patterns of control behind the apparent lack of a coherent overall national language planning policy in Britain and charts some of the ways in which English furthers its dominance over other languages within the areas of English mother-tongue teaching, modern foreign and Welsh language teaching and provision for bilingual pupils.

13. Guari Viswanathan

How do dominant literacies achieve and maintain their place within a national cultural canon? Viswanathan provides a historical account of the English literature canon in India, which Indian citizens were required to study after the English Education Act 1835. She describes the processes involved in the decision to teach English literature in India, the selection of texts to constitute that literature and the way in which these English texts were 'removed from their social formation and assigned functions that obscure the historical forces which produced them'. Viswanathan argues, however, that the introduction of English literature teaching was not simply an unmediated assertion of authority, but rather 'an embattled response to historical and political pressures' which needs to be understood in the light of the interpenetration of social, cultural, political and literary histories.

14. Kathleen Rockhill

Rockhill uses her study of a group of Spanish immigrant women's experience of literacy to critique existing theories and assumptions about literacy and inequality. She suggests that the assumption that literacy gives access to power in the public sphere, and that it can be somehow added on to people, ignores the way in which women in particular are enmeshed in everyday material conditions and social relations. For the women in her study, language, gender and their position within an immigrant community structure the possibilities of literacy, and reproduce specific patterns of inequality which strongly affect their access to, and desire for, particular learning opportunities.

15. Paulo Freire

Freire links literacy directly to the empowerment of oppressed peoples within the Third World. He rejects the 'banking' approach to education where' knowledge and skills are deposited in learners as an investment towards economic advancement. Rather, literacy teaching should involve 'conscientization', through which people learn to read the world as well as the word, and to take action against injustice and tyranny. With this insistence on praxis, the dialectic between words and action, Freire sees within a particular pedagogical approach the potential to change people from objects to subjects within their own history, and, ultimately, to transform all structures of oppression.

Reference

Taylor, D. (1983) *Family Literacy: Young Children Learning to Read and Write.* London: Heinemann Educational.

Acknowledgement

The editor gratefully acknowledges the help and advice she received from Dr Brian Street of the University of Sussex in the compilation of this reader.

1 The Problem of Meaning in Primitive Languages

BRONISLAW MALINOWSKI

I.

In the course of my Ethnographic researches among some Melanesian tribes of Eastern New Guinea, which I conducted exclusively by means of the local language, I collected a considerable number of texts: magical formulae items of folk-lore, narratives, fragments of conversation, and statements of my informants. When, in working out this linguistic material, I tried to translate my texts into English, and incidentally to write out the vocabulary and grammar of the language, I was faced by fundamental difficulties. These difficulties were not removed, but rather increased, when I consulted the extant grammars and vocabularies of Oceanic languages. The authors of these, mainly missionaries who wrote for the practical purpose of facilitating the task of their successors, proceeded by rule of thumb. For instance, in writing a vocabulary they would give the next best approximation in English to a native word.

But the object of a scientific translation of a work is not to give its rough equivalent, sufficient for practical purposes, but to state exactly whether a native word corresponds to an idea at least partially existing for English speakers, or whether it covers an entirely foreign conception. That such foreign conceptions do exist for native languages and in great number, is clear. All words which describe the native social order, all expressions referring to native beliefs, to specific customs, ceremonies, magical rites — all such words are obviously absent from English as from any European language. Such words can only be translated into English, not by giving their imaginary equivalent — a real one obviously cannot be found — but by explaining the meaning of each of them through an exact Ethnographic account of the sociology, culture and tradition of that native community.

But there is an even more deeply reaching, though subtler difficulty: the whole manner in which a native language is used is different from our own.

1

In a primitive tongue, the whole grammatical structure lacks the precision and definiteness of our own, though it is extremely telling in certain specific ways. Again some particles, quite untranslatable into English, give a special flavour to native phraseology. In the structure of sentences, an extreme simplicity hides a good deal of expressiveness, often achieved by means of position and context. Returning to the meaning of isolated words, the use of metaphor, the beginnings of abstraction, of generalisation and a vagueness associated with extreme concreteness of expression — all these features baffle any attempt at a simple and direct translation. The Ethnographer has to convey this deep yet subtle difference of language and of the mental attitude which lies behind it, and is expressed through it. But this leads more and more into the general psychological problem of Meaning.

II.

This general statement of the linguistic difficulties which beset an Ethnographer in his field-work, must be illustrated by a concrete example. Imagine yourself suddenly transported on to a coral atoll in the Pacific, sitting in a circle of natives and listening to their conversation. Let us assume further that there is an ideal interpreter at hand, who, as far as possible, can convey the meaning of each utterance word for word, so that the listener is in possession of all the linguistic data available. Would that make you understand the conversation or even a single utterance? Certainly not.

Let us have a look at such a text, an actual utterance taken down from a conversation of natives in the Trobriand Islands, N.E. New Guinea. In analysing it, we shall see quite plainly how helpless one is in attempting to open up the meaning of a statement by mere linguistic means; and we shall also be able to realise what sort of additional knowledge, besides verbal equivalence, is necessary in order to make the utterance significant.

I adduce a statement in native, giving under each word its nearest English equivalent:

Tasakaulo	*kaymatana*	*yakida;*	
We run	front-wood	ourselves;	
tawoulo	*ovanu;*	*tasivila*	*tagine*
we paddle	in place;	we turn	we see
soda;	*isakaulo*	*ka'u'uya*	
companion ours;	he runs	rear-wood	
oluvieki	*similaveta*	*Pilolu*	
behind	their sea-arm	Pilolu	

The verbatim English translation of this utterance sounds at first like a riddle or a meaningless jumble of words; certainly not like a significant, unambiguous statement. Now if the listener, whom we suppose acquainted with the language, but unacquainted with the culture of the natives, were to understand even the general trend of this statement, he would have first to be informed about the situation in which these words were spoken. He would need to have them placed in their proper setting of native culture. In this case, the utterance refers to an episode in an overseas trading expedition of these natives, in which several canoes take part in a competitive spirit. This last-mentioned feature explains also the emotional nature of the utterance: it is not a mere statement of fact, but a boast, a piece of self-glorification, extremely characteristic of the Trobrianders' culture in general and of their ceremonial barter in particular.

Only after a preliminary instruction is it possible to gain some idea of such *technical terms of boasting and emulation* as *kaymatana* (front-wood) and *ka'u'uya* (rear-wood). The metaphorical use of *wood* for *canoe* would lead us into another field of language psychology, but for the present it is enough to emphasise that 'front' or 'leading canoe' and 'rear canoe' are important terms for a people whose attention is so highly occupied with competitive activities for their own sake. To the meaning of such words is added a specific emotional tinge, comprehensible only against the background of their tribal psychology in ceremonial life, commerce and enterprise.

Again, the sentence where the leading sailors are described as looking back and perceiving their companions lagging behind on the sea-arm of Pilolu, would require a special discussion of the geographical feeling of the natives, of their use of imagery as a linguistic instrument and of a special use of the possessive pronoun (*their* sea-arm Pilolu).

All this shows the wide and complex considerations into which we are led by an attempt to give an adequate analysis of meaning. Instead of translating, of inserting simply an English word for a native one, we are faced by a long and not altogether simple process of describing wide fields of custom, of social psychology and of tribal organisation which correspond to one term or another. We see that linguistic analysis inevitably leads us into the study of all the subjects covered by Ethnographic field-work.

Of course the above given comments on the specific terms (front-wood, rear-wood, their sea-arm Pilolu) are necessarily short and sketchy. But I have on purpose chosen an utterance which corresponds to a set of customs, already described quite fully.[1] The reader of that description will be able to understand thoroughly the adduced text, as well as appreciate the present argument.

Besides the difficulties encountered in the translation of single words, difficulties which lead directly into descriptive Ethnography, there are others, associated with more exclusively linguistic problems, which however can be solved only on the basis of psychological analysis. Thus it has been suggested that the characteristically Oceanic distinction of inclusive and exclusive pronouns requires a deeper explanation than any which would confine itself to merely grammatical relations. Again, the puzzling manner in which some of the obviously correlated sentences are joined in our text by mere juxtaposition would require much more than a simple reference, if all its importance and significance had to be brought out.

In the grammars and interpretations of Melanesian languages, almost all of which have been written by missionaries for practical purposes, the grammatical modifications of verbs have been simply set down as equivalent to Indo-European tenses. When I first began to use the Trobriand language in my field-work, I was quite unaware that there might be some snares in taking savage grammar at its face value and followed the missionary way of using native inflection.

I had soon to learn, however, that this was not correct and I learnt it by means of a practical mistake, which interfered slightly with my field-work and forced me to grasp native flection at the cost of my personal comfort. At one time I was engaged in making observations on a very interesting transaction which took place in a lagoon village of the Trobriands between the coastal fishermen and the inland gardeners. I had to follow some important preparations in the village and yet I did not want to miss the arrival of the canoes on the beach. I was busy registering and photographing the proceedings among the huts, when word went round, 'they have come already' — *boge laymayse.* I left my work in the village unfinished to rush some quarter of a mile to the shore, in order to find, to my disappointment and mortification, the canoes far away, punting slowly along towards the beach! Thus I came some ten minutes too soon, just enough to make me lose my opportunities in the village!

It required some time and a much better general grasp of the language before I came to understand the nature of my mistake and the proper use of words and forms to express the subtleties of temporal sequence. Thus the root *ma* which means *come, move hither,* does not contain the meaning, covered by our word *arrive.* Nor does any grammatical determination give it the special and temporal definition, which we express by, 'they have come, they have arrived'. The form *boge laymayse,* which I heard on that memorable morning in the lagoon village, means to a native 'they have already been moving hither' and not 'they have already come here'.

In order to achieve the spatial and temporal definition which we obtain by using the past definite tense, the natives have recourse to certain concrete and specific expressions. Thus in the case quoted, the villagers, in order to convey the fact that the canoes had arrived, would have used the word *to anchor, to moor.* 'They have already moored their canoes,' *boge aykotasi,* would have meant, what I assumed they had expressed by *boge laymayse.* That is, in this case the natives use a different root instead of a mere grammatical modification.

Returning to our text, we have another telling example of the characteristic under discussion. The quaint expression 'we paddle in place' can only be properly understood by realising that the word *paddle* has here the function, not of describing what the crew are doing, but of indicating their immediate proximity to the village of their destination. Exactly as in the previous example the past tense of the word to come ('they have come') which we would have used in our language to convey the fact of arrival, has another meaning in native and has to be replaced by another root which expresses the idea; so here the native root *wa, to move thither,* could not have been used in (approximately) past definite tense to convey the meaning of 'arrive there', but a special root expressing the concrete act of paddling is used to mark the spatial and temporal relations of the leading canoe to the others. The origin of this imagery is obvious. Whenever the natives arrive near the shore of one of the overseas villages, they have to fold the sail and to use the paddles, since there the water is deep, even quite close to the shore, and punting impossible. So 'to paddle' means 'to arrive at the overseas village'. It may be added that in this expression 'we paddle in place', the two remaining words *in* and *place* would have to be retranslated in a free English interpretation by *near the village.*

With the help of such an analysis as the one just given, this or any other savage utterance can be made comprehensible. In this case we may sum up our results and embody them in a free commentary or paraphrase of the statement:

> A number of natives sit together. One of them, who has just come back from an overseas expedition, gives an account of the sailing and boasts about the superiority of his canoe. He tells his audience how, in crossing the sea-arm of Pilolu (between the Trobriands and the Amphletts), his canoe sailed ahead of all others. When nearing their destination, the leading sailors looked back and saw their comrades far behind, still on the sea-arm of Pilolu.

Put in these terms, the utterance can at least be understood broadly, though for an exact appreciation of the shades and details of meaning a full knowledge of the native customs and psychology, as well as of the general structure of their language, is indispensable.

What I have tried to make clear by analysis of a primitive linguistic text is that language is essentially rooted in the reality of the culture, the tribal life and customs of a people, and that it cannot be explained without constant reference to these broader contexts of verbal utterance.

III.

Returning once more to our native utterance, it needs no special stressing that in a primitive language the meaning of any single word is to a very high degree dependent on its context. The words 'wood', 'paddle', 'place' had to be retranslated in the free interpretation in order to show what is their real meaning, conveyed to a native by the context in which they appear. Again, it is equally clear that the meaning of the expression 'we arrive near the village (of our destination)' literally: 'we paddle in place', is determined only by taking it in the context of the whole utterance. This latter again, becomes only intelligible when it is placed within its *context of situation,* if I may be allowed to coin an expression which indicates on the one hand that the conception of *context* has to be broadened and on the other that the *situation* in which words are uttered can never be passed over as irrelevant to the linguistic expression. We see how the conception of context must be substantially widened, if it is to furnish us with its full utility. In fact is must burst the bonds of mere linguistics and be carried over into the analysis of the general conditions under which a language is spoken. Thus, starting from the wider idea of context, we arrive once more at the results of the foregoing section, namely that the study of any language, spoken by a people who live under conditions different from our own and possess a different culture, must be carried out in conjunction with the study of their culture and of their environment.

A statement, spoken in real life, is never detached from the situation in which it has been uttered. For each verbal statement by a human being has the aim and function of expressing some thought or feeling actual at that moment and in that situation, and necessary for some reason or other to be made known to another person or persons — in order either to serve purposes of common action, or to establish ties of purely social communion, or else to deliver the speaker of violent feelings or passions. Without some imperative stimulus of the moment there can be no spoken statement. In each case, therefore, utterance and situation are bound up inextricably with each other and the context of situation is indispensable for the understanding of the words.

The clear realisation of the intimate connection between linguistic interpretation and the analysis of the culture to which the language belongs, shows convincingly that neither a Word not its Meaning has an independent and self-sufficient existence. The Ethnographic view of language proves the principle of Symbolic Relativity as it might be called, that is that words must be treated only as symbols and that a psychology of symbolic reference must serve as the basis for all science of language. Since the whole world of 'things-to-be expressed' changes with the level of culture, with geographical, social and economic conditions, the consequence is that the meaning of a word must be always gathered, not from a passive contemplation of this word, but from an analysis of its functions, with reference to the given culture.

IV.

So far, I have dealt mainly with the simplest problems of meaning, those associated with the definition of single words and with the lexicographical task of bringing home to a European reader the vocabulary of a strange tongue. And the main result of our analysis was that it is impossible to translate words of a primitive language or of one widely different from our own, without giving a detailed account of the culture of its users and thus providing the common measure necessary for a translation. But though an Ethnographic background is indispensable for a scientific treatment of a language, it is by no means sufficient, and the problem of Meaning needs a special theory of its own. I shall try to show that, looking at language from the Ethnographic perspective and using our conception of *context of situation,* we shall be able to give an outline of a Semantic theory, useful in the work on Primitive Linguistics, and throwing some light on human language in general.

Take for instance language spoken by a group of natives engaged in one of their fundamental pursuits in search of subsistence — hunting, fishing, tilling the soil; or else in one of those activities, in which a savage tribe express some essentially human forms of energy — war, play or sport, ceremonial performance or artistic display such as dancing or singing. The actors in any such scene are all following a purposeful activity, are all set on a definite aim; they all have to act in a concerted manner according to certain rules established by custom and tradition. In this, Speech is the necessary means of communion; it is the one indispensable instrument for creating the ties of the moment without which unified social action is impossible.

Let us now consider what would be the type of talk passing between people thus acting, what would be the manner of its use. To make it quite concrete at first, let us follow up a party of fishermen on a coral lagoon, spying for a shoal of fish, trying to imprison them in an enclosure of large nets, and to drive them into small net-bags — an example which I am choosing also because of my personal familiarity with the procedure.

The canoes glide slowly and noiselessly, punted by men especially good at this task and always used for it. Other experts who know the bottom of the Lagoon, with its plant and animal life, are on the look-out for fish. One of them sights the quarry. Customary signs, or sounds or words are uttered. Sometimes a sentence full of technical references to the channels or patches on the Lagoon has to be spoken; sometimes when the shoal is near and the task of trapping is simple, a conventional cry is uttered not too loudly. Then, the whole fleet stops and ranges itself — every canoe and every man in it performing his appointed task — according to a customary routine. But, of course, the men, as they act, utter now and then a sound expressing keenness in the pursuit or impatience at some technical difficulty, joy of achievement or disappointment at failure. Again, a word of command is passed here and there, a technical expression or explanation which serves to harmonise their behaviour towards other men. The whole group act in a concerted manner, determined by old tribal tradition and perfectly familiar to the actors through life-long experience. Some men in the canoes cast the wide encircling nets into the water, others plunge, and wading through the shallow lagoon, drive the fish into the nets. Others again stand by with the small nets, ready to catch the fish. An animated scene, full of movement follows, and now that the fish are in their power the fishermen speak loudly, and give vent to their feelings. Short, telling exclamations fly about, which might be rendered by such words as: 'Pull in', 'Let go', 'Shift further', 'Lift the net'; or again technical expressions completely untranslatable except by minute description of the instruments used, and of the mode of action.

All the language used during such a pursuit is full of technical terms, short references to surroundings, rapid indications of change — all based on customary types of behaviour, well-known to the participants from personal experience. Each utterance is essentially bound up with the context of situation and with the aim of the pursuit, whether it be the short indications about the movements of the quarry, or references to statements about the surroundings, or the expression of feeling and passion inexorably bound up with behaviour, or words of command, or correlation of action. The structure of all this linguistic material is inextricably mixed up with, and dependent upon, the course of the activity in which the utterances are embedded. The vocabulary, the meaning of the particular words used in their characteristic technicality is not less subordinate to action. For technical language, in matters of practical pursuit, acquires its meaning only through personal participation in this type of pursuit. It has to be learned, not through reflection but through action.

Had we taken any other example than fishing, we would have reached similar results. The study of any form of speech used in connection with vital work would reveal the same grammatical and lexical peculiarities: the dependence of the meaning of each word upon practical experience, and of the structure of each utterance upon the momentary situation in which it is spoken. Thus the consideration of linguistic uses associated with any practical pursuit, leads us to the conclusion that language in its primitive forms ought to be regarded and studied against the background of human activities and as a mode of human behaviour in practical matters.

A narrative is associated also indirectly with one situation to which it refers — in our text with a performance of competitive sailing. In this relation, the words of a tale are significant because of previous experiences of the listeners; and their meaning depends on the context of the situation referred to, not to the same degree but in the same manner as in the speech of action. The difference in degree is important; narrative speech is derived in its function, and it refers to action only indirectly, but the way in which it acquires its meaning can only be understood from the direct function of speech in action.

The case of language used in free, aimless, social intercourse requires special consideration. When a number of people sit together at a village fire, after all the daily tasks are over, or when they chat, resting from work, or when they accompany some mere manual work by gossip quite unconnected with what they are doing — it is clear that here we have to do with another mode of using language, with another type of speech function. Language here is not dependent upon what happens at that moment, it seems to be even deprived of any context of situation. The meaning of any utterance cannot be connected with the speaker's or hearer's behaviour, with the purpose of what they are doing.

A mere phrase of politeness, in use as much among savage tribes as in a European drawing room, fulfils a function to which the meaning of its words is almost completely irrelevant. Enquiries about health, comments on weather, affirmations of some supremely obvious state of things — all such are exchanged, not in order to inform, not in this case to connect people in action, certainly not in order to express any thought. It would be even incorrect, I think, to say that such words serve the purpose of establishing a common sentiment, for this is usually absent from such current phrases of intercourse; and where it purports to exist, as in expressions of sympathy, it is avowedly spurious on one side. What is the *raison d'être*, therefore, of such phrases as 'How do you do?', 'Ah, here you are', 'Where do you come from?', 'Nice day to-day' — all of which serve in one society or another as formulae of greeting or approach?

After the first formula, there comes a flow of language, purposeless expressions of preference or aversion, accounts of irrelevant happenings, comments on what is perfectly obvious. Such gossip, as found in Primitive Societies, differs only a little from our own. Always the same emphasis of affirmation and consent, mixed perhaps with an incidental disagreement which creates the bonds of antipathy. Or personal accounts of the speaker's views and life history, to which the hearer listens under some restraint and with slightly veiled impatience, waiting till his own turn arrives to speak. For in this use of speech the bonds created between hearer and speaker are not quite symmetrical, the man linguistically active receiving the greater share of social pleasure and self-enhancement. But though the hearing given to such utterances is as a rule not as intense as the speaker's own share, it is quite essential for his pleasure, and the reciprocity is established by the change of rôles.

There can be no doubt that we have here a new type of linguistic use — *phatic communion* I am tempted to call it, actuated by the demon of terminological invention — a type of speech in which ties of union are created by a mere exchange of words. Let us look at it from the special point of view with which we are here concerned; let us ask what light it throws on the function or nature of language. Are words in Phatic Communion used primarily to convey meaning, the meaning which is symbolically theirs? Certainly not! They fulfil a social function and that is their principal aim, but they are neither the result of intellectual reflection, nor do they necessarily arouse reflection in the listener. Once again we may say that language does not function here as a means of transmission of thought.

But can we regard it as a mode of action? And in what relation does it stand to our crucial conception of context of situation? It is obvious that the outer situation does not enter directly into the technique of speaking. But what can be considered as *situation* when a number of people aimlessly gossip together? It consists in just this atmosphere of sociability and in the fact of the personal communion of these people. But this is in fact achieved by speech, and the situation in all such cases is created by the exchange of words, by the specific feelings which form convivial gregariousness, by the give and take of utterances which make up ordinary gossip. The whole situation consists in what happens linguistically. Each utterance is an act serving the direct aim of binding hearer to speaker by a tie of some social sentiment or other. Once more language appears to us in this function not as an instrument of reflection but as a mode of action.

I should like to add at once that though the examples discussed were taken from savage life, we could find among ourselves exact parallels to every type of linguistic use so far discussed. The binding tissue of words which unites the crew of a ship in bad weather, the verbal concomitants of a company of soldiers in action, the technical language running parallel to some practical work or sporting pursuit — all these resemble essentially the primitive uses of speech by man in action and our discussion could have been equally well conducted in a modern example.

Note

1. See *Argonauts of the Western Pacific* — An Account of Native Enterprise and Adventure in the Archipelagoes of Melanesian New Guinea, by B. Malinowski, Routledge, 1922.

2 Toward Ethnographies of Communication

DELL HYMES

The term 'ethnography of communication' is intended to indicate the necessary scope, and to encourage the doing, of studies ethnographic in basis, and communicative in the range and kind of patterned complexity with which they deal. That is, the term implies two characteristics that an adequate approach to language must have.

As to scope: one cannot simply take separate results from linguistics, psychology, sociology, ethnology, as given, and seek to correlate them, however partially useful such work may be, if one is to have a theory of language (not just a theory of grammar). One needs fresh kinds of data, one needs to investigate directly the use of language in contexts of situation, so as to discern patterns proper to speech activity, patterns that escape separate studies of grammar, of personality, of social structure, religion, and the like, each abstracting from the patterning of speech activity into some other frame of reference.

As to basis: one cannot take linguistic form, a given code, or even speech itself, as a limiting frame of reference. One must take as context a community, or network of persons, investigating its communicative activities as a whole, so that any use of channel and code takes its place as part of the resources upon which the members draw.

It is not that linguistics does not have a vital role. Analyzed linguistic materials are indispensable, and the logic of linguistic methodology is an influence in the ethnographic perspective. It is rather that it is not linguistics, but ethnography, not language, but communication, which must provide the frame of reference within which the place of language in culture and society is to be assessed. The boundaries of the community within which communication is possible; the boundaries of the situations within which communication occurs; the means and purposes and patterns of selection, their structure and hierarchy — all elements that constitute the communicative economy of a group, are conditioned, to be sure, by properties of the linguistic codes within the group, but are not controlled by them. The same linguistic

11

means may be made to serve various ends; the same communicative ends may be served, linguistically, by various means. Facets of the cultural values and beliefs, social institutions and forms, roles and personalities, history and ecology of a community may have to be examined in their bearing on communicative events and patterns (just as any aspect of a community's life may come to bear selectively on the study of kinship, sex, or role conflict).

It will be found that much that has impinged upon linguistics as variation and deviation has an organization of its own. What seem variation and deviation from the standpoint of a linguist's analysis may emerge as structure and pattern from the standpoint of the communicative economy of the group among whom the analyzed form of speech exists. The structures and patterns that emerge will force reconsideration, moreover, of the analysis of linguistic codes themselves. Just as elements and relations of phonology appear partly in a new light when viewed from the organization of grammar, and just as elements and relations of grammar appear in a new light when viewed from the organization of sememics (Lamb, 1964), so elements and relations of the linguistic code as a whole will appear partly in a new light, viewed from the organization of the elements and relations of the speech act and speech event, themselves part of a system of communicative acts and events characteristic of a group.

To project the ethnography of communication in such a way is tantamount to the belief that there awaits constitution a second descriptive science comprising language, in addition to, and ultimately comprehending, present linguistics — a science that would approach language neither as abstracted form nor as an abstract correlate of a community, but as situated in the flux and pattern of communicative events. It would study communicative form and function in integral relation to each other. In this it would constrast with long held views of linguistics and of what is within linguistics. Some divorce linguistic form from context and function. An old but apt illustration is found in Bloomfield's often cited remark that, if a beggar says 'I'm hungry' to obtain food, and a child says 'I'm hungry' to avoid going to bed, then linguistics is concerned just with what is the same in the two acts. It abstracts, in other words, from context. In contrast, an influential book has characterized pragmatics in a way exactly complementary as 'all those aspects which serve to distinguish one communication event from any other where the sign types may be the same' (Cherry, 1961: 225). It abstracts, in other words, from linguistic form.

Such views are not the only ones to be found, but they have been characteristic of linguistics, on the one hand, and social science, on the other, and most practice has exemplified one or the other. For ethnographies of communication, however, the aim must be not so to divide the communicative act or event, divorcing message-form (Cherry's sign-type) and context of use

from one another. The aim must be to keep the multiple hierarchy of relations among messages and contexts in view (cf. Bateson, 1963). Studies of
social contexts and functions of communication, if divorced from the means
that serve them, are as little to the purpose as are studies of communicative
means, if divorced from the contexts and functions they serve. Methodologi-
cally, of course, it is not a matter of limiting a structural perspective inspired
by linguistics to a particular component of communication, but of extending
it to the whole.

For many people, the place of the ethnography of communication will
appear to be, not in relation to one or more traditions in linguistics, but in
relation to some general perspective on human behavior. For many, the
name of this perspective will be social anthropology, or sociology, or
psychology, or some other disciplinary category. The work required does
fall somewhere into place within the purview of each such discipline, and
there can be no quarrel with any, except to say that the division of the study
of man into departmentalized disciplines seems itself often arbitrary and an
obstacle. What is essential, in any case, is that the distinctive focus of concern advanced here be recognized and cultivated, whatever the disciplinary
label. One way to state the need is to remark that there are anthropological,
sociological, and psychological studies of many kinds, but of ethnographic
analyses of communicative conduct, and of comparative studies based upon
them, there are still few to find.

Fundamental Notions

Among the notions with which a theory must deal are those of ways of
speaking, fluent speaker, speech situation, speech event, speech act, components of speech events and acts, rules (relations) of speaking, and functions of speech.

Ways of speaking

Ways of speaking is used as the most general, indeed, as a primitive term.
The point of it is the heuristic, or regulative, idea, that communicative conduct within a community comprises determinate patterns of speech activity,
such that the communicative competence of persons comprises knowledge
with regard to such patterns. (Speech is taken here as surrogate for all manifestations and derivations of language, including writing, song, speech-
linked whistling, drumming, horn-blowing, etc.)

Ways of speaking can be taken to refer to the relationships among speech
events, acts, and styles, on the one hand, and personal abilities and roles,
contexts and institutions, and beliefs, values, and attitudes, on the other.

Fluent speaker

The aspect of ability that grammars are intended to model presumably is connected with fluency; the kind of person whose abilities are most closely approximated is presumably the fluent speaker. Of course a person may have grammatical knowledge and be unable to use it; but the thrust of linguistics has been toward an image of a person who both has the knowledge and is unimpeded in its use (cf. Chomsky, 1965). The difficulty for an ethnographer is that persons differ in ability, in life, if not in grammars. Even if one abstracts from individual differences, community differences remain. 'Fluency' would appear to mean different profiles of ability in different communities, and indeed would seem not to be the most appropriate label everywhere for the abilities considered those of an ideal speaker (-hearer). We know too little about community ideals for speakers — the lack is great with regard to the complex makeup of American society itself — and too little about the role of such conceptions in acquisition of speech, in what goes on in schools and jobs, in linguistic change. Communities may hold differing ideals of speaking for different statuses and roles and situations. Moreover, the dimensions of ideal speaking may differ — 'knowledge that' such and such is the case in a language vs. 'knowledge how' to accomplish something verbally; memorization vs. improvisation; vocal carrying power and endurance vs. certain qualities of voice; etc. Thus, normative notions of ability, as embodied in kinds of speakers, must be part of ethnography. Knowledge of them is of course indispensable background to study of actual abilities.

Speech community

Speech community is a necessary, primary concept in that, if taken seriously, it postulates the unit of description as a social, rather than linguistic, entity. One starts with a social group and considers the entire organization of linguistic means within it, rather than start with some one partial, named organization of linguistic means, called a 'language'.

Definition of a speech community in terms of a language is inadequate to the bounding of communities, either externally or internally. Externally, the linguistic and communicative boundaries between communities cannot be defined by linguistic features alone (cf. Hymes, 1968). Forms of speech of the same degree of linguistic difference may be counted as dialects of the same language in one region, and as distinct languages in another, depending on the political, not linguistic, history of the regions.

A speech community is defined, then, tautologically but radically, as a community sharing knowledge of rules for the conduct and interpretation of speech. Such sharing comprises knowledge of at least one form of speech, and knowledge also of its patterns of use. Both conditions are necessary.

Since both kinds of knowledge may be shared apart from common member-ship in a community, an adequate theory of language requires additional notions, such as *language field, speech field,* and *speech network,* and requires the contribution of social science in characterising the notions of community, and of membership of a community.

Speech situation

Within a community one readily detects many situations associated with (or marked by the absence of) speech. Such contexts of situation will often be naturally described as ceremonies, fights, hunts, meals, lovemaking, and the like.

In a sociolinguistic description, then, it is necessary to deal with activities which are in some recognizable way bounded or integral. From the stand-point of general social description they may be registered as ceremonies, fishing trips, and the like; from particular standpoints they may be regarded as political, esthetic, etc., situations, which serve as contexts for the manifes-tation of political, esthetic, etc., activity. From the sociolinguistic standpoint they may be regarded as speech situations.

Speech event

The term *speech event* will be restricted to activities, or aspects of activities, that are directly governed by rules or norms for the use of speech. An event may consist of a single speech act, but will often comprise several. Just as an occurrence of a noun may at the same time be the whole of a noun phrase and the whole of a sentence (e.g. 'Fire!'), so a speech act may be the whole of a speech event, and of a speech situation (say, a rite consisting of a single prayer, itself a single invocation). More often, however, one will find a difference in magnitude: a party (speech situation), a conversation during the party (speech event), a joke within the conversation (speech act). It is of speech events and speech acts that one writes formal rules for their occurr-ence and characteristics. Notice that the same type of speech act may recur in different types of speech event, and the same type of speech event in dif-ferent contexts of situation. Thus, a joke (speech act) may be embedded in a private conversation, a lecture, a formal introduction. A private conversa-tion may occur in the context of a party, a memorial service, a pause in changing sides in a tennis match.

Speech act

The *speech act* is the minimal term of the set just discussed, as the remarks on speech events have indicated. It represents a level distinct from the sen-tence, and not identifiable with any single portion of other levels of gram-mar, nor with segments of any particular size defined in terms of other levels of grammar. That an utterance has the status of a command may depend upon a conventional formula ('I hereby order you to leave this building'), intonation ('Go!' vs. 'Go?'), position in a conversational exchange ('Hello' as initiating greeting or as response, as when answering the telephone), and the social relationship obtaining between the parties (as when an utterance that is in form a polite question is in effect a command, when made by a superior to a subordinate). In general the relation between sentence forms and speech acts is of the kind just mentioned: a sentence interrogative in form may be now a request, now a command, now a statement; a request may be manifested by a sentence that is now interrogative, now declarative, now imperative in form; and one and the same sentence may be taken as a promise or as a threat, depending on the norm of interpretation applied to it.

To some extent speech acts may be analyzable by extensions of syntactic and semantic structure, as commonly analyzed in linguistics, but much of the knowledge that speakers share about the status of utterances as acts is immediate and abstract, and having to do with features of interaction and context as well as of grammar.

Components of speech

A descriptive theory requires some schema of the components of speech acts. At present such a schema can be only an etic, heuristic input to descriptions. Later it may assume the status of a theory of universal features and dimensions.

Long traditional in our culture is the threefold division between speaker, hearer, and something spoken about. It has been elaborated in information theory, linguistics, semiotics, literary criticism, and sociology in various ways. In the hands of some investigators various of these models have proven productive, but their productivity has depended upon not taking them literally, let alone using them precisely. All such schemes, e.g. appear to agree either in taking the standpoint of an individual speaker or in postulating a dyad, speaker–hearer (or source–destination, sender–receiver, addressor–addressee). Even if such a scheme is intended to be a model, for descriptive work it cannot be. Some rules of speaking require specification of *three* participants — addressor, addressee, hearer (audience), source, spokesman, addressees, etc.; some of but *one*, indifferent as to role in the speech event; some of *two*, but of speaker and audience (e.g. a child); and so on. In short, serious ethnographic work shows that there is one general, or universal, dimension to be postulated, that of *participant*. The common dyadic model of speaker–hearer specifies sometimes too many, sometimes too few, sometimes the wrong participants. Further ethnographic work will enable us to state the range of actual types of participant relations and to see in differential occurrence something to be explained.

Ethnographic material so far investigated indicates that some sixteen or seventeen components have sometimes to be distinguished. No rule has been found that requires specification of all simultaneously. There are always redundancies, and sometimes a rule requires explicit mention of a relation between only two, message form and some other. (It is a general principle that all rules involve message form, if not by affecting its shape, then by governing its interpretation.) Since each of the components may sometimes be a factor, however, each has to be recognized in the general grid.

(1) *Message form.* The form of the message is fundamental, as has just been indicated. The most common, and most serious, defect in most reports of speaking probably is that the message form, and, hence, the rules governing it, cannot be recaptured. A concern for the details of actual form strikes some as picayune, as removed from humanistic or scientific importance. Such a view betrays an impatience that is a disservice to both humanistic and scientific purposes. It is precisely the failure to unite form and content in the scope of a single focus of study that has retarded understanding of the human ability to speak, and that vitiates many attempts to analyze the significance of behavior. Content categories, interpretive categories, alone do not suffice. It is a truism, but one frequently ignored in research, that *how* something is said is part of *what* is said. Nor can one prescribe in advance the gross size of the signal that will be crucial to content and skill. The more a way of speaking has become shared and meaningful within a group, the more likely that crucial cues will be efficient, i.e. slight in scale.

Only painstaking analysis of message form — how things are said — of a sort that indeed parallels and can learn from the intensity of literary criticism can disclose the depth and adequacy of the elliptical art that is talk.

(2) *Message content.* One context for distinguishing message form from message content would be: 'He prayed, saying ". . ."' (quoting message form) vs. 'He prayed that he would get well' (reporting content only).

Content enters analysis first of all perhaps as a question of *topic*, and of change of topic. Members of a group know what is being talked about, and when what is talked about has changed, and manage maintenance, and change, of topic. These abilities are parts of their communicative competence of particular importance to study of the coherence of discourse.

Message form and message content are central to the speech act and the focus of its 'syntactic structure'; they are also tightly interdependent. Thus they can be dubbed jointly as components of 'act sequence' (mnemonically, A).

(3) *Setting.* Setting, refers to the time and place of a speech act and, in general, to the physical circumstances.

(4) *Scene.* Scene, which is distinct from setting, designates the 'psychological setting', or the cultural definition of an occasion as a certain type of scene. Within a play on the same stage with the same stage set the dramatic time may shift: 'ten years later'. In daily life the same persons in the same setting may redefine their interaction as a changed type of scene, say, from formal to informal, serious to festive, or the like. Speech acts frequently are used to define scenes, and also frequently judged as appropriate or inappropriate in relation to scenes. Settings and scenes themselves, of course, may be judged as appropriate or inappropriate, happy or unhappy, in relation to each other, from the level of complaint about the weather to that of dramatic irony.

Setting and scene may be linked as components of act situation (mnemonically, S). Since 'scene' implies always an analysis of cultural definitions, 'setting' probably is to be preferred as the informal, unmarked term of the two.

(5) *Speaker,* or *sender.*

(6) *Addressor.*

(7) *Hearer,* or *receiver,* or *audience.*

(8) *Addressee.* These four components were discussed in introducing the subject of components of speech.

(9) *Purposes — outcomes.* Conventionally recognized and expected outcomes often enter into the definition of speech events, as among the Waiwai of Venezuela, where the central speech event of the society, the *oho-chant,* has several varieties, according to whether the purpose to be accomplished is a marriage contract, a trade, a communal work task, an invitation to a feast, or a composing of social peace after a death. The rules for participants and settings vary accordingly (Fock, 1965). A taxonomy of speech events among the Yakan of the Philippines (analyzed by Frake, 1972) is differentiated into levels according jointly to topic (any topic, an issue, a disagreement, a dispute) and outcome (no particular outcome, a decision, a settlement, a legal ruling).

(10) *Purposes — goals.* The purpose of an event from a community standpoint, of course, need not be identical to the purposes of those engaged in it. Presumably, both sides to a Yakan litigation wish to win. In a negotiation the purpose of some may be to obtain a favorable settlement, of others simply that there be a settlement.

(11) *Key.* Key is introduced to provide for the tone, manner, or spirit in which an act is done. It corresponds roughly to modality among grammatical categories. Acts otherwise the same as regards setting, participants, message form, and the like may differ in key, as e.g. between *mock: serious* or *perfunctory: painstaking.*

Key is often conventionally ascribed to an instance of some other component as its attribute; seriousness, for example, may be the expected concomitant of a scene, participant, act, code, or genre (say, a church, a judge, a vow, use of Latin, obsequies). Yet there is always the possibility that there is a conventionally understood way of substituting an alternative key. (This possibility corresponds to the general possibility of choosing one speech style or register as against another.) In this respect, ritual remains always informative. Knowing what should happen next, one still can attend to the way in which it happens.

The significance of key is underlined by the fact that, when it is in conflict with the overt content of an act, it often overrides the latter (as in sarcasm). The signalling of key may be nonverbal, as with a wink, gesture, posture, style of dress, musical accompaniment, but it also commonly involves conventional units of speech too often disregarded in ordinary linguistic analysis, such as English aspiration and vowel length to signal emphasis. Such features are often termed *expressive*, but are better dubbed *stylistic* since they need not all depend on the mood of their user.

(12) *Channels.* By choice of channel is understood choice of oral, written, telegraphic, semaphore, or other medium of transmission of speech. With regard to channels, one must further distinguish modes of use. The oral channel, e.g. may be used to sing, hum, whistle, or chant features of speech as well as to speak them.

(13) *Forms of speech.* Earlier discussion of the speech community dealt with the distinction between the provenance of linguistic resources, and the mutual intelligibility, and the use, of some organized set of them. Where common provenance of a stock of lexical and grammatical materials is in question, one can easily continue to speak of *languages* and *dialects.* Where mutual intelligibility is in question, whether due to different provenance or to derivation by addition, deletion, substitution, permutation from a common set of resources, the term *code* is most appropriate; it suggests decoding and intelligibility. Where use is in question, the term *variety* has become fairly well established (Ferguson & Gumperz, 1960), especially for community-wide uses or use in relation to broad domains; for situation-specific use, the British term *register* has gained acceptance.

(14) *Norms of interaction.* All rules governing speaking, of course, have a normative character. What is intended here are the specific behaviors and proprieties that attach — that one must not interrupt, for example, or that one may freely do so; that normal voice should not be used, except when scheduled, in a church service (whisper otherwise); that turns in speaking are to be allocated in a certain way. Norms of interaction obviously implicate analysis of social structure, and social relationships generally, in a community.

(15) *Norms of interpretation.* An account of norms of interaction may still leave open the interpretation to be placed upon them, especially when members of different communities are in communication. Thus it is clear that Arabic and American students differ on a series of interactional norms: Arabs confront each other more directly (face to face) when conversing, sit closer to each other, are more likely to touch each other, look each other more squarely in the eye, and converse more loudly (Watson & Graves, 1966: 976–7). The investigators who report these findings themselves leave open the meanings of these norms to the participants (p. 984).

The problem of *norms of interpretation* is familiar from the assessment of communications from other governments and national leaders. One often looks for friendliness in lessened degree of overt hostility. Relations between groups within a country are often affected by misunderstandings on this score. For white middle-class Americans, for example, normal hesitation behavior involves 'fillers' at the point of hesitation ('uh', etc.). For many blacks, a normal pattern is to recycle to the beginning of the utterance (perhaps more than once). This black norm may be interpreted by whites not as a different norm but as a defect. Norms of interpretation implicate the belief system of a community.

(16) *Genres.* By genres are meant categories such as poem, myth, tale, proverb, riddle, curse, prayer, oration, lecture, commercial, form letter, editorial, etc. From one standpoint the analysis of speech into acts is an analysis of speech into instances of genres. The notion of genre implies the possibility of identifying formal characteristics traditionally recognized. It is heuristically important to proceed as though all speech has formal characteristics of some sort as manifestation of genres; and it may well be true (on genres, see Ben-Amos, 1969).

Genres often coincide with speech events, but must be treated as analytically independent of them. They may occur in (or as) different events. The sermon as a genre is typically identical with a certain place in a church service, but its properties may be invoked, for serious or humorous effect, in other situations.

Rules (relations) of speaking

In discovering the local system of speaking, certain familiar guidelines are, of course, to be used. One must determine the local taxonomy of terms as an essential, though never perfect, guide. A shift in any of the components of speaking may mark the presence of a rule (or structured relation), e.g. from normal tone of voice to whisper, from formal English to slang, correction, praise, embarrassment, withdrawal, and other evaluative responses to speech may indicate the violation or accomplishment of a rule. In general, one can think of any change in a component as a potential locus for application for a 'sociolinguistic' commutation test: What relevant contrast, if any, is present?

The heuristic set of components should be used negatively as well as positively, i.e. if a component seems irrelevant to certain acts or genres, that should be asserted, and the consequences of the assertion checked.

Many generalizations about rules of speaking will take the form of statements of relationship among components. It is not yet clear that there is any priority to be assigned to particular components in such statements. So far as one can tell at present, any component may be taken as starting point, and the others viewed in relation to it. When individual societies have been well analyzed, hierarchies of precedence among components will very likely appear and be found to differ from case to case. Such differences in hierarchy of components will then be an important part of the taxonomy of sociolinguistic systems. For one group, rules of speaking will be heavily bound to setting; for another primarily to participants; for a third, perhaps to topic.

Functions of speech

Functions themselves may be statable in terms of relations among components, such that poetic function, e.g. may require a certain relationship among choice of code, choice of topic, and message form in a given period or society.

It would be misleading, however, to think that the definition of functions can be reduced to or derived from other components. Such a thought would be a disabling residue of behavior ideology. Ultimately, the functions served in speech must be derived directly from the purposes and needs of human persons engaged in social action, and are what they are: talking to seduce, to stay awake, to avoid a war. The formal analysis of speaking is a means to the understanding of human purposes and needs, and their satisfaction; it is an indispensable means, but only a means, and not that understanding itself.

References

Bateson, G. (1963) Exchange of information about patterns of human behavior. In W. Field and W. Abbott (eds) *Information Storage and Neural Control.* Springfield: Charles C. Thomas.

Ben-Amos, D. (1969) Analytical categories and ethnic genres. *Genre* 2, 275–301.

Cherry, E. C. (1961) *On Human Communication. A Review, a Survey and a Criticism.* New York: Science Editions.

Chomsky, N. (1965) *Aspects of the Theory of Syntax.* Cambridge, MA: MIT Press.

Ferguson, C. A. and Gumperz, J. J. (eds) (1960) Linguistic diversity in South Asia: Studies in regional, social and functional variation. Research Center in Anthropology, Folklore, and Linguistics, Publication 13, *International Journal of American Linguistics* 26 (3), Part III. Bloomington: Indiana University Research Center.

Fock, N. (1965) Cultural aspects of the oho institution among the Waiwai. *Proceedings of the 36th International Congress of Americanists, 1964* (pp. 136–40). Copenhagen: Munksgaard.

Frake, C. O. (1972) Struck by speech. The Yakan concept of litigation. In J. J. Gumperz and D. Hymes (eds) *Directions in Sociolinguistics: The Ethnography of Communication* (pp. 109–29). New York: Holt Rinehart and Winston.

Hymes, D. (1968) Linguistic problems in defining the concept of the 'tribe'. In J. Helm (ed.) Essays on the problem of tribe. *Proceedings of the American Ethnological Society, 1967* (pp. 23–48). Seattle: University of Washington Press.

Lamb, S. (1964) The sememic approach to structural semantics. *American Anthropologist* 66 (3), 57–78.

Watson, O. M. and Graves, T. D. (1966) Quantitative research in proxemic behavior. *American Anthropologist* 68, 971–85.

3 Language as Social Semiotic

M. A. K. HALLIDAY

1 Introductory

Sociolinguistics sometimes appears to be a search for answers which have no questions. Let us therefore enumerate at this point some of the questions that do seem to need answering.

(1) How do people decode the highly condensed utterances of everyday speech, and how do they use social system for doing so?

(2) How do people reveal the ideational and interpersonal environment within which what they are saying is to be interpreted? In other words, how do they construct the social contexts in which meaning takes place?

(3) How do people relate the social context to the linguistic system? In other words, how do they deploy their meaning potential in actual semantic exchanges?

(4) How and why do people of different social class or other subcultural groups develop different dialectal varieties and different orientations towards meaning?

(5) How far are children of different social groups exposed to different verbal patterns of primary socialization, and how does this determine their reactions to secondary socialization especially in school?

(6) How and why do children learn the functional–semantic system of the adult language?

(7) How do children, through the ordinary everyday linguistic interaction of family and peer group, come to learn the basic patterns of the culture: the social structure, the systems of knowledge and of values, and the diverse elements of the social semiotic?

2 Elements of Sociosemiotic Theory of Language

There are certain general concepts which seem to be essential ingredients in a sociosemiotic theory of language. These are the text, the situation, the text variety or register, the code (in Bernstein's sense), the linguistic system (including the semantic system), and the social structure.

2.1 Text

Let us begin with the concept of *text,* the instances of linguistic interaction in which people actually engage: whatever is said, or written, in an operational context, as distinct from a citational context like that of words listed in a dictionary.

For some purposes it may suffice to conceive of a text as a kind of 'supersentence', a linguistic unit that is in principle greater in size than a sentence but of the same kind. It has long been clear, however, that discourse has its own structure that is not constituted out of sentences in combination; and in a sociolinguistic perspective it is more useful to think of text as *encoded* in sentences, not as composed of them. (Hence what Cicourel (1969) refers to as omissions by the speaker are not so much omissions as encodings, which the hearer can decode because he shares the principles of realization that provide the key to the code.) In other words, a text is a semantic unit; it is the basic unit of the semantic process.

At the same time, text represents choice. A text is 'what is meant', selected from the total set of options that constitute what can be meant. In other words, text can be defined as actualized meaning potential.

The meaning potential, which is the paradigmatic range of semantic choice that is present in the system, and to which the members of a culture have access in their language, can be characterized in two ways, corresponding to Malinowski's distinction between the 'context of situation' and the 'context of culture' (1923, 1935). Interpreted in the context of culture, it is the entire semantic system of the language. This is a fiction, something we cannot hope to describe. Interpreted in the context of situation, it is the particular semantic system, or set of subsystems, which is associated with a particular type of situation or social context. This too is a fiction; but it is something that may be more easily describable (cf. 2.5 below). In sociolinguistic terms the meaning potential can be represented as the range of options that is characteristic of a specific situation type.

2.2 Situation

The situation is the environment in which the text comes to life. This is a well-established concept in linguistics, going back at least to Wegener (1885). It played a key part in Malinowski's ethnography of language, under the name of 'context of situation'; Malinowski's notions were further developed and made explicit by Firth (1957: 182), who maintained that the context of situation was not to be interpreted in concrete terms as a sort of audiovisual record of the surrounding 'props' but was, rather, an abstract representation of the environment in terms of certain general categories having relevance to the text. The context of situation may be totally remote from what is going on round about during the act of speaking or of writing.

It will be necessary to represent the situation in still more abstract terms if it is to have a place in a general sociolinguistic theory; and to conceive of it not as situation but as situation *type,* in the sense of what Bernstein refers to as a 'social context'. This is, essentially, a semiotic structure. It is a constellation of meanings deriving from the semiotic system that constitutes the culture.

If it is true that a hearer, given the right information, can make sensible guesses about what the speaker is going to mean — and this seems a necessary assumption, seeing that communication does take place — then this 'right information' is what we mean by the social context. It consists of those general properties of the situation which collectively function as the determinants of text, in that they specify the semantic configurations that the speaker will typically fashion in contexts of the given type.

However, such information relates not only 'downward' to the text but also 'upward' to the linguistic system and to the social system. The 'situation' is a theoretical sociolinguistic construct; it is for this reason that we interpret a particular situation type, or social context, as a semiotic structure. The semiotic structure of a situation type can be represented as a complex of three dimensions: the ongoing social activity, the role relationships involved, and the symbolic or rhetorical channel. We refer to these respectively as 'field', 'tenor' and 'mode' (following Halliday, *et al.*, 1964, as modified by Spencer & Gregory, 1964; and cf. Gregory, 1967). The field is the social action in which the text is embedded; it includes the subject-matter, as one special manifestation. The tenor is the set of role relationships among the relevant participants; it includes levels of formality as one particular instance. The mode is the channel or wavelength selected, which is essentially the function that is assigned to language in the total structure of the situation; it includes the medium (spoken or written), which is explained as a functional variable.

Field, tenor and mode are not kinds of language use, nor are they simply components of the speech setting. They are a conceptual framework for representing the social context as the semiotic environment in which people exchange meanings. Given an adequate specification of the semiotic properties of the context in terms of field, tenor and mode we should be able to make sensible predications about the semantic properties of texts associated with it. To do this, however, requires an intermediary level — some concept of text variety, or register.

2.3 Register

The term 'register' was first used in this sense, that of text variety, by Reid (1956); the concept was taken up and developed by Jean Ure (Ure &

Ellis, 1972), and interpreted within Hill's (1958) 'institutional linguistic' framework by Halliday *et al.* (1964). The register is the semantic variety of which a text may be regarded as an instance.

Like other related concepts, such as 'speech variant' and '(sociolinguistic) code' (Ferguson, 1971, chs. 1 and 2; Gumperz, 1971, part I), register was originally conceived of in lexicogrammatical terms. Halliday *et al.* (1964) drew a primary distinction between two types of language variety: dialect, which they defined as variety according to the user, and register, which they defined as variety according to the use. The dialect is what a person speaks, determined by who he is; the register is what a person is speaking, determined by what he is doing at the time. This general distinction can be accepted, but, instead of characterizing a register largely by its lexicogrammatical properties, we shall suggest, as with text, a more abstract definition in semantic terms. (See Table 1.)

A register can be defined as the configuration of semantic resources that the member of a culture typically associates with a situation type. It is the meaning potential that is accessible in a given social context. Both the situation and the register associated with it can be described to varying degress of specificity; but the existence of registers is a fact of everyday experience — speakers have no difficulty in recognizing the semantic options and combinations of options that are 'at risk' under particular environmental conditions. Since these options are realized in the form of grammar and vocabulary, the register is recognizable as a particular selection of words and structures. But it is defined in terms of meanings, it is not an aggregate of conventional forms of expression superposed on some underlying content by 'social factors' of one kind or another. It is the selection of meanings that constitutes the variety to which a text belongs.

2.4 Code

'Code' is used here in Bernstein's sense; it is the principle of semiotic organization governing the choice of meanings by a speaker and their interpretation by a hearer. The code controls the semantic styles of the culture.

Codes are not varieties of language, as dialects and registers are. The codes are, so to speak, 'above' the linguistic system; they are types of social semiotic, or symbolic orders of meaning generated by the social system (cf. Hasan, 1973). The code is actualized in language through the register, since it determines the semantic orientation of speakers in particular social contexts; Bernstein's use of 'variant' (as in 'elaborated variant') refers to those characteristics of a register which derive from the form of the code. When the semantic systems of the language are activated by the situational determinants of text — the field, tenor and mode — this process is regulated by the codes.

Hence the codes transmit, or control the transmission of, the underlying patterns of a culture or subculture, acting through the socializing agencies of family, peer group and school. As a child comes to attend to and interpret meanings, in the context of situation and in the context of culture, at the same time he takes over the code. The culture is transmitted to him with the code acting as a filter, defining and making accessible the semiotic principles of his own subculture, so that as he learns the culture he also learns the grid, or subcultural angle on the social system. The child's linguistic experience reveals the culture to him through the code, and so transmits the code as part of the culture.

2.5 The linguistic system

Within the linguistic system, it is the *semantic system* that is of primary concern in a sociolinguistic context. The 'ideational', 'interpersonal' and 'textual' functional components of the semantic system are the modes of meaning that are present in every use of language in every social context. A text is a product of all three; it is a polyphonic composition in which different semantic melodies are interwoven, to be realized as integrated lexicogrammatical structures. Each functional component contributes a band of structure to the whole.

The ideational function represents the speaker's meaning potential as an observer. It is the content function of language, language as 'about something'. This is the component through which the language encodes the cultural experience, and the speaker encodes his own individual experience as a member of the culture. It expresses the phenomena of the environment: the things — creatures, objects, actions, events, qualities, states and relations — of the world and of our own consciousness, including the phenomenon of language itself; and also the 'metaphenomena', the things that are already encoded as facts and as reports. All these are part of the ideational meaning of language.

The interpersonal component represents the speaker's meaning potential as an intruder. It is the participatory function of language, language as doing something. This is the component through which the speaker intrudes himself into the context of situation, both expressing his own attitudes and judgements and seeking to influence the attitudes and behaviour of others. It expresses the role relationships associated with the situation, including those that are defined by language itself, relationships of questioner–respondent, informer–doubter and the like. These constitute the interpersonal meaning of language.

The textual component represents the speaker's text-forming potential; it is that which makdes language relevant. This is the component which provides the texture; that which makes the difference between language that is suspended *in vacuo* and language that is operational in a context of situation. It expresses the relation of the language to its environment, including both the verbal environment — what has been said or written before — and the nonverbal, situational environment. Hence the textual component has an enabling function with respect to the other two; it is only in combination with textual meanings that ideational and interpersonal meanings are actualized.

These components are reflected in the lexicogrammatical system in the form of discrete networks of options. In the clause, for example, the ideational function is represented by transitivity, the interpersonal by mood and modality, and the textual by a set of systems that have been referred to collectively as 'theme'. Each of these three sets of options is characterized by strong internal but weak external constraints: for example, any choice made in transitivity has a significant effect on other choices within the transitivity systems, but has very little effect on choices within the mood or theme systems. Hence the functional organization of meaning in language is built in to the core of the linguistic system, as the most general organizing principle of the lexicogrammatical stratum.

2.6 Social structure

Of the numerous ways in which the social structure is implicated in a sociolinguistic theory, there are three which stand out. In the first place, it defines and gives significance to the various types of social context in which meanings are exchanged. The different social groups and communication networks that determine what we have called the 'tenor' — the status and role relationships in the situation — are obviously products of the social structure; but so also in a more general sense are the types of social activity that constitute the 'field'. Even the 'mode', the rhetorical channel with its associated strategies, though more immediately reflected in linguistic patterns, has its origin in the social structure; it is the social structure that generates the semiotic tensions and the rhetorical styles and genres that express them (Barthes, 1970).

Secondly, through its embodiment in the types of role relationship within the family, the social structure determines the various familial patterns of communication; it regulates the meanings and meaning styles that are associated with given social contexts, including those contexts that are critical in the processes of cultural transmission. In this way the social structure determines, through the intermediary of language, the forms taken by the socialization of the child. (See Bernstein, 1971; 1975.)

Thirdly, and most problematically, the social structure enters in through the effects of social heirarchy, in the form of caste or class. This is obviously the background to social dialects, which are both a direct manifestation of

social hierarchy and also a symbolic expression of it, maintaining and rein-
forcing it in a variety of ways: for example, the association of dialect with
register — the fact that certain registers conventionally call for certain
dialectal modes — expresses the relation between social classes and the division of labour. In a more pervasive fashion, the social structure is present in
the forms of semiotic interaction, and becomes apparent through incon-
gruities and disturbances in the semantic system. Linguistics seems now to
have largely abandoned its fear of impurity and come to grips with what is
called 'fuzziness' in language; but this has been a logical rather than a
sociological concept, a departure from an ideal regularity rather than an
organic property of sociosemiotic systems. The 'fuzziness' of language is in
part an expression of the dynamics and the tensions of the social system. It
is not only the text (what people mean) but also the semantic system (what
they can mean) that embodies the ambiguity, antagonism, imperfection,
inequality and change that characterize the social system and social structure. This is not often systematically explored in linguistics, though it is
familiar enough to students of communication and of general semantics, and
to the public at large. It could probably be fruitfully approached through an
extension of Bernstein's theory of codes (cf. Douglas, 1972). The social
structure is not just an ornamental background to linguistic interaction, as it
has tended to become in sociolinguistic discussions. It is an essential element
in the evolution of semantic systems and semantic processes.

3 A Sociolinguistic View of Semantics

In this section we shall consider three aspects of sociological semantics:
the semantics of situation types, the relation of the situation to the semantic
system, and the sociosemantics of language development. The discussion
will be illustrated from a sociolinguistic study of early language development.

3.1 The semantics of situation types

A sociological semantics implies not so much a general description of the
semantic system of a language but rather a set of context-specific semantic
descriptions, each one characterizing the meaning potential that is typically
associated with a given situation type. In other words, a semantic description
is the description of a register.

The sociolinguistic notion of a situation type, or social context, is variable
in generality, and may be conceived of as covering a greater or smaller
number of possible instances. So the sets of semantic options that constitute
the meaning potential associated with a situation type may also be more or
less general. What characterizes this potential is its truly 'sociolinguistic'
nature. A semantics of this kind forms the interface between the social

system and the linguistic system; its elements realize social meanings and are realized in linguistic forms. Each option in the semantic network, in other words, is interpreted in the semiotics of the situation and is also represented in the lexicogrammar of the text. (Note that this is not equivalent to saying that the entire semiotic structure of the situation is represented in the semantic options, and hence also in the text, which is certainly not true.)

Figure 1 shows an outline semantic network for a particular situation type, one that falls within the general context of child play; more specifically, it is that of a small child manipulating vehicular toys in interaction with an adult. The network specifies some of the principal options, together with their possible realizations. The options derive from the general functional components of the semantic system (2.5 above) and are readily interpretable in terms of the grammar of English; we have not attempted to represent the meaning potential of the adult in the situation, but only that of the child. The networks relate, in turn, to a general description of English, modified to take account of the child's stage of development.

3.2 Structure of the situation, and its relation to the semantic system

The semiotic structure of a situation type can be represented in terms of the three general concepts of field, tenor and mode (cf. 2.2 above). The 'child play' situation type that was specified by the semantic networks in Figure 1 might be characterized, by reference to these concepts, in something like the following manner:

Field
Child at play: manipulating movable objects (wheeled vehicles) with related fixtures, assisted by adult; concurrently associating (i) similar past events, (ii) similar absent objects; also evaluating objects in terms of each other and of processes.

Tenor
Small child and parent interacting: child determining course of action, (i) announcing own intentions, (ii) controlling actions of parent; concurrently sharing and seeking corroboration of own experience with parent.

Mode
Spoken, alternately monologue and dialogue, task-oriented; pragmatic, (i) referring to processes and objects of situation, (ii) relating to and furthering child's own actions, (iii) demanding other objects; interposed with narrative and exploratory elements.

Below is a specimen of a text having these semiotic properties. It is taken from a study of the language development of one subject. Nigel, from nine months to three and a half years; the passage selected is from age 1;11.

(Note: ` = falling tone; ´ = rising tone; ˘ = fall–rise tone; tonic nucleus falls on syllables having tone marks; tone group boundaries within an utterance shown by . . . For analysis of intonation, cf. Halliday, 1967a.)

Nigel: *[small wooden train in hand, approaching track laid along a plank sloping from chair to floor]* Here the ràilway line . . . but it not for the tràin to go on that.

Father: Isn't it?

Nigel: Yès tiś. . . . I wonder the train will carry the lòrry *[puts train on lorry (sic)]*.

Father: I wonder.

Nigel: Oh yes it wíll. . . . I don't wànt to send the train on this flóor . . . you want to send the train on the ràilway line *[runs it up plank onto chair]* . . . but it doesn't go very well on the chǎir. . . . *[makes train go round in circles]* The train all round and ròund . . . it going all round and ròund . . . *[tries to reach other train]* have that tráin . . . have the blue tráin ('give it to me') *[Father does so]* . . . send the blue train down the ráilway line . . . *[plank falls of chair]* lèt me put the railway line on the cháir ('you put the railway line on the chair!') *[Father does so]* . . . *[looking at blue train]* Daddy put sèllotape on it ('previously') . . . there a very fierce lìon in the train . . . Daddy go and see if the lion still thére . . . Have your éngine ('give me my engine').

Father: Which engine? The little black engine?

Nigel: Yés . . . Daddy go and find it fór you . . . Daddy go and find the black éngine for you.

Nigel's linguistic system at this stage is in a state of transition, as he approximates more and more closely to the adult language, and it is unstable at various points. He is well on the way to the adult system of mood, but has not quite got there — he has not quite grasped the principle that language can be used as a *substitute* for shared experience, to impart information not previously known to the hearer; and therefore he has not yet learnt the general meaning of the yes/no question. He has a system of person, but alternates between *I/me* and *you* as the expression of the first person 'I'. He has a transitivity system, but confuses the roles of agent (actor) and medium (goal) in a non-middle (two-participant) process. It is worth pointing out perhaps that adult linguistic systems are themselves unstable at many points — a good example being transitivity in English, which is in a state of considerable flux; what the child is approximating to, therefore, is not something fixed and harmonious but something shifting, fluid and full of indeterminacies.

What does emerge from a consideration of Nigel's discourse is how, through the internal organization of the linguistic system, situational features determine text. It we describe the semiotic structure of the situation in terms of features of field, tenor and mode, and consider how these various features relate to the systems making up the semantic networks shown in Figure 1, we arrive at something like the picture presented in Table 1.

Table 1 Determination of semantic features by elements of semiotic structures of situation (text in 3.2)

	Situational	Semantic	
Field	manipulation of objects assistance of adult movable objects and fixtures movability of objects & their relation to fixtures recall of similar events evaluation	process type and participant structure benefactive type of relevant object type of location and movement past time modulation	**Ideational**
Tenor	interaction with parent determination of course of action enunciation of intention control of action sharing of experience seeking corroboration of experience	person mood and polarity demand, 'I want to' demand, 'I want you to' statement/question, monologue statement/question, dialogue	**Interpersonal**

Mode	dialogue
	reference to situation
	textual cohesion: objects
	textual cohesion: processes
	furthering child's actions
	
	orientation to task
	spoken mode
		ellipsis (question-answer)
		exophoric reference
		anaphoric reference
		conjunction
		theme (in conjunction with transitivity
		   and mood; typically, parent or child
		   in demands, child in two-participant
		   statements, object in one-participant
		   statements)
		lexical collocation and repetition
		information structure
			Textual

There is thus a systematic correspondence between the semiotic structure of the situation type and the functional organization of the semantic system. Each of the main areas of meaning potential tends to be determined or activated by one particular aspect of the situation:

Semantic components		*Situational elements*
ideational	systems activated by features of	field
interpersonal	"	tenor
textual	"	mode

Figure 1 Semantic systems and their realizations, as represented in Nigel's speech (see Section 3.2 for text)

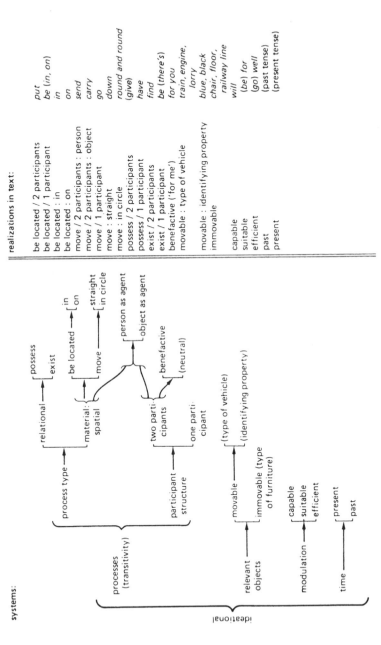

(a) Ideational systems and their realizations

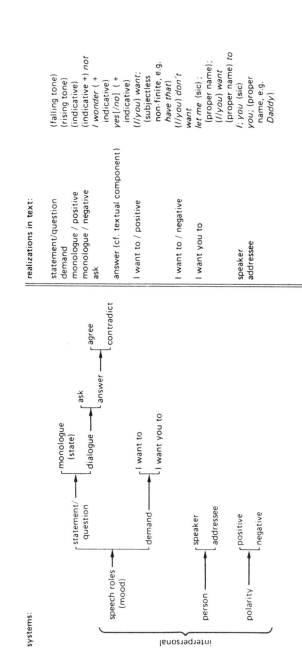

(b) Interpersonal systems and their realizations

realizations in text:

person theme : child	I/you (initial); (subjectless non-finite)
person theme : parent	(proper name initial)
object theme	(object name initial)
exophoric : demonstrative	this, that, the, here
exophoric : possessive	your ('my')
anaphoric	it, that, the
adversative	but; (fall-rise tone)
ellipsis : 'yes/no'	yes [no]
ellipsis : modal	(modal element, e.g. it is, it will)
lexical : repetition of items	(e.g. train ... train)
lexical : collocations	(e.g. chair ... floor; train ... railway line
information structure : text units	organization in tone groups)
information structure : given—new	(location of tonic nucleus)

systems:

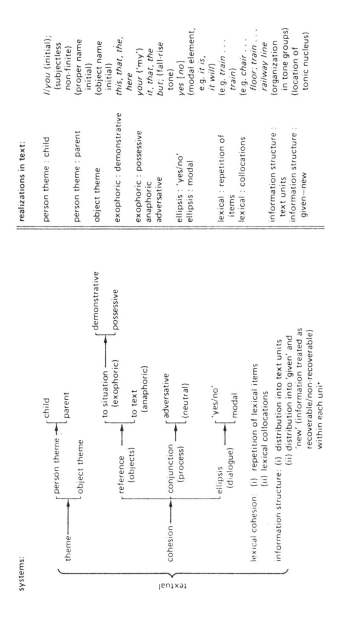

theme — person theme — child / parent; object theme

cohesion — reference (objects) — to situation (exophoric) — demonstrative / possessive; to text (anaphoric)
— conjunction (process) — adversative / (neutral)
— ellipsis (dialogue) — 'yes/no' / modal

lexical cohesion: (i) repetition of lexical items (ii) lexical collocations

information structure: (i) distribution into text units (ii) distribution into 'given' and 'new' (information treated as recoverable/non-recoverable) within each unit

textual

(c) Textual systems and their realizations

In other words, the type of symbolic activity (field) tends to determine the range of meaning as content, language in the observer function (ideational); the role relationships (tenor) tend to determine the range of meaning as participation, language in the intruder function (interpersonal); and the rhetorical channel (mode) tends to determine the range of meaning as texture, language in its relevance to the environment (textual). There are of course many indeterminate areas — though there is often some system even in the indeterminacy: for example, the child's evaluation of objects lies on the borderline of 'field' and 'tenor', and the system of 'modulation' likewise lies on the borderline of the ideational and interpersonal components of language (Halliday, 1969). But there is an overall pattern. This is not just a coincidence: presumably the semantic system evolved as symbolic interaction among people in social contexts, so we should expect the semiotic structure of these contexts to be embodied in its internal organization. By taking account of this we get an insight into the form of relationship among the three concepts of situation, text and semantic system. The semiotic features of the situation activate corresponding portions of the semantic system, in this way determining the register, the configuration of potential meanings that is typically associated with this situation type, and becomes actualized in the text that is engendered by it.

3.3 Sociosemantics of language development

A child learning his mother tongue is learning how to mean; he is building up a meaning potential in respect of a limited number of social functions. These functions constitute the semiotic environment of a very small child, and may be thought of as universals of human culture.

The meanings the child can express at this stage derive very directly from the social functions. For example, one of the functions served by the child's 'proto-language' is the regulatory function, that of controlling the behaviour of other people; and in this function he is likely to develop meanings such as 'do that some more' (continue or repeat what you've just been doing), and 'don't do that'. How does he get from these to the complex and functionally remote meanings of the adult semantic system?

These language-engendering functions, or 'proto-contexts', are simultaneously the origin both of the social context and of the semantic system. The child develops his ability to mean by a gradual process of generalization and abstraction, which in the case of Nigel appeared to go somewhat along the following lines. Out of six functions of his proto-language (instrumental, regulatory, interactional, personal, heuristic and imaginative), he derived a simple but highly general distinction between language as a means of doing and language as a means of knowing — with the latter, at this stage, interpretable functionally as 'learning'. As he moved into the phase of transition into the adult system, at around 18 months, he assigned every utterance to one or other of these generalized functional categories, encoding the distinction by means of intonation: all 'learning' utterances were on a falling tone, and all 'doing' utterances on a rising tone. As forms of interaction, the latter required a response (increasingly, as time went on, a *verbal* response) while the former did not.

From the moment when this semantic principle was adopted, however, it ceased to satisfy, since Nigel already needed a semiotic system which would enable him to do both these things at once — to use language in both the learning mode and the doing mode within a single utterance. Without this ability he could not engage in true dialogue; the system could not develop a dynamic for adoption and assignment of semiotic roles in verbal interaction. At this point, two steps were required, or really one complex step, for effectively completing the transition to the adult system. One was a further abstraction of the basic functional opposition, such that it came to be incorporated into his semantic system, as the two components of 'ideational' and 'interpersonal'; in the most general terms, the former developed from the 'learning' function, the latter from the 'doing' function. The other step was the introduction of a lexicogrammar, or syntax, making it possible for these two modes of meaning to be expressed simultaneously in the form of integrated lexicogrammatical structures.

The term 'sociosemantics of language development' refers to this process, whereby the original social functions of the infant's proto-language are reinterpreted, first as 'macro-functions', and then as 'meta-functions', functional components in the organization of the semantic system. These components, as remarked earlier (2.5), are clearly seen in the adult language; the options show a high degree of mutual constraint within one component but a very low degree of constraint between components. At the same time, looked at from another point of view, what the child has done is finally to dissociate the concept of 'function' from that of 'use'; the functions evolve into components of the semantic system, and the uses into what we are calling social contexts or situation types. For a detailed treatment of this topic see Halliday (1975a).

4 Towards a General Sociolinguistic Theory

In this final section we shall try to suggest how the main components of the sociolinguistic universe relate to one another, the assumption being that this network of relations is the cornerstone of a general sociolinguistic theory.

4.1 Meaning and text

The *text* is the linguistic form of social interaction. It is a continuous progression of meanings, coming both simultaneously and in succession. The meanings are the selections made by the speaker from the options that constitute the *meaning potential*; text is the actualization of this meaning potential, the process of semantic choice.

The selections in meaning derive from diferent functional origins, and are mapped onto one another in the course of their realization as lexicogrammatical structure. In our folk linguistic terminology, the 'meaning' is represented as 'wording' — which in turn is expressed as 'sound' ('pronouncing') or as 'spelling'. The folk linguistic, incidentally, shows our awareness of the tri-stratal nature of language.

4.2 Text and situation

A text is embedded in a context of *situation*. The context of situation of any text is an instance of a generalized social context or situation type. The situation type is not an inventory of ongoing sights and sounds but a semiotic structure; it is the ecological matrix that is constitutive of the text.

Certain types of situation have in their semiotic structure some element which makes them central to the processes of cultural transmission; these are Bernstein's 'critical socializing contexts'. Examples are those having a regulative component (where a parent is regulating the child's behaviour), or an instructional component (where the child is being explicitly taught).

4.3 Situation as semiotic structure

The semiotic structure of the situation is formed out of the three socio-semiotic variables of field, tenor and mode. These represent in systematic form the type of activity in which the text has significant function (field), the status and role relationships involved (tenor) and the symbolic mode and rhetorical channels that are adopted (mode). The field, tenor and mode act collectively as determinants of the text through their specification of the register (4.5 below); at the same time they are systematically associated with the linguistic system through the functional components of the semantics (4.4).

4.4 Situation and semantic system

The semiotic components of the situation (field, tenor and mode) are systematically related to the functional components of the semantics (ideational, interpersonal and textual); *field* to the *ideational* component, representing the 'content' function of language, the speaker as observer; *tenor* to the *interpersonal* component, representing the 'participation' function of language, the speaker as intruder; and *mode* to the *textual* component, representing the 'relevance' function of language, without which the other two do not become actualized. There is a tendency, in other words, for the field of social action to be encoded linguistically in the form of ideational meanings, the role relationships in the form of interpersonal meanings, and the symbolic mode in the form of textual meanings.

4.5 Situation, semantic system and register

The semiotic structure of a given situation type, its particular pattern of field, tenor and mode, can be thought of as resonating in the semantic system and so activating particular networks of semantic options, typically options from within the corresponding semantic components (4.4). This process specifies a range of meaning potential, or *register*; the semantic configuration that is typically associated with the situation type in question.

4.6 Register and code

The specification of the register by the social context is in turn controlled and modified by the *code*: the semiotic style, or 'sociolinguistic coding orientation' in Bernstein's term, that represents the particular subcultural angle on the social system. This angle of vision is a function of the social structure. It reflects, in our society, the pattern of social hierarchy, and the resulting tensions between an egalitarian ideology and a hierarchical reality. The code is transmitted initially through the agency of family types and family role systems, and subsequently reinforced in the various peer groups of children, adolescents and adults.

4.7 Language and the social system

The foregoing synthesis presupposes an interpretation of the social system as a *social semiotic*: a system of meanings that constitutes the 'reality' of the culture. This is the higher-level system to which language is related: the semantic system of language is a realization of the social semiotic. There are many other forms of its symbolic realization besides language; but language is unique in having its own semantic stratum.

This takes us back to the 'meaning potential' of 4.1. The meaning potential of language, which is realized in the lexicogrammatical system, itself realizes meanings of a higher order; not only the semiotic of the particular social context, its organization as field, tenor and mode, but also that of the total set of social contexts that constitutes the social system. In this respect language is unique among the modes of expression of social meanings: it operates on both levels, having meaning both in general and in particular at the same time. This property arises out of the functional organization of the semantic system, whereby the meaning potential associated with a particular social context is derived from corresponding sets of generalized options in the semantic system.

4.8 Language and the child

A child begins by creating a proto-language of his own, a meaning potential in respect of each of the social functions that constitute his developmental semiotic. In the course of maturation and socialization he comes to take over the adult language. The text-in-situation by which he is surrounded is filtered through his own functional-semantic grid, so that he processes just as much of it as can be interpreted in terms of his own meaning potential at the time.

As a strategy for entering the adult system he generalizes from his initial set of functions an opposition between language as doing and language as learning. This is the developmental origin of the interpersonal and ideational components in the semantic system of the adult language. The concept of function is now abstracted from that of use, and has become the basic principle of the linguistic organization of meaning.

4.9 The child and the culture

As a child learns language, he also learns *through* language. He interprets text not only as being specifically relevant to the context of situation but also as being generally relevant to the context of culture. It is the linguistic system that enables him to do this; since the sets of semantic options which are characteristic of the situation (the register) derive from generalized functional components of the semantic system, they also at the same time realize the higher order meanings that constitute the culture, and so the child's focus moves easily between microsemiotic and macrosemiotic environment.

So when Nigel's mother said to him 'Leave that stick outside; stop teasing the cat; and go and wash your hands. It's time for tea', he could not only understand the instructions but could also derive from them information about the social system: about the boundaries dividing social space, and 'what goes where'; about the continuity between the human and the animal world; about the regularity of cultural events; and more besides. He does not, of course, learn all this from single instances, but from the countless sociosemiotic events of this kind that make up the life of social man. And as a corollary to this, he comes to rely heavily on the social system for the decoding of the meanings that are embodied in such day-to-day encounters.

In one sense a child's learning of this mother tongue is a process of progressively freeing himself from the constraints of the immediate context — or, better, of progressively redefining the context and the place of language within it — so that he is able to learn through language, and interpret an exchange of meanings in relation to the culture as a whole. Language is not the only form of the realization of social meanings, but it is the only form of it that has this complex property: to mean, linguistically, is at once both to reflect and to act — and to do both these things both in particular and in general at the same time. So it is first and foremost through language that the culture is transmitted to the child, in the course of every day interaction in the key socializing agencies of family, peer group and school. This process, like other semiotic processes, is controlled and regulated by the code; and so, in the course of it, the child himself also takes over the coding orientation, the subcultural semiotic bias is a feature of all social structures except those of a (possibly non-existent) homogeneous type, and certainly of all complex societies of a pluralistic and hierarchical kind.

4.10 Summary

Social interaction typically takes a linguistic form, which we call *text*. A text is the product of infinitely many simultaneous and successive choices in meaning, and is realized as lexicogrammatical structure, or 'wording'. The environment of the text is the context of situation, which is an instance of a social context, or *situation type*. The situation type is a semiotic construct which is structured in terms of *field, tenor* and *mode*: the text-generating activity, the role relationships of the participants, and the rhetorical modes they are adopting. These situational variables are related respectively to the *ideational, interpersonal* and *textual* components of the *semantic system*: meaning as content (the observer function of language), meaning as participation (the intruder function) and meaning as texture (the relevance function). They are related in the sense that each of the situational features typically calls forth a network of options from the corresponding semantic component; in this way the semiotic properties of a particular situation type, its structure in terms of field, tenor and mode, determine the semantic configuration or *register* — the meaning potential that is characteristic of the situation type in question, and is realized as what is known as a 'speech variant'. This process is regulated by the *code*, the semiotic grid or principles of the organization of social meaning that represent the particular subcultural angle on the social system. The subcultural variation is in its turn a product of the *social structure*, typically the social hierarchy acting through the distribution of family types having different familial role systems. A child, coming into the picture, interprets text-in-situation in terms of his generalized functional categories of *learning (mathetic)* and *doing (pragmatic)*; from here by a further process of abstraction he constructs the functionally organized semantic system of the adult language. He has now gained access to the social semiotic; this is the context in which he himself will learn to mean, and in which all his subsequent meaning will take place.

I have been attempting here to interrelate the various components of the sociolinguistic universe, with special reference to the place of language within it. It is for this reason that I have adopted the mode of interpretation of the social system as a semiotic, and stressed the systematic aspects of it: the concept of system itself, and the concept of function within a system. It is all the more important, in this context, to avoid any suggestion of an idealized social functionalism, and to insist that the social system is not something static, regular and harmonious, nor are its elements held poised in some perfect pattern of functional relationships.

A 'sociosemiotic' perspective implies an interpretation of the shifts, the irregularities, the disharmonies and the tensions that characterize human interaction and social processes. It attempts to explain the semiotic of the social structure, in its aspects both of persistence and of change, including the semantics of social class, of the power system, of heirarchy and of social conflict. It attempts also to explain the linguistic processes whereby the members construct the social semiotic, whereby social reality is shaped, constrained and modified — processes which far from tending towards an ideal construction, admit and even institutionalize myopia, prejudice and misunderstanding (Berger & Luckmann, 1966, ch. 3).

The components of the sociolinguistic universe themselves provide the sources and conditions of disorder and of change. These may be seen in the text, in the situation, and in the semantic system, as well as in the dynamics of cultural transmission and social learning. All the lines of determination are *ipso facto* also lines of tension, not only through indeterminacy in the transmission but also through feedback. The meaning of the text, for example, is fed back into the situation, and becomes part of it, changing it in the process; it is also fed back, through the register, into the semantic system, which it likewise affects and modifies. The code, the form in which we conceptualize the injection of the social structure into the semantic process, is itself a two-way relation, embodying feedback from the semantic configurations of social interaction into the role relationships of the family and other social groups. The social learning processes of a child, whether those of learning the language or of learning the culture, are among the most permeable surfaces of the whole system, as one soon becomes aware in listening to the language of young children's peer groups — a type of semiotic context which has hardly begun to be seriously studied. In the light of the role of language in social processes, a sociolinguistic perspective does not readily accommodate strong boundaries. The 'sociolinguistic order' is neither an ideal order nor a reality that has no order at all; it is a human artefact having some of the properties of both.

References

Barthes, R. (1970) L'ancienne rhétorique. *Communications* 16.

Berger, P. L. and Luckmann, T. (1966) *The Social Construction of Reality: A Treatise in the Sociology of Knowledge*. New York: Doubleday.

Bernstein, B. (1971) *Class, Codes and Control 1: Theoretical Studies towards a Sociology of Language*. London: Routledge & Kegan Paul.

— (1975) *Class, Codes and Control 3: Towards a Theory of Educational Transmissions*. London: Routledge & Kegan Paul.

Cicourel, A. V. (1969) Generative semantics and the structure of social interaction. In *International Days of Sociolinguistics*.

Douglas, M. (1972) Speech, class and Basil Bernstein. London: *The Listener* 2241.

Ferguson, C. A. (1971) *Language Structure and Language Use: Essays Selected and Introduced by Anwar S. Dil*. Stanford, California: Stanford University Press.

Firth, J. R. (1957) *Papers in Linguistics (1934–1951)*. London: Oxford University Press.

Gregory, M. (1967) Aspects of varieties differentiation. *Journal of Linguistics* 3.

Gumperz, J. (1971) *Language in Social Groups: Essays Selected and Introduced by Anwar S. Dil*. Stanford: University Press.

Halliday, M. A. K., McIntosh, A. and Strevens, P. (1964) *The Linguistic Sciences and Language Teaching*. Longman Linguistics Library, London: Longman.

Halliday, M. A. K. (1967) *Grammar, Society and the Noun*. London: H. K. Lewis (for University College London).

— (1969) Functional diversity in language, as seen from a consideration of modality and mood in English. *Foundations of Language* 6.

— (1975) *Learning How to Mean: Exploration in the Development of Language*. (Explorations in Language Study). London: Edward Arnold.

Hasan, R. (1973) Code, register and social dialect. In B. Bernstein (ed.) *Class Codes and Control 2: Applied Studies towards a Sociology of Language*. London: Routledge & Kegan Paul.

Hill, T. (1958) Institutional Linguistics. *Orbis* 7.

Malinowski, B. (1923) The problem of meaning in primitive languages. Supplement 1 to C. K. Ogden and I. A. Richards *The Meaning of Meaning*. International Library of Psychology, Philosophy and Scientific Method, London: Kegan Paul.

— (1935) *Coral Gardens and their Magic, 2*. London: Allen and Unwin.

Reid, T. B. W. (1956) Linguistics, structuralism, philology. *Archivum Linguisticum* 8.

Spencer, J. and Gregory, M. J. (1964) An approach to the study of style. In Enkvist, *et al. Linguistics and Style* (Language and Language Learning 6). London: Oxford University Press.

Ure, J. and Ellis, J. (1974) El registro en la lingüistica descriptiva y en la sociologia lingüistica. *La sociolingüistica actual: algunos de sus problemas, planteamientos y soluciones*. Oscar Uribe-Villegas (ed.). Mexico: Universidad Nacional Autonoma de Mexico, 115–64. English version: Register in descriptive linguistics and linguistic sociology. *Issues in sociolinguistics*. Oscar Uribe-Villegas (ed.). The Hague: Mouton.

Wegener, P. (1885) *Untersuchungen über die Grundfragen der Sprachlebens*. Halle.

4 Language and Ideology[1]

V. N. VOLOSINOV

The Ideological Sign and Consciousness

Everything ideological possesses *meaning*: it represents, depicts, or stands for something lying outside itself. In other words, it is a *sign. Without signs, there is no ideology.* The ideological chain stretches from individual consciousness to individual consciousness, connecting them together. Signs emerge, after all, only in the process of interaction between one individual consciousness and another. And the individual consciousness itself is filled with signs. Consciousness becomes consciousness only once it has been filled with ideological (semiotic) content, consequently, only in the process of social interaction.

The only possible objective definition of consciousness is a sociological one. Consciousness cannot be derived directly from nature, as has been and still is being attempted by naive mechanistic materialism and contemporary objective psychology (of the biological, behavioristic, and reflexological varieties). Ideology cannot be derived from consciousness, as is the practice of idealism and psychologistic positivism. Consciousness takes shape and being in the material of signs created by an organized group in the process of its social intercourse. The individual consciousness is nurtured on signs; it derives its growth from them; it reflects their logic and laws. The logic of consciousness is the logic of ideological communication, of the semiotic interaction of a social group. If we deprive consciousness of its semiotic, ideological content, it would have absolutely nothing left. Consciousness can harbor only in the image, the word, the meaningful gesture, and so forth. Outside such material, there remains the sheer physiological act unilluminated by consciousness, i.e. without having light shed on it, without having meaning given to it, by signs.

All that has been said above leads to the following methodological conclusion: *the study of ideologies does not depend on psychology to any extent and need not be grounded in it.* It is rather the reverse: *objective psychology must be grounded in the study of ideologies.* The reality of ideological phenomena is the objective reality of social signs. The laws of this reality are the laws of semiotic communication and are directly determined by the total aggregate of social and economic laws. Ideological reality is the immediate superstructure over the economic basis. Individual consciousness is not the architect of the ideological superstructure, but only a tenant lodging in the social edifice of ideological signs.

With our preliminary argument disengaging ideological phenomena and their regulatedness from individual consciousness, we tie them in all the more firmly with conditions and forms of social communication. The reality of the sign is wholly a matter determined by that communication. After all, the existence of the sign is nothing but the materialization of that communication. Such is the nature of all ideological signs.

But nowhere does this semiotic quality and the continuous, comprehensive role of social communication as conditioning factor appear so clearly and fully expressed as in language. *The word is the ideological phenomenon par excellence.*

The entire reality of the word is wholly absorbed in its function of being a sign. A word contains nothing that is indifferent to this function, nothing that would not have been engendered by it. A word is the purest and most sensitive medium of social intercourse.

This indicatory, representative power of the word as an ideological phenomenon and the exceptional distinctiveness of its semiotic structure would already furnish reason enough for advancing the word to a prime position in the study of ideologies. It is precisely in the material of the word that the basic, general-ideological forms of semiotic communication could best be revealed.

One other property belongs to the word that is of the highest order of importance and is what makes the word the primary medium of the individual consciousness. Although the reality of the word, as is true of any sign, resides between individuals, a word, at the same time, is produced by the individual organism's own means without recourse to any equipment or any other kind of extracorporeal material. This has determined the role of word as *the semiotic material of inner life — of consciousness* (inner speech). Indeed, the consciousness could have developed only by having at its disposal material that was pliable and expressible by bodily means. And the word was exactly that kind of material. The word is available as the sign for, so to speak, inner employment: it can function as a sign in a state short of outward expression. For this reason, the problem of individual consciousness as the *inner word* (as an *inner sign* in general) becomes one of the most vital problems in philosophy of language.

It is clear, from the very start, that this problem cannot be properly approached by resorting to the usual concept of word and language as worked out in nonsociological linguistics and philosophy of language. What is needed is profound and acute analysis of the word as social sign before its function as the medium of consciousness can be understood.

It is owing to this exclusive role of the word as the medium of consciousness that *the word functions as an essential ingredient accompanying all ideological creativity whatsoever.* The word accompanies and comments on each and every ideological act. The processes of understanding any ideological phenomenon at all (be it a picture, a piece of music, a ritual, or an act of human conduct) cannot operate without the participation of inner speech. All manifestations of ideological creativity — all other nonverbal signs — are bathed by, suspended in, and cannot be entirely segregated or divorced from the element of speech.

This does not mean, of course, that the word may supplant any other ideological sign. None of the fundamental, specific ideological signs is replaceable wholly by words. It is ultimately impossible to convey a musical composition or pictorial image adequately in words. Words cannot wholly substitute for a religious ritual; nor is there any really adequate verbal substitute for even the simplest gesture in human behavior. To deny this would lead to the most banal rationalism and simplisticism. Nonetheless, at the very same time, every single one of these ideological signs, though not supplantable by words, has support in and is accompanied by words, just as is the case with singing and its musical accompaniment.

No cultural sign, once taken in and given meaning, remains in isolation: it becomes part of the *unity of the verbally constituted consciousness.* It is in the capacity of the consciousness to find verbal access to it. Thus, as it were, spreading ripples of verbal responses and resonances form around each and every ideological sign. Every *ideological refraction of existence in process of generation,* no matter what the nature of its significant material, *is accompanied by ideological refraction in word* as an obligatory concomitant phenomenon. Word is present in each and every act of understanding and in each and every act of interpretation.

The Social Ubiquity of the Word

The problem of the interrelationship of the basis and superstructures — a problem of exceptional complexity, requiring enormous amounts of preliminary data for its productive treatment — can be elucidated to a significant degree through the material of the word.

Looked at from the angle of our concerns, the essence of this problem comes down to *how* actual existence (the basis) determines sign and *how* sign reflects and refracts existence in its process of generation.

The properties of the word as an ideological sign are what make the word the most suitable material for viewing the whole of this problem in basic terms. What is important about the word in this regard is not so much its sign purity as its *social ubiquity*. The word is implicated in literally each and every act or contact between people — in collaboration on the job, in ideological exchanges, in the chance contacts of ordinary life, in political relationships, and so on. Countless ideological threads running through all areas of social intercourse register effect in the word. It stands to reason, then, that the word is the most sensitive *index of social changes,* and what is more, of changes still in the process of growth, still without definitive shape and not as yet accommodated into already regularized and fully defined ideological systems. The word is the medium in which occur the slow quantitative accretions of those changes which have not yet achieved the status of a new ideological quality, not yet produced a new and fully-fledged ideological form. The word has the capacity to register all the transitory, delicate, momentary phases of social change.

Production relations and the sociopolitical order shaped by those relations determine the full range of verbal contacts between people, all the forms and means of their verbal communication — at work, in political life, in ideological creativity. In turn, from the conditions, forms, and types of verbal communication derive not only the forms but also the themes of speech performances.

Social psychology is first and foremost an atmosphere made up of multifarious *speech performances* that engulf and wash over all persistent forms and kinds of ideological creativity: unofficial discussions, exchanges of opinion at the theater or a concert or at various types of social gatherings, purely chance exchanges of words, one's manner of verbal reaction to happenings in one's life and daily existence, one's inner-word manner of identifying oneself and identifying one's position in society, and so on. Social psychology exists primarily in a wide variety of forms of the 'utterance', of little *speech genres* of internal and external kinds — things left completely unstudied to the present day. All these speech performances, are, of course, joined with other types of semiotic manifestation and interchange — with miming, gesturing, acting out, and the like.

All these forms of speech interchange operate in extremely close connection with the conditions of the social situation in which they occur and exhibit an extraordinary sensitivity to all fluctuations in the social atmosphere. And it is here, in the inner workings of this verbally materialized social psychology, that the barely noticeable shifts and changes that will later find expression in fully fledged ideological products accumulate.

From what has been said, it follows that social psychology must be studied from two different viewpoints: first, from the viewpoint of content, i.e. the themes pertinent to it at this or that moment in time; and second, from the viewpoint of the forms and types of verbal communication in which the themes in question are implemented (i.e. discussed, expressed, questioned, pondered over, etc.).

Each period and each social group has had and has its own repertoire of speech forms for ideological communication in human behavior. Each set of cognate forms, i.e. each behavioral speech genre, has its own corresponding set of themes.

An interlocking organic unity joins the form of communication (for example, on-the-job communication of the strictly technical kind), the form of the utterance (the concise, businesslike statement) and its theme. Therefore, *classification of the forms of utterance must rely upon classification of the forms of verbal communication.* The latter are entirely determined by production relations and the sociopolitical order. Were we to apply a more detailed analysis, we would see what enormous significance belongs to *the hierarchical factor* in the processes of verbal interchange and what a powerful influence is exerted on forms of utterance by the hierarchical organization of communication. Language etiquette, speech tact, and other forms of adjusting an utterance to the hierarchical organization of society have tremendous importance in the process of devising the basic behavioral genres.

Every sign, as we know, is a construct between socially organized persons in the process of their interaction. Therefore, *the forms of signs are conditioned above all by the social organization of the participants involved and also by the immediate conditions of their interaction.* When these forms change, so does sign. And it should be one of the tasks of the study of ideologies to trace this social life of the verbal sign. Only so approached can the *problem of the relationship between sign and existence* find its concrete expression; only then will the process of the causal shaping of the sign by existence stand out as a process of genuine existence-to-sign transit, of genuine dialectical refraction of existence in the sign.

To accomplish this task certain basic, methodological prerequisites must be respected:

(1) *Ideology may not be divorced from the material reality of sign* (i.e. by locating it in the 'consciousness' or other vague and elusive regions).

(2) *The sign may not be divorced from the concrete forms of social intercourse* (seeing that the sign is part of organized social intercourse and cannot exist, as such, outside it, reverting to a mere physical artifact).

(3) *Communication and the forms of communication may not be divorced from the material basis.*

The Evaluative Accentuation of the Sign

Every ideological sign — the verbal sign included — in coming about through the process of social intercourse, is defined by the *social purview* of the given time period and the given social group. So far, we have been speaking about the form of the sign as shaped by the forms of social interaction. Now we shall deal with its other aspect — the *content* of the sign and the evaluative accentuation that accompanies all content.

Every stage in the development of a society has its own special and restricted circle of items which alone have access to that society's attention and which are endowed with evaluative accentuation by that attention. Only items within that circle will achieve sign formation and become objects in semiotic communication. What determines this circle of items endowed with value accents?

In order for any item, from whatever domain of reality it may come, to enter the social purview of the group and elicit ideological semiotic reaction, it must be associated with the vital socioeconomic prerequisites of the particular group's existence; it must somehow, even if only obliquely, make contact with the bases of the group's material life.

Individual choice under these circumstances, of course, can have no meaning at all. The sign is a creation between individuals, a creation within a social milieu. Therefore the item in question must first acquire interindividual significance, and only then can it become an object for sign formation. In other words, *only that which has acquired social value can enter the world of ideology, take shape, and establish itself there.*

For this reason, all ideological accents, despite their being produced by the individual voice (as in the case of word) or, in any event, by the individual organism — all ideological accents are social accents, ones with claim to *social recognition* and, only thanks to that recognition, are made outward use of in ideological material.

Let us agree to call the entity which becomes the object of a sign the *theme* of the sign. Each fully fledged sign has its theme. And so, every verbal performance has its theme.

An ideological theme is always socially accentuated. Of course, all the social accents of ideological themes make their way also into the individual consciousness (which, as we know, is ideological through and through) and there take on the semblance of individual accents, since the individual consciousness assimilates them as its own. However, the source of these accents is not the individual consciousness. Accent, as such, is inter-individual. The animal cry, the pure response to pain in the organism, is bereft of accent; it is a purely natural phenomenon. For such a cry, the social atmosphere is irrelevant, and therefore it does not contain even the germ of sign formation.

The theme of an ideological sign and the form of an ideological sign are inextricably bound together and are separable only in the abstract. Ulti-mately, the same set of forces and the same material prerequisites bring both the one and the other to life.

Indeed, the economic conditions that inaugurate a new element of reality into the social purview, that make it socially meaningful and 'interesting', are exactly the same conditions that create the forms of ideological com-munication (the cognitive, the artistic, the religious, and so on), which in turn shape the forms of semiotic expression.

Thus, the themes and forms of ideological creativity emerge from the same matrix and are in essence two sides of the same thing.

The process of incorporation into ideology — the birth of theme and birth of form — is best followed out in the material of the word. This process of ideological generation is reflected two ways in language: both in its large-scale, universal-historical dimensions as studied by semantic paleontology, which has disclosed the incorporation of undifferentiated chunks of reality into the social purview of prehistoric man, and in its small-scale dimensions as constituted within the framework of contemporaneity, since, as we know, the word sensitively reflects the slightest variations in social existence.

The Class Struggle and the Dialectics of Signs

Existence reflected in sign is not merely reflected but *refracted*. How is this refraction of existence in the ideological sign determined? By an inter-secting of differently oriented social interests within one and the same sign community, i.e. *by the class struggle.*

Class does not coincide with the sign community, i.e. with the commun-ity, which is the totality of users of the same set of signs for ideological com-munication. Thus various different classes will use one and the same lan-guage. As a result, differently oriented accents intersect in every ideological sign. Sign becomes an arena of the class struggle.

This social *multiaccentuality* of the ideological sign is a very crucial aspect. By and large, it is thanks to this intersecting of accents that a sign maintains its vitality and dynamism and the capacity for further development. A sign that has been withdrawn from the pressures of the social struggle — which, so to speak, crosses beyond the pale of the class struggle — inevitably loses force, degenerating into allegory and becoming the object not of live social intelligibility but of philological comprehension. The historical memory of mankind is full of such worn out ideological signs incapable of serving as arenas for the clash of live social accents. However, inasmuch as they are remembered by the philologist and the historian, they may be said to retain the last glimmers of life.

The very same thing that makes the ideological sign vital and mutable is also, however, that which makes it a refracting and distorting medium. The ruling class strives to impart a supraclass, eternal character to the ideological sign, to extinguish or drive inward the struggle between social value judgments which occurs in it, to make the sign uniaccentual.

In actual fact, each living ideological sign has two faces, like Janus. Any current curse word can become a word of praise, any current truth must inevitably sound to many other people as the greatest lie. This *inner dialectic quality* of the sign comes out fully in the open only in times of social crises or revolutionary changes. In the ordinary conditions of life, the contradiction embedded in every ideological sign cannot emerge fully because the ideological sign in an established, dominant ideology is always somewhat reactionary and tries, as it were, to stabilize the preceding factor in the dialectical flux of the social generative process, so accentuating yesterday's truth as to make it appear today's. And that is what is responsible for the refracting and distorting peculiarity of the ideological sign within the dominant ideology.

Theme and Meaning

A definite and unitary meaning, a unitary significance, is a property belonging to any utterance *as a whole.* Let us call the significance of a whole utterance its *theme.*[2] The theme must be unitary, otherwise we would have no basis for talking about any one utterance. The theme of an utterance itself is individual and unreproducible, just as the utterance itself is individual and unreproducible. The theme is the expression of the concrete, historical situation that engendered the utterance. The utterance 'What time is it?' has a different meaning each time it is used, and hence, in accordance with our terminology, has a different theme, depending on the concrete historical situation ('historical' here in microscopic dimensions) during which it is enunciated and of which, in essence, it is a part.

It follows, then, that the theme of an utterance is determined not only by the linguistic forms that comprise it — words, morphological and syntactic structure, sounds, and intonation — but also by extraverbal factors of the situation. Should we miss these situational factors, we would be as little able to understand an utterance as if we were to miss its most important words. The theme of an utterance is concrete — as concrete as the historical instant to which the utterance belongs. *Only an utterance taken in its full, concrete scope as an historical phenomenon possesses a theme.* That is what is meant by the theme of an utterance.

However, if we were to restrict ourselves to the historical unreproducibility and unitariness of each concrete utterance and its theme, we would be poor dialecticians. Together with theme or, rather, within the theme, there is also the *meaning* that belongs to an utterance. By meaning, as distinguished from theme, we understand all those aspects of the utterance that are *reproducible* and *self-identical* in all instances of repetition. Of course, these aspects are abstract: they have no concrete, autonomous existence in an artificiality isolated form, but, at the same time, they do constitute an essential and inseparable part of the utterance. The theme of an utterance is, in essence, indivisible. The meaning of an utterance, on the contrary, does break down into a set of meanings belonging to each of the various linguistic elements of which the utterance consists. The unreproducible theme of the utterance 'What time is it?' taken in its indissoluble connection with the concrete historical situation, cannot be divided into elements. The meaning of the utterance 'What time is it?' — a meaning that, of course, remains the same in all historical instances of its enunciation — is made up of the meanings of the words, forms of morphological and syntactic union, interrogative intonations, etc., that form the construction of the utterance.

Theme is a complex, dynamic system of signs that attempts to be adequate to a given instant of generative process. Theme is reaction by the consciousness in its generative process to the generative process of existence. Meaning is *the technical apparatus for the implementation of theme.* Of course, no absolute, mechanistic boundary can be drawn between theme and meaning. There is no theme without meaning and no meaning without theme. Moreover, it is even impossible to convey the meaning of a particular word (say, in the course of teaching another person a foreign language) without having made it an element of theme, i.e. without having constructed an 'example' utterance. On the other hand, a theme must base itself on some kind of fixity of meaning; otherwise it loses its connection with what came before and what comes after — i.e. it altogether loses its significance.

The distinction between theme and meaning acquires particular clarity in connection with the *problem of understanding,* which we shall now briefly touch upon.

We have already had occasion to speak of the philological type of passive understanding, which excludes response in advance. Any genuine kind of understanding will be active and will constitute the germ of a response. Only active understanding can grasp theme — a generative process can be grasped only with the aid of another generative process.

To understand another person's utterance means to orient oneself with respect to it, to find the proper place for it in the corresponding context. For each word of the utterance that we are in process of understanding, we, as it were, lay down a set of our own answering words. The greater their number and weight, the deeper and more substantial our understanding will be.

Thus each of the distinguishable significative elements of an utterance and the entire utterance as a whole entity are translated in our minds into another, active and responsive, context. *Any true understanding is dialogic in nature.* Understanding is to utterance as one line of a dialogue is to the next. Understanding strives to match the speaker's word with a *counter word.* Only in understanding a word in a foreign tongue is the attempt made to match it with the 'same' word in one's own language.

Therefore, there is no reason for saying that meaning belongs to a word as such. In essence, meaning belongs to a word in its position between speakers; that is, meaning is realized only in the process of active, responsive understanding. Meaning does not reside in the word or in the soul of the speaker or in the soul of the listener. Meaning is the *effect of interaction between speaker and listener produced via the material of a particular sound complex.* It is like an electric spark that occurs only when two different terminals are hooked together. Those who ignore theme (which is accessible only to active, responsive understanding) and who, in attempting to define the meaning of a word, approach its lower, stable, self-identical limit, want, in effect, to turn on a light bulb after having switched off the current. Only the current of verbal intercourse endows a word with the light of meaning.

The Interrelationship between Meaning and Evaluation

Any word used in actual speech possesses not only theme and meaning in the referential, or content, sense of these words, but also value judgment: i.e. all referential contents produced in living speech are said or written in conjunction with a specific *evaluative accent.* There is no such thing as word without evaluative accent.

What is the nature of this accent, and how does it relate to the referential side of meaning?

The most obvious, but, at the same time, the most superficial aspect of social value judgement incorporated in the word is that which is conveyed with the help of *expressive intonation.* In most cases, intonation is determined by the immediate situation and often by its most ephemeral circumstances. To be sure, intonation of a more substantial kind is also possible. Here is a classic instance of such a use of intonation in real-life speech. Dostoevskij, in *Diary of a Writer,* relates the following story.

> One Sunday night, already getting on to the small hours, I chanced to find myself walking alongside a band of six tipsy artisans for a dozen paces or so, and there and then I became convinced that all thoughts, all feelings, and even whole trains of reasoning could be expressed merely by using a certain noun, a noun, moreover, of utmost simplicity in itself [Dostoevskij has in mind here a certain widely used obscenity. — V.V.]. Here is what happened. First, one of these fellows voices this noun shrilly and emphatically by way of expressing his utterly disdainful denial of some point that had been in general contention just prior. A second fellow repeats this very same noun in response to the first fellow, but now in an altogether different tone and sense — to wit, in the sense that he fully doubted the veracity of the first fellow's denial. A third fellow waxes indignant at the first one, sharply and heatedly sallying into the conversation and shouting at him that very same noun, but now in a pejorative, abusive sense. The second fellow, indignant at the third for being offensive, himself sallies back in and cuts the latter short to the effect: 'What the hell do you think you're doing, butting in like that?! Me and Fil'ka were having a nice quiet talk and just like that you come along and start cussing him out!' And in fact, this whole train of thought he conveyed by emitting just that very same time-honored word, that same extremely laconic designation of a certain item, and nothing more, save only that he also raised his hand and grabbed the second fellow by the shoulder. Thereupon, all of a sudden a fourth fellow, the youngest in the crowd, who had remained silent all this while, apparently having just struck upon the solution to the problem that had originally occasioned the dispute, in a tone of rapture, with one arm half-raised, shouts — What do you think: 'Eureka!'? 'I found it, I found it!'? No, nothing at all like 'Eureka', nothing like 'I found it'. He merely repeats that very same unprintable noun, just that one single word, just that one word alone, but with rapture, with a squeal of ecstacy, and apparently somewhat excessively so, because the sixth fellow, a surly character and the oldest in the bunch, didn't think it seemly and in a trice stops the young fellow's rapture cold by turning on him and repeating in a gruff and expostulatory bass — yes, that very same noun whose usage is forbidden in the company of ladies, which, however, in this case clearly and precisely denoted: 'What the hell are you shouting for, you'll burst a blood vessel!' And so, without having uttered one other word, they repeated just this one, but obviously beloved, little word of theirs six times in a row, one after the other, and they understood one another perfectly.[3]

All six 'speech performances' by the artisans are different, despite the fact that they all consisted of one and the same word. That word, in this instance, was essentially only a vehicle for intonation. The conversation was conducted in intonations expressing the value judgements of the speakers. These value judgments and their corresponding intonations were wholly determined by the immediate social situation of the talk and therefore did not require any referential support. In living speech, intonation often does have a meaning quite independent of the semantic composition of speech. Intonational material pent up inside us often does find outlet in linguistic constructions completely inappropriate to the particular kind of intonation involved. In such a case, intonation does not impinge upon the intellectual, concrete, referential significance of the construction. We have a habit of expressing our feelings by imparting expressive and meaningful intonation to some word that crops up in our mind by chance, often a vacuous interjection or adverb. Almost everybody has his favorite interjection or adverb or sometimes even a semantically full-fledged word that he customarily uses for purely intonational resolution of certain trivial (and sometimes not so trivial) situations and moods that occur in the ordinary business of life. There are certain expressions like 'so-so', 'yes-yes', 'now-now', 'well-well' and so on that commonly serve as 'safety valves' of that sort. The doubling usual in such expressions is symptomatic; i.e. it represents an artificial prolongation of the sound image for the purpose of allowing the pent up intonation to expire fully. Any one such favorite little expression may, of course, be pronounced in an enormous variety of intonations in keeping with the wide diversity of situations and moods that occur in life.

In all these instances, theme, which is a property of each utterance (each of the utterances of the six artisans had a theme proper to it), is implemented entirely and exclusively by the power of expressive intonation without the aid of word meaning or grammatical coordination. This sort of value judgment and its corresponding intonation cannot exceed the narrow confines of the immediate situation and the small, intimate social world in which it occurs. Linguistic evaluation of this sort may rightly be called an accompaniment, an accessory phenomenon, to meaning in language.

However, not all linguistic value judgments are like that. We may take any utterance whatsoever, say, an utterance that encompasses the broadest possible semantic spectrum and assumes the widest possible social audience, and we shall still see that, in it, an enormous importance belongs to evaluation. Naturally, value judgment in this case will not allow of even minimally adequate expression by intonation, but it will be the determinative factor in the choice and deployment of the basic elements that bear the meaning of the utterance. No utterance can be put together without value judgment. Every utterance is above all an *evaluative orientation*. Therefore, each element in a living utterance not only has a meaning but also has a value. Only the abstract element, perceived within the system of language and not within the structure of an utterance, appears devoid of value judgment. Focusing their attention on the abstract system of language is what led most linguists to divorce evaluation from meaning and to consider evaluation an accessory factor of meaning, the expression of a speaker's individual attitude towards the subject matter of his discourse.

A change in meaning is, essentially, always a *reevaluation:* the transposition of some particular word from one evaluative context to another. A word is either advanced to a higher rank or demoted to a lower one. The separation of word meaning from evaluation inevitably deprives meaning of its place in the living social process (where meaning is always permeated with value judgment), to its being ontologized and transformed into ideal Being divorced from the historical process of Becoming.

Precisely in order to understand the historical process of generation of theme and of the meanings implementing theme, it is essential to take social evaluation into account. The generative process of signification in language is always associated with the generation of the evaluative purview of a particular social group, and the generation of an evaluative purview — in the sense of the totality of all those things that have meaning and importance for the particular group — is entirely determined by expansion of the economic basis. As the economic basis expands, it promotes an actual expansion in the scope of existence which is accessible, comprehensible, and vital to man. The prehistoric herdsman was virtually interested in nothing, and virtually nothing had any bearing on him. Man at the end of the epoch of capitalism is directly concerned about everything, his interests reaching the remotest corners of the earth and even the most distant stars. This expansion of evaluative purview comes about dialectically. New aspects of existence, once they are drawn into the sphere of social interest, once they make contact with the human word and human emotion, do not coexist peacefully with other elements of existence previously drawn in, but engage them in a struggle, reevaluate them, and bring about a change in their position within the unity of the evaluative purview. This dialectical generative process is reflected in the generation of semantic properties in language. A new significance emanates from an old one, and does so with its help, but this happens so that the new significance can enter into contradiction with the old one and restructure it.

The outcome is a constant struggle of accents in each semantic sector of existence. There is nothing in the structure of signification that could be said to transcend the generative process, to be independent of the dialectical expansion of social purview. Society in process of generation expands its perception of the generative process of existence. There is nothing in this that could be said to be absolutely fixed. And that is how it happens that meaning — an abstract, self-identical element — is subsumed under theme and torn apart by theme's living contradictions so as to return in the shape of a new meaning with a fixity and self-identity only for the while, just as it had before.

Notes

1. This chapter is compiled from extracts from *Marxism and the Philosophy of Language.*
2. The term is, or course, a provisional one. *Theme* in our sense embraces its implementation as well; therefore, our concept must not be confused with that of a theme in a literary work. The concept of 'thematic unity' would be closer to what we mean.
3. *Polnoe sobranie sočinenij F. M. Dostoevskogo* (The Complete Works of F. M. Dostoevskijl), Vol. IX, pp. 274–5, 1906.

5 Family Literacy: Conservation and Change in the Transmission of Literacy Styles and Values

DENNY TAYLOR

Early in the study, I was impressed by the way the parents moved easily between the past and present as they talked about their own experiences of learning to read and write and the experiences of their children. In each family, some rituals and routines of written language usage appear to conserve family traditions of literacy, while others appear to change the patterns of the past. The patterns of family literacy are constantly evolving to accomodate the everyday experiences of both parents and children; the introduction of a younger sibling can lead to the systematic restructuring of the routine. In analyzing the data it has become increasingly evident that the most significant 'mode' of transmitting literacy styles and values occurs indirectly, at the very margins of awareness (Leichter, 1974) through the continuously diffuse use of written language in the ongoing life of the family. The direct transmission of literacy styles and values through specific encounters occurs less frequently, and such didactic occasions are spasmodic, usually occurring in response to some school-related situation.

Memories of the Past and Interpretations of the Present

Parents' memories

Reminiscing, Laura Lindell spoke of 'the long trek' to Maine her family had made when she was two years of age, and she spoke of the funny things that had happened. She explained, 'There was an out house and I had my potty chair and I used it one day without the pot and was amazed!' It would seem that such memories remain clear as the years pass. Jessie Dawson spoke of the flowered wallpaper in her bedroom, and Lee Farley of the swing that had seemed to go 'two miles high'. Dan Dawson spoke of planting radishes with his father, and Nina Simms of her predilection for getting lost. She recounted gleefully:

> There was a snowstorm and I was gone again as usual. Finally my father goes to the police station and there I am on the captain's desk eating lollipops and ice cream and all bundled up. The policeman says to me, 'Is this your father?' And I say 'No!' (Laughs.) So my father was ready to choke me and he had to show all kinds of identification that he was my father and then carry me home in the snow.

Memories of 'literate things' were much slower to surface. All of the parents had some memories of print being a part of family life and of their parents' involvement with print (such as reading the newspapers), but few could remember specific occasions designed to introduce them to written language. Lee Farley said that both his parents had read a lot, and Leo Langdon presented a similar picture, but both men emphasized that they had not been read to by their parents.

Leo Langdon stated that he had no recollection of having any books except when he went to school.

> I don't remember my parents reading to me and I'm not saying they didn't but I have no real recollection. I remember, it's funny when you start thinking about it, I remember my grandparents. My grandmother used to read the comics to me . . . but I remember and the reason I remember is because at times people would say, 'Do you remember your grandmother reading comics to you?' or something like that. They would say that to me, and that's probably why I remember.

Similarly, Joe King, who spoke of his parents as immigrants and of his background as 'impoverished', said that his mother had read to him: 'the sense I have is that my mother used to read to me all the time, but it's a sense I have and I've been told that.' Barry Lindell's memories of his early years were difficult to face, and he spoke of trying to suppress as much as he could. He commented, 'None of the people in my family were very good readers . . . it wasn't important.' Barry said that no one had read to him, adding, 'It's absolutely amazing that with the amount of reading I do now that I did virtually none and my parents did very little.' Although Barry's impression was that his family did not read, he did speak of his father reading the newspaper 'regularly every night'. Only Laura Lindell and Jessie Dawson spoke of being read to on a regular basis. Laura listened to her father reading adventure stories to her brothers, while Jessie was read to 'just about every day' by her mother as well as by her grandmother and her aunts, who had helped raise her after her parents' divorce. For Dan Dawson, there was little regularity in his early years, but there was a time when he too had been read to by his father and grandfather. Dan spoke of the afternoon when his grandfather returned home with a new book: 'He taught me to read, it seemed to me, in one afternoon.' For many of the parents, their memories of being read to were locked inside stories of long-forgotten books. Donna King spoke of reading *Peter Rabbit* to her children and realizing the story was familiar to her; Jill Langdon spoke of a book she had found at the library and of the repetitive line 'Scat, scat, go away little cat', which she had loved as a child; and Karen Farley spoke of rediscovering *Little House,* which she vaguely remembered her mother reading to her as a small child.' For these parents, recollections were triggered by the books they read their children. Listening to stories was deeply embedded in the recesses of the past and much more difficult to retrieve than the memories of observing their parents read. Although Karen Farley had few memories of being read to as a child, she had very clear memories of seeing her father reading engineering books and of enjoying the feeling of the bumpy leather on the spines of the texts.

School memories

Only Jessie Dawson and Karen Farley had pleasant memories of their first-grade year. Jessie spoke of sitting in a circle with a book in her lap:

> We sat in a circle with the teacher and we had flash cards she would hold up and we would be told what the words were and we would go through an exercise where they were shown to us again and we could call them out as we saw them. Then she would put that away and we would open the book and there would be those words and you could read them. I remember very clearly sitting in that circle.

Karen Farley recalled the excitement of getting a new reader, and she spoke of how happy she was when she was allowed to take a book home, because it seemed like homework. Laura Lindell's memories were very different. When I asked her if she remembered being taught to read in school, she said, 'No. I don't remember it because I remember feeling bored by their way of doing it with the traditional Dick and Jane and Sally the little sister and Puff and Spot and all the happy clean faces.' Dan Dawson also remembered thinking of it as 'kind of dull'. Barry Lindell learned to read easily in school, but remembered it as an anxious time. He said that one of the things that bothered him was that so many of the children could not read; he added, 'They would falter over little words and I would get very anxious and want to go over and read it for them.'

Leo Langdon spoke of his 'mixed emotions' about the parochial grammar school he attended and of the harsh discipline which he so clearly remembers. Leo said he had great difficulty learning to read and had been in sixth grade when he finally began to read. However, Leo emphasized that it was not until he was in the army that he became a reader. Stuck in West Germany with time on his hands, he occupied himself reading the paperbacks other men left lying around. Lee Farley spoke of learning to read as probably the worst experience of his entire life, and speaking of some of the ways that reading was taught he said:

> Oh, I can remember those agonies but I don't know when that was, of passing the story around the room deal. 'OK, Johnny, you read the first four sentences.' (Groans and pretends to read.) 'Your turn Lee.' And you go (strangled sound) (laughs), you just choke right there. God, I read badly. To this day I have difficulty spelling anything except my name. That was probably the worst experience of my life . . . I think probably that is the most humiliating, embarrassing, and most horrible thing that teachers do to kids. Maybe it was just because I was the one who couldn't do it. 'It's your turn to read', and you didn't even know what page they were on. (Laughs.) I was off someplace but even if I knew what page they were on and you read over a word and you botch the word and you didn't know what it was or they make you 'sound it out'. You didn't even know what it sounded like. Yuk. No (laughs), I don't remember enjoying that ever.

Like Leo, Lee was an adult when he became a reader. Stimulated by his desire for a career in banking, Lee began to read the relevant literature, and today the *Wall Street Journal* is his standard fare.

Throughout the discussions of their childhood experiences, the parents often referred to the experiences of their children, and they found it as difficult to talk about their children's preschool involvement with written language as it was to speak of their own preschool experiences. Occasionally they mentioned their early interest in writing and drawing, and the interest of their children in such activities, but it was only when examples of the children's work were collected for this study that they became aware of the amount of drawing and writing that was taking place on a daily basis.

The only activity which was repeatedly mentioned by the parents was the reading of stories to their children, and in this context the literacy styles and values that they wished to impart to their children were in some ways made 'visible'. On different occasions, Laura Lindell spoke of her great interest in books, her father's love of literature, and her children's enjoyment of books. She attributed her children's interest to the fact that they had always listened to stories at bedtime, and speaking of their early years she said, 'They loved finding out what was between the covers; if they ripped them it didn't matter; they ate them and they teethed on them.' Barry also spoke of when the children had been babies, and he emphasized that they had read to them 'as soon as their eyes could focus'. Based upon the many occasions that Laura and Barry have talked about reading stories, it would seem that Laura is conserving patterns of literate language use while Barry is attempting to change the patterns of his past.

The Juxtapositioning of Childhood Experiences

The conservation of literacy styles and values occurs almost automatically, and only when the parent is intent on change is a conscious effort involved. Laura never spoke of reading to her children because her father had read to her, but Barry did speak of not being read to as a child and of how important he felt it was for his children to listen to stories. Similarly, Karen Farley read stories to her children, and the only linkages she made with her own childhood were her comments when she found that a story she was reading to her children was one she had heard as a child, whereas Lee Farley was conscious of wishing to provide alternate experiences for his children. Speaking of his own experiences, he stated:

> Yes, the books were around, yes, we read, but I don't remember anybody sitting down and saying, 'Gee, isn't this fun?' as opposed to 'You've got to do it!' And it's something, when I work with her (Kathy) I (say), 'Hey, let's try this! Won't this be fun!'

As Lee spoke, it was clear that he wanted to change patterns of his past, and as he stated when speaking of Kathy, 'Maybe I know that because I hated it so badly I'm going to guarantee her that she doesn't know that I disliked it so much.'

Parents vis-à-vis one another

In each of the families, the evolution of literacy transmission is highly dependent on the childhood experiences of the parents and evolves through the interplay of their individual biographies and educative styles. Yet, although each of the parents was aware of the background of his or her partner, they had not specifically discussed with each other the literate experiences that they wanted for their children. Without implying any general statement of harmony, it appeared that the parents had evolved complementary roles without planning explicit strategies. Laura Lindell commented that 'it had just happened that way'. She said that she had naturally given the children books when they were 'at the eating stage', and that she thought Barry had taken his cues from her. Karen Farley said that there were so many other things that they had to deal with on a daily basis that 'reading had never been an issue', and she added that if at some time in the future one of the children were to have a problem, she was sure that they would discuss it. Once, Karen was talking about the activities that her children enjoyed in the magazine *Cricket*, and I asked her if she ever helped them with these activities. She replied:

> It's hard, I think it's very hard to find the time. Mainly when they do it is when Lee comes home . . . I do the more practical things, but when

he comes home he's fresh for them, and they're so anxious to show him and he even gets a kick out of doing these things.

The mediation of past experiences: An idiosyncratic process

In looking at the ways the parents shared literate experiences with their children, it was found that through the interplay of the personal biographies and educative styles of the parents comparable childhood experiences were mediated in different ways. The childhood experiences of Leo Langdon were very similar to those of Lee Farley. Both men had found it difficult to learn to read and had spoken of the social humiliation of the experience, and both men wished to ensure that their children did not suffer similar experiences. However, this is where the similarities end, for the men have evolved very different styles in working with their children. Lee Farley is actively intent upon making it fun for his children to play with print, while Leo Langdon is attempting to ensure that his children are not pressured into learning to read before they are ready. He has bided his time, and it was only when Ken was in first grade and learning to read without any difficulty that he began to participate in his reading and writing activities.

The different approaches that Lee Farley and Leo Langdon evolved in their transmission of literary skills and values illustrate that the mediation of past experiences is an idiosyncratic process which can result in very different experiences for individual children who are nevertheless successful in learning to read.

The Parents' Mediation of the Literate Experiences of their Children

There are also differences within each family in the ways the parents mediate the literate experiences of individual children. The first born appears to be influenced to a large degree by the experiences of the parents, whereas the second child is greatly affected by the family's interpretations of the experiences of the first born and by the interaction which takes place between the children. The process is both active and reactive, as all family members are influenced by the changing dynamics of family life, triggered by the inclusion of another child within the group.

First borns

Parents spoke of reading to the first-born child from a very early age, and they emphasized the active role that the child had taken in the story-reading occasion. Karen Farley's comments about reading to Kathy illustrates the ways the personal agendas of parent and child come together in the newness of the situation. Karen related:

Well, she had always been read to and I seemed to spend a great deal of time with her because I was so concerned about being a new mother, doing things with her the whole time . . . I don't know, so much of it is Kathy. She had that ability to catch on to things quickly, to absorb it, and to play it back.

Donna King also emphasized the active role Bonnie had played during the story-sharing occasions, and she recalled that from a very young age Bonnie would come to her with a book for her to read. However, not all the children were so inclined toward listening to stories. Jessie Dawson remembered that Sissie did not like to sit still for long and although she liked picture books she had a very short attention span, and so Jessie could not read to her as much as she would have liked. From Jessie's comments, it would seem that Sissie was quite active in shaping the literate experiences that she shared with her mother.

Siblings

During the many discussions that focused on the children, the parents spoke of their subsesquent children as fitting into the established patterns of family life. Laura Lindell spoke of Sandy learning by 'osmosis', and she emphasized that she 'just had to adapt'. Karen Farley, speaking of Nan, said, 'I just think of her as being very calm and of fitting into the group and of going along with it.' Jessie Dawson spoke specifically of reading when she said that Ellie had naturally listened to stories; she explained 'We had developed a habit of reading when Ellie was born. Sissie was nine and Hannah was six.' In such ways, the established patterns were conserved, but also changes were made, some of them quite basic. Caring for two children requires considerable orchestration, and each family mentioned that in the rush of coping, the second child received less parental attention than the first child had. Jill Langdon made this point when she said, 'I can remember times when Steven cried and I was going to tend to him and something else would come up, Ken would be running outside, and by the time I'd straightened that out the baby maybe had stopped crying.'

Other changes were stimulated by the children themselves. The parents spoke of the differences they perceived, juxtaposing the characteristics of their children as they described the differences. Azar Simms talked of Andrew and Carol in this way. He said he felt that Andrew had an excellent attention span. He laughed and went on to say that Andrew was like a spider, that he would spend hours tying all sorts of objects together — chairs, tables, and so on — until the whole room was tied in knots. Azar then spoke of Carol, and he stated that she did not have such an attention span and that she would often flit from one thing to another.

The parents also made sharp contrasts between their children in literate areas. Joe King shared his observation of Donna reading to Bonnie, and he explained that she sat quietly, intently listening to the stories. Characterizing the experience that Donna and Bonnie had shared, he said, 'It's almost a hypnotic effect . . . You don't even need to listen to the words; it's like a mother talking to a child; it's that kind of rapport.' Of James, Joe related that he enjoyed talking about the story more than listening to the printed words, and he added that James let him 'know what was happening' in more ways than Bonnie, who had always been content to sit and listen.

In talking of their children, the parents hinted at the difficulties which arose as they tried to balance the conservation of the pattern established by the family with the changes necessitated by the needs of individual children. Nina Simms presented an example at the beginning of the study when she expressed her concern at Andrew's lack of interest in such activities as coloring and painting. Nina said that, although she provided him with the materials as she had done for Carol, Andrew preferred to build and play with trucks. These difficulties are also illustrated by the comments of Lee Farley when he was speaking of Kathy and her younger sister Debbie. In his attempts to ensure that Kathy enjoyed her early experiences of written language, Lee played many games with her, but Debbie was not interested in these games. While conserving his need to provide his children with good experiences of print, Lee was forced to change his strategies. What worked with Kathy was not working with Debbie. Lee commented:

> She's not showing the interest in it and the last thing I feel inspired to do is ram it down her throat kind of routine: 'Here. Sit down we'll look at words!' (said crossly). I mean, fine, when we look at words we'll look at words. When the opportunity is there we'll do it but she doesn't want to play the game. For Kathy it was a challenge, it was a game, a new word. Debbie doesn't quite see it that way so OK, we'll try a little different approach. I don't know what.

It would seem that while Lee was conscious of wanting to provide Debbie with the same guarantee that he offered to Kathy, he realized that it must be couched in different terms and with different provisions. Restructuring was necessary. During the year following this conversation, Lee played few games with Debbie, but he continued to read to her on a regular basis. Interestingly, when Debbie was five and in her last year of nursery school she became interested in playing with print at school, and both Lee and Karen supported her in these activities.

On another level, it is not only the difference between children which contributes to the different ways in which the parents worked with their children. This is well illustrated by Donna King's remarks when she listened to an audio recording of a story she had read with James. She said:

I sure was frustrated with him. I don't know, in a sense I'm not sure whether it's a difference in him or in terms of what I've gotten used to. I have a sense that in general I've gotten used to reading to Bonnie, and reading the story. I'm more impatient about looking at the pictures and talking about the pictures and so forth than I might have been with her when she was at that age or at that stage in terms of looking at pictures and talking about them.

Donna's comments emphasize the ways the parents changed as they engaged in, moved through, and combined educational experiences over time (Leichter, 1973, 1978).

Siblings vis-à-vis one another

In *The Sibling,* Sutton-Smith and Rosenberg (1970) write 'siblings make each other different' (p. 2). In each family, the parents spoke of how their children influenced one another. Again, the data suggest that both older and younger siblings are active and reactive in shaping the literate experiences of each other. The parents emphasized the amount of time their children spent together. Jill Langdon spoke of Steven's relationship with Ken, his older brother. Speaking of Steven as a baby, she said, 'He had someone else to watch and watching Ken was much more interesting than watching me. He would do things that were much more interesting to a child than the things that I do.' Karen Farley made similar comments, while Donna King emphasized that although James had missed having his parents to himself, he enjoyed his interactions with his sister Bonnie, and that he had many experiences which Bonnie as a first born had missed.

Parents spoke of the younger children listening to their older sibling(s) read. Beth and Sarah Lindell both read stories to Sandy, and Sissie and Hannah Dawson read to Ellie. Nina Simms said that when she was busy, she often asked Carol to read to Andrew, and once when Carol was reading stories to me Andrew joined us, listening to the story and echoing his sister's words as she spoke. Kathy Farley reads to Debbie at bedtime. Debbie has often spoken of her sister reading to her, and Karen has spoken of Kathy reading to Nan. Two years ago, Karen spoke of Kathy propping Nan up in her pumpkin seat when she was only six months old so that she could see the pictures as Kathy read her a story. However, the data indicate that although emphasis was given to older siblings reading stories to younger siblings, this did not occur as regularly as the reading of stories by parents. The children read together spasmodically, and these events were influenced by many factors, including whether the older child wanted to read and the younger child wanted to listen and finding time for such an activity in the bustle of daily living.

On another level, the children were interacting with print daily, but the extent of this activity was only hinted at by the parents. Parents occasionally mentioned that individual children liked to draw or write, and they some-times spoke of them writing with or to friends. But much went by unnoticed, and it was only when examples of the children's work were collected that the extent of their involvement became evident and this part of their lives became available for discussion. However, it should be emphasized that the children are interacting with print on a daily basis and that siblings and friends are mediating each other's literate experiences.

The Family's Mediation of School Experience of Learning to Read and Write

For the families taking part in this study, the sum total of their literate experiences comes into play in the mediation of each child's learning to read and write in school. The experiences of the parents, the experiences of brothers and sisters, and the child's own experiences form a filter through which learning at school must pass. In each of the families, the parents were critical of the schools their children attended and of the methods by which they were taught; however, they were also supportive of the schools. I mentioned this interpretation to the parents. During my discussion with Jill Langdon she elaborated on her and her husband's criticisms of the teachers and the teaching methods — while at the same time being supportive of the system. Jill explained that at the beginning of Ken's second-grade year she had been quite concerned because she disliked the teacher. She said that the teacher had a voice 'like gravel' which 'grated on you', and she added that the teacher did not have a good relationship with the children. Jill then spoke of how Leo had impressed upon her that she should not let Ken know she was upset because it would confuse him. Jill said Leo had emphasized their supporting the school as it was important for Ken to feel that his school learning was important.

The parents also played an active role in school activites. Most of the parents attended school meetings on a regular basis, and the mothers worked for the schools in voluntary capacities, assisting in libraries, producing flyers, taking part in safety programs, and working as members of the various committees of the parent associations. Within this framework they mediated their children's school experiences of learning to read and write.

Negotiating the present in light of the past

Recollections of the past gained meaning in the present as the parents negotiated their children's early school experiences. Most of the parents spoke of their first-grade year as an unsettling time for them, and they portrayed it as such for their children. Barry Lindell spoke of the difficult move that Sandy had made from kindergarten to first grade, while Karen Farley commented at the end of Kathy's first-grade year that there were times when she could have cried because dealing with Kathy was so difficult. Nina Simms expressed the problem in terms of the work that first-grade children are expected to do; she said, 'They're expected to read, they're expected to write, and they're expected to do math. It's a lot and too much for some kids.' Other parents spoke of the length of the day and the amount of time the children were expected to sit. First grade was portrayed by the parents as a period of transition. New schedules, new rules, and new work were a part of the school situation with which the first grader had to contend. While it was a new experience for the child, it was a familiar experience for the parents. It had happened to them in their own childhoods, and for some it had happened more recently through the experiences of their older children.

Parents spoke of their children's experiences whithin the context of their own experience. This is well illustrated by Leo Langdon's comments on the discussion he had with Jill when they were deciding on a school for Ken. He said they had discussed sending Ken to a parochial school, but because of his experience and because Jill had gone to a public school, they had decided against it. Leo emphasized, 'I did not particularly want to send my child to a parochial school because of the experiences I had.' As Ken entered first grade, Leo and Jill continued their discussion. On one occasion, Jill spoke specifically of reading. She explained:

> My husband and I have been talking about this a lot now because we are starting in with this with Ken. I don't remember how we started but I can remember once we knew some words and could read the 'Dick and Jane' books; I can remember going around the room and everybody reading a sentence from the book. That I can remember. And one thing we've been talking about is right now the way our schools are set up the children are placed in levels because it's the Ginn method of reading, and my husband doesn't really think that this whole level thing is good. He feels it makes the child feel that there's someone else smarter than they are or they're behind. I said that when I was in first grade I could remember we knew who was not reading because we would have this reading a sentence and it would always be the same person who would stumble on words so I said I didn't think that was right either because that makes that person feel awful.

Leo also spoke of this issue commenting, 'It just upset me that they were putting pressure on the children.' The situation was complicated for Leo and Jill by the school's insistence that the children in Ken's first-grade year participate in a series of reading tests which were being given throughout the school. The children had spent two weeks in first grade when they were tested. Ken came home upset. Leo recalled:

He was upset that he couldn't read the instructions and couldn't read the words he was supposed to read to get the right answers and I immediately became upset about it because I told him he didn't have to know how to read yet, he was only in the first grade for the second week and that he shouldn't be upset about it and he got over that.

In mediating Ken's early experiences of reading in first grade, Leo and Jill worked to minimize the pressure they felt was being exerted within the school situation. They faced a specific problem, and in so doing they combined their personal experiences as they searched for some way of easing Ken into his first-grade year. They had established a home environment for Ken and Steven in which the children were not pushed toward academic activities. Of reading, Jill had commented that they read stories 'to enjoy now, not to pressure them into anything else'. But the pressure had come, and they had an urgent need to deal with it. Leo explained to Ken that it was OK that he was not reading in his second week of first grade, while Jill downplayed the idea of levels, emphasizing that it did not matter which level you were in as long as you were working. The Langdon parents spent an anxious few weeks as Ken got deeper into first grade. Ken started to read. He was reading well. That Christmas Leo commented:

But I'm amazed today, Ken comes home with books and he can actually read the books, actually read them and I'm so impressed because I can remember when I was in first grade I could not read a book. He's motivated to read, he wants to read.

Teaching in school and learning at home

Within the context of the family, the transmission of literary styles and values is a diffuse experience, often occurring at the margins of awareness. Even when parents quite consciously introduced their children to print, the words were locked into the context of the situation. The label on the shampoo bottle, the recipe for carrot bread, and the neon signs in the street were not constructed to specifically teach reading; they were part of the child's world, and the child learned of their purpose as well as of their meaning. However, the data also indicate that 'shifts' occurred in the parents' approaches to the transmission of literacy styles and values, and these shifts coincided with the child's beginning to learn to read and write in school. Leo and Jill Langdon had not consciously tried to teach their children to read, but in the middle of Ken's first-grade year, it became clear that he was learning to read without difficulty. He was interested in words; he was inquisitive about the words in his own home. At that time Leo and Jill began to participate in his reading activities. He explained, 'A couple of months ago I went over to see his teacher and I had spoken to her and told her how well he was doing, how we felt. I asked her if he could bring books home so that we could help him and he could read and she said "sure".' Ken took home the books and read them to his family and Leo decided to ask for more. Jill listens to him read whenever she can, and Leo helps him read words and sentences out of the magazines in their home. Ken is motivated to learn, and Leo and Jill are determined to help him while they continue to downplay the competition at school.

The active role that the child plays in bringing specific written language activities into the home was noted in each of the families. Sensitive to the child's response to school-related activities, the parents joined with the child in incorporating them into the life of the family. Like Ken Langdon, the Lindell children demonstrated their interest in written language. The Lindells spoke of the times when their children had become interested in words. Laura and Barry had played word games with their children during their kindergarten and first-grade years. Laura spoke of the children coming home from school and wanting to play with words. Barry created word games to play with them. Speaking of one game he had played with Sandy, he said, 'Fill-in-the-blank-space type thing; that helps an awful lot and in fact it becomes addictive. We'll play it for hours.' Now, Sandy is in third grade and no longer interested in such games. Both Laura and Barry have emphasized that they played these games spasmodically, depending on the interest of the children. Laura explained that so much of it had come from them, and she added, 'It's like everything else; sometimes in your life you'll do something very intensively, like for a couple of weeks, and maybe not at all for a long time.'

The Influence of the Older Children's School Experiences on their Younger Siblings

The experiences of the older children reflect upon and, in some ways, shape the experiences of the younger children. While parents spoke of spending less time with their younger chidlren, they also spoke of trying to provide them with experiences which they had not given their older children. Jill Langdon spoke of teaching Steven to differentiate between left and right because Ken had been expected to understand these concepts when he had entered first grade; Donna King spoke of teaching James his address and telephone number as Bonnie had been expected to know this information when she began school. This was not confined to the younger children's pre-school years; their parents continued to mediate their experiences in light of those of their older siblings. Laura Lindell said that she was much more prepared to intervene for Sandy than she had been for Sarah and Beth. Laura did intervene for Sandy. Sandy had been in first grade for two weeks when Laura went to see the teacher. Laura explained that Sandy was bored with all the 'getting to know each other' activities of the first two weeks. Laura asked the teacher to give Sandy some work that was in keeping with what she had been doing at the end of her kindergarten year.

The older children also influence the experiences of their young siblings more directly. From simple exposure to the activities of their older brothers and sisters, school is a part of the climate in which the younger children grow. School is a part of the family life, and it shapes the lives of younger children in ways their older siblings missed. Leo Langdon spoke of Steven being present when Ken was reading to them during his first-grade year. He stated, 'He's there, he hears it, it's going on.' Donna King talked of Bonnie playing with James, showing him how to write letters while they were playing. She commented that Bonnie had focused on letters that were possibly easier to form, such as H, A, and E, rather than working through the alphabet. Karen Farley spoke of Kathy doing more interesting things with Debbie, and she emphasized that in these games Kathy was able to share with Debbie many school-related literate experiences that would have smacked of teaching if she (Karen) had attempted them. Debbie demonstrated her awareness of Kathy's school activities several times, speaking of the homework Kathy brought home from school. Once Debbie explained that Kathy had to write something about the news she had watched on television. I asked Debbie if she had helped Kathy with her homework. She replied she had not, and then she added as an afterthought, 'But I watched!' Perhaps it was Debbie's awareness of her sister's homework that led her to speak of her own writing activities as homework, for every afternoon before her nap Debbie would sit at the desk in her bedroom practicing the letters of the alphabet in a book Karen had bought her. Ellie Dawson also watched. Both Sissie and Hannah talked of Ellie joining them in their rooms when they did their homework. Ellie would draw while they worked.

Conclusions

In his 1925 Lowell Letures, Alfred North Whitehead stated, 'mere change without conservation is a passage from nothing to nothing,' while 'conservation without change cannot conserve. For after all, there is a flux of circumstance, and the freshness of being evaporates under mere repetition.' This is the essence of my interpretation.

Neisser, writing of memory, states, 'Much of that formative past is now tacit rather than explicit knowledge: I do not dwell on it, and I cannot recall it as such, the specifics are beyond recall, although their resultant is here in person' (1979, p. 13). In the ongoing dialogue with the families, I was continuously impressed by the way the parents' interpretations of the present were bound by their recollections of the past. The conservation of past literate experiences was noted in the many implicit linkages between the past and present, as parents spoke of their childhood experiences and then later described similar experiences they had shared with their children. Implicit linking was also evidenced in the reading of stories, as some of the parents found that the stories they shared with their children were stories they had listened to when they were young.

In addition to the implicit linking of the past with the present, many ties were made directly as the memories of the parents were juxtaposed with the present-day experiences of the children. On such occasions, the parents were deliberately intent upon providing alternate experiences for their children. In considering the present data, when the parents were intent on change, the course of action they chose was closely related to their need to provide for their children experiences they had missed. Thus the interplay of the individual biographies and educative styles of the parents becomes the dominant factor in shaping the literate experiences of the children within the home. And yet, from the very beginning, the children are active and reactive in the sharing of literate experiences with their parents. Dewey speaks of the continuous alteration of such patterns by children as 'unconscious and unintended'. He speaks of immature and undeveloped activity succeeding in modifying 'adult organized activity accidently and surreptitiously' (1922, p. 92). Undoubtedly, each child brings a new dimension to the transmission of literacy style and values within the family.

References

Dewey, J. (1922) *Human Nature and Conduct.* New York: Random House. Reprinted 1957.
Leichter, H. J. (1973) The concept of educative style. *Teachers College Record* 75, 239–50.
— (1974) The family as educator. *Teachers College Record* 76, 175–217. Reprinted in H. J. Leichter, H. J. (ed.) *The Family as Educator.* New York Teachers College Press, 1977.
— (1978) Families and communities as educators: Some concepts of relationship. *Teachers College Records* 79, 567–658.
Neisser, U. (1979) Memory: What are the important questions? In M. M. Gruneburg, P. M. Morris and R. N. Sykes (eds) *Practical Applications of Memory.* London: Academic Press.
Sutton-Smith, B. and Rosenberg, B. G. (1970) *The Sibling.* New York: Holt, Rinehart & Winston.
Whitehead, A. N. (1925) Requisites for social progress. In *Science and the Modern World.* New York: The Free Press. Reprinted 1967.

6 What No Bedtime Story Means: Narrative Skills at Home and School

SHIRLEY BRICE HEATH

In the preface to *S/Z* Roland Barthes' work on ways in which readers read, Richard Howard writes: 'We require an education in literature . . . in order to discover that *what we have assumed* — with the complicity of our teachers — *was nature is in fact culture, that what was given is no more than a way of taking*' (emphasis not in the original; Howard 1974: ix).[1] This statement reminds us that the *culture* children learn as they grow up is, in fact, 'ways of taking' meaning from the environment around them. The means of making sense from books and relating their contents to knowledge about the real world is but one 'way of taking' that is often interpreted as 'natural' rather than learned. The quote also reminds us that teachers (and researchers alike) have not recognized that ways of taking from books are as much a part of learned behavior as are ways of eating, sitting, playing games, and building houses.

As school-oriented parents and their children interact in the pre-school years, adults give their children, through modelling and specific instruction, ways of taking from books which seem natural in school and in numerous institutional settings such as banks, post offices, businesses, or government offices. These *mainstream* ways exist in societies around the world that rely on formal educational systems to prepare children for participation in settings involving literacy. In some communities these ways of schools and institutions are very similar to the ways learned at home; in other communities the ways of school are merely an overlay on the home-taught ways and may be in conflict with them.[2]

Yet little is actually known about what goes on in story-reading and other literacy-related interactions between adults and preschoolers in communities around the world. Specifically, though there are numerous diary accounts and experimental studies of the preschool reading experiences of mainstream middle-class children, we know little about the specific literacy features of the environment upon which the school expects to draw. Just

73

how does what is frequently termed 'the literate tradition' envelope the child in knowledge about interrelationships between oral and written language, between knowing something and knowing ways of labelling and displaying it? We have even less information about the variety of ways children from *non-mainstream* homes learn about reading, writing, and using oral language to display knowledge in their preschool environment. The general view has been that whatever it is that mainstream school-oriented homes have, these other homes do not have it; thus these children are not from the literate tradition and are not likely to succeed in school.

A key concept for the empirical study of ways of taking meaning from written sources across communities is that of *literacy events*; occasions in which written language is integral to the nature of participants' interactions and their interpretive processes and strategies. Familiar literacy events for mainstream preschoolers are bedtime stories, reading cereal boxes, stop signs, and television ads, and interpreting instructions for commercial games and toys. In such literacy events, participants follow socially established rules for verbalizing what they know from and about the written material. Each community has rules for socially interacting and sharing knowledge in literacy events.

This paper briefly summarizes the ways of taking from printed stories families teach their preschoolers in a cluster of mainstream school-oriented neighborhoods of a city in the Southeastern region of the United States. We then describe two quite different ways of taking used in the homes of two English-speaking communities in the same region that do not follow the school-expected patterns of bookreading and reinforcement of these patterns in oral storytelling. Two assumptions underlie this paper and are treated in detail in the ethnography of these communities (Heath 1983):

(1) Each community's ways of taking from the printed word and using this knowledge are interdependent with the ways children learn to talk in their social interactions with caregivers.

(2) There is little or no validity to the time-honored dichotomy of 'the literate tradition' and 'the oral tradition'.

This paper suggests a frame of reference for both the community patterns and the paths of development children in different communities follow in their literacy orientations.

Mainstream School-Oriented Bookreading

Children growing up in mainstream communities are expected to develop habits and value which attest to their membership in a 'literate society'. Children learn certain customs, beliefs, and skills in early enculturation experiences with written materials: the bedtime story is a major literacy event which helps set patterns of behavior that recur repeatedly through the life of mainstream children and adults.

In both popular and scholarly literature, the 'bedtime story' is widely accepted as a given — a natural way for parents to interact with their child at bedtime. Commercial publishing houses, television advertising, and children's magazines make much of this familiar ritual, and many of their sales pitches are based on the assumption that in spite of the intrusion of television into many patterns of interaction between parents and children, this ritual remains. Few parents are fully conscious of what bedtime storyreading means as preparation for the kinds of learning and displays of knowledge expected in school. Ninio & Bruner (1978), in their longitudinal study of one mainstream middle class mother–infant dyad in joint picture-book reading, strongly suggest a universal role of bookreading in the achievement of labelling by children.

In a series of 'reading cycles', mother and child alternate turns in a dialogue: the mother directs the child's attention to the book and/or asks what-questions and/or labels items on the page. The items to which the what-questions are directed and labels given are two-dimensional representations of three-dimensional objects, so that the child has to resolve the conflict between perceiving these as two-dimensional objects and as representations of a three dimensional visual setting. The child does so 'by assigning a privileged, autonomous status to picture as visual objects' (1978: 5). The arbitrariness of the picture, its decontextualization, and its existence as something which cannot be grasped and manipulated like its 'real' counterparts is learned through the routines of structured interactional dialogue in which mother and child take turns playing a labelling game. In a 'scaffolding' dialogue (cf. Cazden, 1979), the mother points and asks 'What is x?' and the child vocalizes and/or gives a nonverbal signal of attention. The mother then provides verbal feedback and a label. Before the age of two, the child is socialized into the 'initiation–reply–evaluation sequences' repeatedly described as the central structural feature of classroom lessons (e.g. Sinclair & Coulthard, 1975; Griffin & Humphrey, 1978; Mehan, 1979). Teachers ask their students questions which have answers prespecified in the mind of the teacher. Students respond, and teachers provide feedback, usually in the form of an evaluation. Training in ways of responding to this pattern begins very early in the labelling activities of mainstream parents and children.

Mainstream ways

This patterning of 'incipient literacy' (Scollon & Scollon, 1979) is similar in many ways to that of the families of fifteen primary-level school teachers in

Maintown, a cluster of middle-class neighborhoods in a city of the Piedmont Carolinas. These families (all of whom identify themselves as 'typical', 'middle-class', or 'mainstream'), had preschool children, and the mother in each family was either teaching in local public schools at the time of the study (early 1970s), or had taught in the academic year preceding participation in the study. Through a research dyad approach, using teacher-mothers as researchers with the ethnographer, the teacher-mothers audio-recorded their children's interactions in their primary network — mothers, fathers, grandparents, maids, siblings, and frequent visitors to the home. Children were expected to learn the following rules in literacy events in these nuclear households:

(1) As early as six months of age, children *give attention to books and infor-mation derived from books*. The rooms contain bookcases and are decorated with murals, bedspreads, mobiles, and stuffed animals which represent characters found in books. Even when these characters have their origin in television programs, adults also provide books which either repeat or extend the characters' activities on television.

(2) Children, from the age of six months, *acknowledge questions about books*. Adults expand nonverbal responses and vocalizations from infants into fully formed grammatical sentences. When children begin to verbalize about the contents of books, adults extend their questions from simple requests for labels (What's that? Who's that?) to ask about the attributes of these items (What does the doggie say? What color is the ball?).

(3) From the time they start to talk, children *respond to conversational allu-sions to the content of books; they act as question–answerers who have a knowledge of books*. For example, a fuzzy black dog on the street is likened by an adult to Blackie in a child's book: 'Look, there's a Blackie. Do you think *he's* looking for a boy?'. Adults strive to maintain with children a running commentary on any event or object which can be book-related, thus modelling for them the extension of familiar items and events from books to new situational contexts.

(4) Beyond two years of age, children *use their knowledge of what books do to legitimate their departures from 'truth'*. Adults encourage and reward 'book talk', even when it is not directly relevant to an ongoing conversa-tion. Children are allowed to suspend reality, to tell stories which are not true, to ascribe fiction-like features to everyday objects.

(5) Preschool children *accept book and book-related activities as entertain-ment*. When preschoolers are 'captive audiences' (e.g. waiting in a doc-tor's office, putting a toy together, or preparing for bed), adults reach for books. If there are no books present, they talk about other objects as though they were pictures in books. For example, adults point to

items, and ask children to name, describe, and compare them to familiar objects in their environment. Adults often ask children to state their likes or dislikes, their view of events, and so forth, at the end of the captive audience period. These affective questions often take place while the next activity is already underway (e.g. moving toward the doctor's office, putting the new toy away, or being tucked into bed), and adults do not insist on answers.

(6) Preschoolers *announce their own factual and fictive narratives* unless they are given in response to direct adult elicitation. Adults judge as most acceptable those narratives which open by orienting the listener to setting and main character. Narratives which are fictional are usually marked by formulaic openings, a particular prosody, or the borrowing of episodes in story books.

(7) When children are about three years old, adults discourage the highly interactive participative role in bookreading children have hitherto played and children *listen and wait as an audience.* No longer does either adult or child repeatedly break into the story with questions and comments. Instead, children must listen, store what they hear, and on cue from the adult, answer a question. Thus, children begin to formulate 'practice' questions as they wait for the break and the expected formulaic-type questions from the adult. It is at this stage that children often choose to 'read' to adults rather than to be read to.

A pervasive pattern of all these features is the authority which books and book-related activities have in the lives of both the preschoolers and members of their primary network. Any initiation of a literacy event by a preschooler makes an interruption, an untruth, a diverting of attention from the matter at hand (whether it be an uneaten plate of food, a messy room, or an avoidance of going to bed) acceptable. Adults jump at openings their children give them for pursuing talk about books and reading.

In this study, writing was found to be somewhat less acceptable as an 'anytime activity', since adults have rigid rules about times, places, and materials for writing. The only restrictions on bookreading concern taking good care of books: they should not be wet, torn, drawn on, or lost. In their talk to children about books, and in their explanations of why they buy children's books, adults link school success to 'learning to love books', 'learning what books can do for you', and 'learning to entertain yourself and to work independently'. Many of the adults also openly expressed a fascination with children's books 'nowadays'. They generally judged them as more diverse, wide-ranging, challenging, and exciting than books they had as children.

The mainstream pattern

A close look at the way bedtime story routines in Maintown taught children how to take meaning from books raises a heavy sense of the familiar in all of us who have acquired mainstream habits and values. Throughout a lifetime, any school-successful individual moves through the same processes described above thousands of times. Reading for comprehension involves an internal replaying of the same types of questions adults ask children of bedtime stories. We seek *what-explanations,* asking what the topic is, establishing it as predictable and recognizing it in new situational contexts by classifying and categorizing it in our mind with other phenomena. The what-explanation is replayed in learning to pick out topic sentences, write outlines, and answer standardized tests which ask for the correct titles to stories, and so on. In learning to read in school, children move through a sequence of skills designed to teach what-explanations. There is a tight linear order of instruction which recapitulates the bedtime story pattern of breaking down the story into small bits of information and teaching children to handle sets of related skills in isolated sequential hierarchies.

In each individual reading episode in the primary years of schooling, children must move through what-explanations before they can provide *reason-explanations* or *affective commentaries.* Questions about why a particular event occurred or why a specific action was right or wrong come at the end of primary-level reading lessons, just as they come at the end of bedtime stories. Throughout the primary grade levels, what-explanations predominate, reason-explanations come with increasing frequency in the upper grades, and affective comments most often come in the extra-credit portions of the reading workbook or at the end of the list of suggested activities in text books across grade levels. This sequence characterizes the total school career. High school freshmen who are judged poor in compositional and reading skills spend most of their time on what-explanations and practice in advanced versions of bedtime story questions and answers. They are given little or no chance to use reason-giving explanations or assessments of the actions of stories. Reason-explanations result in configurational rather than hierarchical skills, are not predictable, and thus do not present content with a high degree of redundancy. Reason-giving explanations tend to rely on detailed knowledge of a specific domain. This detail is often unpredictable to teachers, and is not as highly valued as is knowledge which covers a particular area of knowledge with less detail but offers opportunity for extending the knowledge to larger and related concerns. For example, a primary-level student whose father owns a turkey farm may respond with reason-explanations to a story about a turkey. His knowledge is intensive and covers details perhaps not known to the teacher and not judged as relevant to the story. The knowledge is unpredictable and questions about it do not continue to repeat the common core of content knowledge of the story. Thus such configured knowledge is encouraged only for the 'extras' of reading — an extra-credit oral report or a creative picture and story about turkeys. This kind of knowledge is allowed to be used once the hierarchical what-explanations have been mastered and displayed in a particular situation and, in the course of one's academic career, only when one has shown full mastery of the hierarchical skills and subsets of related skills which underlie what-explanations. Thus, reliable and successful participation in the ways of taking from books that teachers view as natural must, in the usual school way of doing things, precede other ways of taking from books.

Close analyses of how mainstream school-oriented children come to learn to take from books at home suggest that such children learn not only how to take meaning from books, but also how to talk about it. In doing the latter, they repeatedly practice routines which parallel those of classroom interaction. By the time they enter school, they have had continuous experience as information-givers; they have learned how to perform in those interactions which surround literate sources throughout school. They have had years of practice in interaction situations that are the heart of reading — both learning to read and reading to learn in school. They have developed habits of performing which enable them to run through the hierarchy of preferred knowledge about a literate source and the appropriate sequence of skills to be displayed in showing knowledge of a subject. They have developed ways of decontextualizing and surrounding with explanatory prose the knowledge gained from selective attention to objects.

They have learned to listen, waiting for the appropriate cue which signals it is their turn to show off this knowledge. They have learned the rules for getting certain services from parents (or teachers) in the reading interaction (Merritt, 1979). In nursery school, they continue to practice these interaction patterns in a group rather than in a dyadic situation. There they learn additional signals and behaviors necessary for getting a turn in a group, and responding to a central reader and to a set of centrally defined reading tasks. In short, most of their waking hours during the preschool years have enculturated them into:

(1) all those habits associated with what-explanations,

(2) selective attention to items of the written text, *and*

(3) appropriate interactional styles for orally displaying all the know-how of their literate orientation to the environment.

This learning has been finely tuned and its habits are highly interdependent. Patterns of behaviors learned in one setting or at one stage reappear again and again as these children learn to use oral and written language in literacy events and to bring their knowledge to bear in school-acceptable ways.

Alternative Patterns of Literacy Events

But what corresponds to the mainstream pattern of learning in communities that do not have this finely tuned, consistent, repetitive, and continuous pattern of training? Are there ways of behaving which achieve other social and cognitive aims in other sociocultural groups?

The data below are summarized from an ethnography of two communities — Roadville and Trackson — located only a few miles from Maintown's neighborhoods in the Piedmont Carolinas. Roadville is a white working-class community of families steeped for four generations in the life of the textile mill. Trackton is a working-class black community whose older generations have been brought up on the land, either farming their own land or working for other landowners. However, in the past decade, they have found work in the textile mills. Children of both communities are unsuccessful in school; yet both communities place a high value on success in school, believing earnestly in the personal and vocational rewards school can bring and urging their children 'to get ahead' by doing well in school. Both Roadville and Trackton are literate communities in the sense that the residents of each are able to read printed and written materials in their daily lives, and on occasion they produce written messages as part of the total pattern of communication in the community. In both communities, children go to school with certain expectancies of print and, in Trackton especially, children have a keen sense that reading is something one does to learn something one needs to know (Heath, 1980). In both groups, residents turn from spoken to written uses of language and vice versa as the occasion demands, and the two modes of expression seem to supplement and reinforce each other. Nonetheless there are radical differences between the two communities in the ways in which children and adults interact in the preschool years; each of the two communities also differs from Maintown. Roadville and Trackton view children's learning of language from two radically different perspectives: in Trackton, children 'learn to talk', in Roadville, adults 'teach them how to talk'.

Roadville

In Roadville, babies are brought home from the hospital to rooms decorated with colorful, mechanical, musical, and literacy-based stimuli. The walls are decorated with pictures based on nursery rhymes, and from an early age, children are held and prompted to 'see' the wall decorations. Adults recite nursery rhymes as they twirl the mobile made of nursery-rhyme characters. The items of the child's environment promote exploration of colors, shapes, and textures: a stuffed ball with sections of fabrics of different colors and textures is in the crib; stuffed animals vary in texture, size, and shape. Neighbors, friends from church, and relatives come to visit and talk to the baby, and about him to those who will listen. The baby is fictionalized in the talk to him: 'But this baby wants to go to sleep, doesn't he? Yes, see those little eyes gettin' heavy.' As the child grows older, adults pounce on word-like sounds and turn them into 'words', repeating the 'words', and expanding them into well-formed sentences. Before they can talk, children are introduced to visitors and prompted to provide all the expected politeness formulas, such as 'Bye-bye', 'Thank you', and so forth. As soon as they can talk, children are reminded about these formulas, and book or television characters known to be 'polite' are involved as reinforcement.

In each Roadville home, preschoolers first have cloth books, featuring a single object on each page. They later acquire books which provide sounds, smells, and different textures or opportunities for practicing small motor skills (closing zippers, buttoning buttons, etc.). A typical collection for a two-year-old consisted of a dozen or so books — eight featured either the alphabet or numbers, others were books of nursery rhymes, simplified Bible stories, or 'real-life' stories about boys and girls (usually taking care of their pets or exploring a particular feature of their environment). Books based on Sesame Street characters were favorite gifts for three- and four-year-olds.

Reading and reading-related activities occur most frequently before naps or at bedtime in the evening. Occasionally an adult or older child will read to a fussy child while the mother prepares dinner or changes a bed. On weekends, fathers sometimes read with their children for brief periods of time, but they generally prefer to play games or play with the children's toys in their interactions.

Bookreading time focuses on letters of the alphabet, numbers, names of basic items pictured in books, and simplified retellings of stories in the words of the adult. If the content or story plot seems too complicated for the child, the adult tells the story in short, simple sentences, frequently laced with requests that the child give what-explanations.

In Roadville's literacy events, the rules for cooperative discourse around print are repeatedly practiced, coached, and rewarded in the preschool years. Adults in Roadville believe that instilling in children the proper use of words and understanding of the meaning of the written word are important for both their educational and religious success. Adults repeat aspects of the learning of literacy events they have known as children. In the words of one Roadville parent: 'It was then that I began to learn . . . when my daddy kept insisting I *read* it, *say* it right. It was then that I *did* right, in his view.'

The path of development for such performance can be described in three overlapping stages. In the first, children are introduced to discrete bits and pieces of books — separate items, letters of the alphabet, shapes, colors, and commonly represented items in books for children (apple, baby, ball, etc.). The latter are usually decontextualized, not pictured in their ordinary contexts, and they are represented in two-dimensional flat line drawings. During this stage, children must participate as predictable information-givers and respond to questions that ask for specific and discrete bits of information about the written matter. In these literacy events, specific features of the two-dimensional items in books which are different from their 'real' counterparts are not pointed out. A ball in a book is flat; a duck in a book is yellow and fluffy; trucks, cars, dogs, and trees talk in books. No mention is made of the fact that such features do not fit these objects in reality. Children are not encouraged to move their understanding of books into other situational contexts or to apply it in their general knowledge of the world about them.

In the second stage, adults demand an acceptance of the power of print to entertain, inform, and instruct. When [children can] no longer participate by contributing their knowledge at any point in the literacy event, they learn to recognize bookreading as a performance. The adult exhibits the book to [the child; the child is] to be entertained, to learn from the information conveyed in the material, and to remember the book's content for the sequential follow-up questioning, as opposed to ongoing cooperative participatory questions.

In the third stage, [children are] introduced to preschool workbooks which provided story information and are asked questions or provided exercises and games based on the content of the stories or pictures. Follow-the-number coloring books and preschool 'push-out and paste' workbooks on shapes, colors, and letters of the alphabet reinforce repeatedly that the written word can be taken apart into small pieces and one item linked to another by following rules. [Children are given] practice in the linear, sequential nature of books: begin at the beginning, stay in the lines for coloring, draw straight lines to link one item to another, write your answers on lines, keep your letters straight, match the cutout letter to diagrams of letter shapes.

The differences between Roadville and Maintown are substantial. Roadville adults do not extend either the content or the habits of literacy events beyond bookreading. They do not, upon seeing an item or event in the real world, remind children of a similar event in a book and launch a running commentary on similarities and differences. When a game is played or a chore done, adults do not use literate sources. Mothers cook without written recipes most of the time; if they use a recipe from a written source, they do so usually only after confirmation and alteration by friends who have tried the recipe. Directions to games are read, but not carefully followed, and they are not talked about in a series of questions and answers which try to establish their meaning. Instead, in the putting together of toys or the playing of games, the abilities or preferences of one party prevail. For example, if an adult knows how to put a toy together, he does so; he does not talk about the process, refer to the written material and 'translate' for the child, or try to sequence steps so the child can do it.[3]

Adults at tasks do not provide a verbal commentary on what they are doing. They do not draw the attention of the child to specific features of the sequences of skills or the attributes of items. They do not ask questions of the child, except questions which are directive or scolding in nature. Explanations which move beyond the listing of names of items and their features are rarely offered by adults. Children do not ask questions of the type 'But I don't understand. What is that?' They appear willing to keep trying, and if there is ambiguity in a set of commands, they ask a question such as 'You want me to do this?' (demonstrating their current efforts), or they try to find a way of diverting attention from the task at hand.

Roadville parents provide their children with books; they read to them and ask questions about the books' contents. They choose books which emphasize nursery rhymes, alphabet learning, animals, and simplified Bible stories, and they require their children to repeat from these books and to answer formulaic questions about their contents. Roadville adults also ask questions about oral stories which have a point relevant to some marked behavior of a child. They use proverbs and summary statements to remind their children of stories and to call on them for simple comparisons of the stories' contents to their own situations. Roadville parents coach children in their telling of a story, forcing them to tell about an incident as it has been pre-composed or pre-scripted in the head of the adult. Thus, in Roadville, children come to know a story as either an accounting from a book, or a factual account of a real event in which some type of marked behavior occurred and there is a lesson to be learned. Any fictionalized account of a real event is viewed as a *lie*; reality is better than fiction. Roadville's church and community life admit no story other than that which meets the definition internal to the group. Thus children cannot decontextualize their knowledge or fictionalize events known to them and shift them about into other frames.

When these children go to school they perform well in the initial stages of each of the three early grades. They often know portions of the alphabet, some colors and numbers, can recognize their names, and tell some their address and their parents' names. They will sit still and listen to a story, and they know how to answer questions asking for what-explanations. They do well in reading workbook exercises which ask for identification of specific portions of words, items from the story, or the linking of two items, letters, or parts of words on the same page. When the teacher reaches the end of story-reading or the reading circle and asks questions such as 'What did you like about the story?', relatively few Roadville children answer. If asked questions such as 'What would you have done if you had been Billy [story's main character]?', Roadville children most frequently say 'I don't know' or shrug their shoulders.

Near the end of each year, and increasingly as they move through the early primary grades, Roadville children can handle successfully the initial stages of lessons. But when they move ahead to extra-credit items or to activities considered more advanced and requiring more independence, they are stumped. They turn frequently to teachers asking 'Do you want me to do this? What do I do here?' If asked to write a creative story or tell it into a tape recorder, they retell stories from books; they do not create their own. They rarely provide emotional or personal commentary on their accounting of real events or book stories. They are rarely able to take knowledge learned in one context and shift it to another; they do not compare two items or events and point out similarities and differences. They find it difficult either to hold one feature of an event constant and shift all others or to hold all features constant but one. For example, they are puzzled by questions such as 'What would have happened if Billy had not told the policemen what happened?' They do not know how to move events or items out of a given frame. To a question such as 'What habits of the Hopi Indians might they be able to take with them when they move to a city?', they provide lists of features of life of the Hopi on the reservation. They do not take these items, consider their appropriateness in an urban setting, and evaluate the hypothetical outcome. In general, they find this type of question impossible to answer, and they do not know how to ask teachers to help them take apart the questions to figure out the answers. Thus their initial successes in reading, being good students, following orders, and adhering to school norms of participating in lessons begin to fall away rapidly about the time they enter the fourth grade. As the importance and frequency of questions and reading habits with which they are familiar decline in the higher grades, they have no way of keeping up or of seeking help in learning what it is they do not even know they don't know.

Trackton

Babies in Trackton come home from the hospital to an environment which is almost entirely human. There are no cribs, car beds, or car sets, and only an occasional high chair or infant seat. Infants are held during their waking hours, occasionally while they sleep, and they usually sleep in the bed with parents until they are about two years of age. They are held, their faces fondled, their cheeks pinched, and they eat and sleep in the midst of human talk and noise from the television, stereo, and radio. Encapsulated in an almost totally human world, they are in the midst of constant human communication, verbal and nonverbal. They literally feel the body signals of shifts in emotion of those who hold them almost continuously; they are talked about and kept in the midst of talk about topics that range over any subject. As children make cooing or babbling sounds, adults refer to this as 'noise', and no attempt is made to interpret these sounds as words or communicative attempts on the part of the baby. Adults believe they should not have to depend on their babies to tell them what they need or when they are uncomfortable; adults know, children only 'come to know'.

When a child can crawl and move about on his own, he plays with the household objects deemed safe for him — pot lids, spoons, plastic food containers. Only at Christmastime are there special toys for very young children; these are usually trucks, balls, doll babies, or plastic cars, but rarely blocks, puzzles, or books. As children become completely mobile, they demand ride toys or electronic and mechanical toys they see on television. They never request nor do they receive manipulative toys, such as puzzles, blocks, take-apart toys or literacy-based items, such as books or letter games.

Adults read newspapers, mail, calendars, circulars (political and civic-events related), school materials sent home to parents, brochures advertising new cars, television sets, or other products, and the Bible and other church-related materials. There are no reading materials especially for children (with the exception of children's Sunday School materials), and adults do not sit and read to children. Since children are usually left to sleep whenever and wherever they fall asleep, there is no bedtime or naptime as such. At night, they are put to bed when the adults go to bed or whenever the person holding them gets tired. Thus, going to bed is not framed in any special routine. Sometimes in a play activity during the day, an older sibling will read to a younger child, but the latter soon loses interest and squirms away to play. Older children often try to 'play school' with younger children, reading to them from books and trying to ask questions about what they have read. Adults look on these efforts with amusement and do not try to convince the small child to sit still and listen.

Signs from very young children of attention to the nonverbal behaviors of others are rewarded by extra fondling, laughter, and cuddling from adults. For example, when an infant shows signs of recognizing a family member's voice on the phone by bouncing up and down in the arms of the adult who is talking on the phone, adults comment on this to others present and kiss and nudge the child. Yet when children utter sounds or combinations of sounds which could be interpreted as words, adults pay no attention. Often by the time they are twelve months old, children approximate words or phrases of adults' speech; adults respond by laughing or giving special attention to the child and crediting him with 'sounding like' the person being imitated. When children learn to walk and imitate the walk of members of the community, they are rewarded by comments on their activities: 'He walks just like Toby when he's tuckered out.'

Children between the ages of twelve and twenty-four months often imitate the tune or 'general Gestalt' (Peters, 1977) of complete utterances they hear around them. They pick up and repeat chunks (usually the ends) of phrasal and clausal utterances of speakers around them. They seem to remember fragments of speech and repeat these without active production. In this first stage of language learning, the repetition stage, they imitate the intonation contours and general shaping of the utterances they repeat. Lem 1;2 in the following example illustrates this pattern:

Mother: [talking to neighbor on porch while Lem plays with a truck on the porch nearby] But they won't call back, won't happen =
Lem: = call back
Neighbor: Sam's going over there Saturday, he'll pick up a form =
Lem: = pick up on, pick up on [Lem here appears to have heard *form* as *on*]

The adults pay no attention to Lem's 'talk', and their talk, in fact, often overlaps his repetitions.

In the second stage, repetition with variations, Trackton children manipulate pieces of conversation they pick up. They incorporate chunks of language from others into their own ongoing dialogue, applying productive rules, inserting new nouns and verbs for those used in the adults' chunks. They also play with rhyming patterns and varying intonation contours.

Mother: She went to the doctor again.
Lem (2;2): [in a sing-song fashion] went to de doctor, doctor, tractor, dis my tractor, doctor on a tractor, went to de doctor.

Lem creates a monologue, incorporating the conversation about him into his own talk as he plays. Adults pay no attention to his chatter unless it gets so noisy as to intefere with their talk.

In the third stage, participation, children begin to enter the ongoing conversations about them. They do so by attracting the adult's attention with a tug on the arm or pant leg, and they help make themselves understood by providing nonverbal reinforcements to help recreate a scene they want the listener to remember. For example, if adults are talking, and a child interrupts with seemingly unintelligible utterances, the child will make gestures, extra sounds, or act out some outstanding features of the scene he is trying to get the adult to remember. Children try to create a context, a scene, for the understanding of their utterance.

This third stage illustrates a pattern in the children's response to their environment and their ways of letting others know their knowledge of the environment. Once they are in the third stage, their communicative efforts are accepted by community members, and adults respond directly to the child, instead of talking to others about the child's activities as they have done in the past. Children continue to practice for conversational participation by playing, when alone, both parts of dialogues, imitating gestures as well as intonation patterns of adults. By 2;6 all children in the community can imitate the walk and talk of others in the community, or frequent visitors such as the man who comes around to read the gas meters. They can feign anger, sadness, fussing, remorse, silliness, or any of a wide range of expressive behaviors. They often use the same chunks of language for varying effects, depending on nonverbal support to give the language different meanings or case it in a different key (Hymes, 1974). Girls between three and four years of age take part in extraordinarily complex stepping and clapping patterns and simple repetitions of hand clap games played by older girls. From the time they are old enough to stand alone, they are encouraged in their participation by siblings and older children in the community. These games require anticipation and recognition of cues for upcoming behaviors, and the young girls learn to watch for these cues and to come in with the appropriate words and movements at the right time.

Preschool children are not asked for what-explanations of their environment. Instead, they are asked a preponderance of analogical questions which call for non-specific comparisons of one item, event, or person with another: 'What's that like?' Other types of questions ask for specific information known to the child but not the adults: 'Where'd you get that from?' 'What do you want?' 'How come you did that?' (Heath, 1982). Adults explain their use of these types of questions by expressing their sense of children: they are 'comers', coming into their learning by experiencing what knowing about things means. As one parent of a two-year-old boy put it: 'Ain't no use me tellin' 'im: learn this, learn that, what's this, what's that? He just gotta learn, gotta know; he see one thing one place one time, he know how it go, see sump'n like it again, maybe it be the same, maybe it won't.' Children are expected to learn how to know when the form belies the meaning, and to know contexts of items and to use their understanding of these contexts to draw parallels between items and events. Parents do not believe they have a tutoring role in this learning; they provide the experiences on which the child draws and reward signs of their successfully coming to know.

Trackton children's early stories illustrate how they respond to adult views of them as 'comers'. The children learn to tell stories by drawing heavily on their abilities to render a context, to set a stage, and to call on the audience's power to join in the imaginative creation of story. Between the ages of two and four years, the children, in a monologue-like fashion, tell stories

about things in their lives, events they see and hear, and situations in which
they have been involved. They produce these spontaneously during play
with other children or in the presence of adults. Sometimes they make an
effort to attract the attention of listeners before they begin the story, but
often they do not. Lem, playing off the edge of the porch, when he was about
two and a half years of age, heard a bell in the distance. He stopped, looked
at Nellie and Benjy, his older siblings, who were nearby and said:

Way
Far
Now
It a church bell
Ringin'
Dey singin'
Ringin'
You hear it?
I hear it
Far
Now

Lem had been taken to church the previous Sunday and had been much impressed by the church bell. He had sat on his mother's lap and joined in the singing, rocking to and fro on her lap, and clapping his hands. His story, which is
like a poem in its imagery and line-like prosody, is in response to the current
stimulus of a distant bell. As he tells the story, he sways back and forth.

This story, somewhat longer than those usually reported from other
social groups for children as young as Lem,[4] has some features which have
come to characterize fully-developed narratives or stories. It capitulates in
its verbal outline the sequence of events being recalled by the storyteller. At
church, the bell rang while the people sang. In the line 'It a church bell', Lem
provides his story's topic, and a brief summary of what is to come. This line
serves a function similar to the formulae often used by older children to open
a story: 'This is a story about (a church bell)', Lem gives only the slightest
hint of story setting or orientation to the listener; where and when the story
took place are capsuled in 'Way, Far'. Preschoolers in Trackton almost
never hear 'Once upon a time there was a . . . .' stories, and they rarely provide definitive orientations for their stories. They seem to assume listeners
'Know' the situation in which the narrative takes place. Similarly, preschoolers in Trackton do not close off their stories with formulaic endings. Lem
poetically balances his opening and closing in an inclusion, beginning 'Way,
Far, Now' and ending 'Far, Now'. The effect is one of closure, but there is
no clearcut announcement of closure. Throughout the presentation of
action and result of action in their stories, Trackton preschoolers invite the
audience to respond or evaluate the story's actions. Lem asks 'You hear it?'
which may refer either to the current stimulus or to yesterday's bell, since

Lem does not productively use past tense endings for any verbs at this stage in his language development.

Preschooler storytellers have several ways of inviting audience evaluation and interest. They may themselves express an emotional response to the story's actions; they may have another character or narrator in the story do so often using alliterative language play; or they may detail actions and results through direct discourse or sound effects and gestures. All these methods of calling attention to the story and its telling distinguish the speech event as a story, an occasion for audience and storyteller to interact pleasantly, and not simply to hear an ordinary recounting of events or actions.

Trackton children must be aggressive in inserting their stories into an ongoing stream of discourse. Storytelling is highly competitive. Everyone in a conversation may want to tell a story, so only the most aggressive wins out. The content ranges widely, and there is 'truth' only in the universals of human experience. Fact is often hard to find, though it is usually the seed of the story Trackton stories often have no point — no obvious beginning or ending; they go on as long as the audience enjoys and tolerates the story-teller's entertainment.

Trackton adults do not separate out the elements ofthe environment around their children to tune their attentions selectively. They do not simplify their language, focus on single-word utterances by young children, label items or features of objects in either books or the environment at large. Instead, children are continuously contextualized, presented with almost continuous communication. From this ongoing, multiple-channeled stream of stimuli, they must themselves select, practice, and determine rules of production and structuring. For language, they do so by first repeating, catching chunks of sounds, intonation contours, and practicing these without specific reinforcement or evaluation. But practice material and models are continuously available. Next the children seem to begin to sort out the productive rules for speech and practice what they hear about them with variation. Finally, they work their way into conversations, hooking their meanings for listeners into a familiar context by recreating scenes through gestures, special sound effects, etc. These characteristics continue in their story-poems and their participation in jump-rope rhymes. Because adults do not select out, name, and describe features of the environment for the young, children must perceive situations, determine how units of the situations are related to each other, recognize these relations in other situations, and reason through what it will take to show their correlation of one situation with another. The children can answer questions such as 'What's that like?' ('It's like Doug's car') but they can rarely name the specific feature or features which make two items or events alike. For example, in the case of saying a car seen on the street is 'like Doug's car', a child may be basing the analogy on the fact that this car has a flat tyre and Doug's also had one last week. But the child does not name (and is not asked to name) what is alike between the two cars.

Children seem to develop connections between situations or items not by specification of labels and features in the situations, but by configuration links. Recognition of similar general shapes or patterns of links seen in one situation and connected to another, seem to be the means by which children set scenes in their nonverbal representations of individuals, and later in their verbal chunking, then segmentation and production of rules for putting together isolated units. They do not decontextualize; instead they heavily contextualize nonverbal and verbal language. They fictionalize their 'true stories', but they do so by asking the audience to identify with the story through making parallels from their own experiences. When adults read, they often do so in a group. One person, reading aloud, for example, from a brochure on a new car decodes the text, displays illustrations and photographs, and listeners relate the text's meaning to their experiences asking questions and expressing opinions. Finally, the group as a whole synthesizes the written text and the negotiated oral discourse to construct a meaning for the brochure (Heath, 1982).

When Trackton children go to school, they face unfamiliar types of questions which ask for what-explanations. They are asked as individuals to identify items by name, and to label features such as shape, color, size, number. The stimuli to which they are to give these responses are two-dimensional flat representations which are often highly stylized and bear little resemblance to the 'real' items. Trackton children generally score in the lowest percentile range on the Metropolitan Reading Readiness tests. They do not sit at their desks and complete reading workbook pages: neither do they tolerate questions about reading materials which are structured along the usual lesson format. Their contributions are in the form of 'I had a duck at my house one time', 'Why'd he do that?' or they imitate the sound effects teachers may produce in stories they read to the children. By the end of the first three primary grades, their general language arts scores have been consistently low, except for those few who have begun to adapt to and adopt some of the behaviors they have had to learn in school. But the majority not only fail to learn the content of lessons, they also do not adopt the social interactional rules for school literacy events. Print in isolation bears little authority in their world. The kinds of questions asked of reading books are unfamiliar. The children's abilities to metaphorically link two events or situations and to recreate scenes are not tapped in the school; in fact, *these abilities often cause difficulties,* because they enable children to see parallels teachers did not intend, and indeed, may not recognize until the children point them out (Heath, 1978).

By the end of the lessons or by the time in their total school career when reason-explanations and affective statements call for the creative comparison of two or more situations, it is too late for many Trackton children. They have not picked up along the way the composition and comprehension skills they need to translate their analogical skills into a channel teachers can accept. They seem not to know how to take meaning from reading; they do not observe the rules of linearity in writing, and their expression of themselves on paper is very limited. Orally taped stories are often much better, but these rarely count as much as written compositions. Thus, Trackton children continue to collect very low or failing grades, and many decide by the end of the sixth grade to stop trying and turn their attention to the heavy peer socialization which usually begins in these years.

From Community to Classroom

A recent review of trends in research on learning pointed out that 'learning to read through using and learning from language has been less systematically studied than the decoding process' (Glaser, 1979: 7). Put another way, how children learn to use language to read to learn has been less systematically studied than decoding skills. Learning how to take meaning from writing before one learns to read involves repeated practice in using and learning from language through appropriate participation in literacy events such as exhibitor/questioner and spectator/respondent dyads (Scollon & Scollon, 1979) or group negotiation of the meaning of a written text. Children have to learn to select, hold, and retrieve content from books and other written or printed texts in accordance with their community's rules or 'ways of taking', and the children's learning follows community paths of language socialization. In each society, certain kinds of childhood participation in literacy events may precede others, as the developmental sequence builds toward the whole complex of home and community behaviors characteristic of the society. The ways of taking employed in the school may in turn build directly on the preschool development, may require substantial adaptation of the preschool development, may require substantial adaption on the part of the children, or may even run directly counter to aspects of the community's pattern.

In the early reading stages, and in later requirements for reading to learn at more advanced stages, children from the three communities respond differently, because they have learned different methods and degrees of taking from books. In comparison to Maintown children, the habits Roadville children learned in bookreading and toy-related episodes have not continued for them through other activities and types of reinforcement in their environment. They have had less exposure to both the content of books and ways of learning from books than have mainstream children. Thus their need in schools is not necessarily for an intensification of presentation of labels, a slowing down of the sequence of introducing what-explanations in connection with bookreading. Instead they need *extension of these habits to other domains* and to opportunities for practicing habits such as producing running commentaries, creating exhibitor/questioner and spectator/respondent roles. Perhaps most important, Roadville children need to have articulated for them *distinctions in discourse strategies and structures.* Narratives of real events have certain strategies and structures; imaginary tales, flights of fancy, and affective expressions have others. Their community's view of narrative discourse style is very narrow and demands a passive role in both creation of and response to the account of events. Moreover, these children have *to be reintroduced in a participant frame of reference to a book.* Though initially they were participants in bookreading, they have been trained into passive roles since the age of three years, and they must learn once again to be active information-givers, taking from books and linking that knowledge to other aspects of their environment.

Trackton students present an additional set of alternatives for procedures in the early primary grades. Since they usually have few of the expected 'natural' skills of taking meaning from books, they must not only learn these, but also *retain their analogical reasoning practices* for use in some of the later stages of learning to read. They must *learn to adapt the creativity in language, metaphor, fictionalization, recreation of scenes and exploration of functions and settings of items they bring to school.* These children already use narrative skills highly rewarded in the upper primary grades. They distinguish a fictionalized story from a real-life narrative. They know that telling a story can be in many ways related to play; it suspends reality, and frames an old event in a new context; it calls on audience participation to recognize the setting and participants. They must now *learn as individuals to recount factual events in a straightforward way* and *recognize appropriate occasions for reason-explanations and affective expressions.* Trackton children seem to have skipped learning to label, list features, and give what-explanations. Thus they need to *have the mainstream or school habits presented in familiar activities with explanations related to their own habit of taking meaning* from the environment. Such 'simple', 'natural' things as distinctions between two-dimensional and three-dimensional objects may need to be explained to help Trackton children learn the stylization and decontextualization which characterizes books.

To lay out in more specific detail how Roadville and Trackton's ways of knowing can be used along with those of mainstreamers goes beyond the scope of this paper. However, it must be admitted that a range of alternatives to ways of learning and displaying knowledge characterizes all highly school-successful adults in the advanced stages of their careers. Knowing more about how these alternatives are learned at early ages in different sociocultural conditions can help the school to provide opportunities for *all* students to avail themselves of these alternatives early in their school careers.

Notes

1. First presented at the Terman Conference on Teaching at Stanford University, 1980, this paper has benefitted from cooperation with M. Cochran-Smith of the University of Pennsylvania. She shares an appreciation of the relevance of Roland Barthes' work for studies of the socialization of young children into literacy; her research (1981) on the story-reading practices of a mainstream school-oriented nursery school provides a much needed detailed account of early school orientation to literacy.
2. Terms such as *mainstream* or *middle-class* cultures or social groups are frequently used in both popular and scholarly writings without careful definition. Moreover, numerous studies of behavioral phenomena (for example, mother–child interactions in language learning) either do not specify that the subjects being described are drawn from mainstream groups or do not recognize the importance of this limitation. As a result, findings from this group are often regarded as universal. For a discussion of this problem, see Chanan & Gilchrist, 1974; Payne & Bennett, 1977. In general, the literature characterizes this group as school-oriented, aspiring toward upward mobility through formal institutions, and providing enculturation which positively values routines of promptness, linearity (in habits ranging from furniture arrangement to entrance into a movie theatre), and evaluative and judgmental responses to behaviors which deviate from their norms.

    In the United States, mainstream families tend to locate in neighborhoods and suburbs around cities. Their social interactions center not in their immediate neighborhoods, but around voluntary associations across the city. Thus a cluster of mainstream families (and not a community — which usually implies a specific geographic territory as the locus of a majority of social interactions) is the unit of comparison used here with the Trackton and Roadville communities.
3. Behind this discussion are findings from cross-cultural psychologists who have studied the links between verbalization of task and demonstration of skills in a hierarchical sequence, e.g. Childs & Greenfield, 1980; see Goody, 1979 on the use of questions in learning tasks unrelated to a familiarity with books.
4. Cf. Umiker-Sebeok's (1979) descriptions of stories of mainstream middle-class children, ages 3–5 and Sutton-Smith, 1981.

References

Basso, K. (1974) The ethnography of writing. In R. Bauman and J. Sherzer (eds) *Explorations in the Ethnography of Speaking.* Cambridge University Press.

Cazden, C. B. (1979) Peekaboo as an instructional model: Discourse development at home and at school. *Papers and Reports in Child Language Development* 17, 1–29.

Chanan, G. and Gilchrist, L. (1974) *What School is For.* New York: Praeger.

Childs, C. P. and Greenfield, P. M. (1980) Informal modes of learning and teaching. In N. Warren (ed.) *Advances in Cross-Cultural Psychology* Vol. 2. London: Academic Press.

Cochran-Smith, M. (1981) The making of a reader. Ph.D. dissertation. University of Pennsylvania.
Cohen, R. (1968) The relation between socio-conceptual styles and orientation to school requirements. *Sociology of Education* 41, 201–20.
— (1969) Conceptual styles, culture conflict, and nonverbal tests of intelligence. *American Anthropologist* 71 (5), 828–56.
— (1971) The influence of conceptual rule-sets on measures of learning ability. In C. L. Brace, G. Gamble and J. Bond (eds) *Race and Intelligence* (Anthropological Studies, No. 8, American Anthropological Association) 41–57.
Glaser, R. (1979) Trends and research questions in psychological research on learning and schooling. *Educational Researcher* 8 (10), 6–13.
Goody, E. (1979) Towards a theory of questions. In E. N. Goody (ed.) *Questions and Politeness: Strategies in Social Interaction.* Cambridge University Press.
Griffin, P. and Humphrey, F. (1978) Task and talk. In *The Study of Children's Functional Language and Education in the Early Years.* Final report to the Carnegie Corporation of New York, Arlington, VA: Center for Applied Linguistics.
Heath, S. (1978) *Teacher Talk: Language in the Classroom* (Language in Education 9). Arlington, VA: Center for Applied Linguistics.
— (1980) The functions and uses of literacy. *Journal of Communication* 30 (1), 123–33.
— (1982) Questioning at home and at school: A comparative study. In G. Spindler (ed.) *Doing Ethnography: Educational Anthropology in Action.* New York: Holt, Rinehart & Winston.
— (1982) Protean shapes: Ever-shifting oral and literate traditions. In D. Tannen (ed.) *Spoken and Written Language: Exploring Orality and Literacy.* Norwood, NJ: Ablex.
— (1983) *Ways with Words: Language, Life and Work in Communities and Classrooms.* Cambridge: Cambridge University Press.
Howard, R. (1974) A note on S/Z. In R. Barthes *Introduction to S/Z.* Trans. Richard Miller. New York: Hill and Wang.
Hymes, D. H. (1973) On the origins and foundations of inequality among speakers. In E. Haugen and M. Bloomfield (eds) *Language as a Human Problem.* New York: W. W. Norton & Co.
— (1974) Models of the interaction of language and social life. In J. J. Gumperz and D. Hymes (eds) *Directions in Sociolinguistics.* New York: Holt, Rinehart & Winston.
Kagen, J., Sigel, I. and Moss, H. (1963) Psychological significance of styles of conceptualization. In J. Wright and J. Kagen (eds) *Basic Cognitive Processes in Children* (Monographs of the Society for Research in Child Development) 28 (2), 73–112.
Mehan, H. (1979) *Learning Lessons.* Cambridge, MA: Harvard University Press.
Merritt, M. (1979) Service-like events during individual work time and their contribution to the nature of the rules for communication. NIE Report EP 78-0436.
Ninio, A. and Bruner, J. (1978) The achievement and antecedents of labelling. *Journal of Child Language* 5, 1–15.
Payne, C. and Bennett, C. (1977) 'Middle class aura' in public schools. *The Teacher Educator* 13 (1), 16–26.
Peters, A. (1977) Language learning strategies. *Language* 53, 560–73.
Scollon, R. and Scollon, S. (1979) The literate two-year old: The fictionalization of self. *Working Papers in Sociolinguistics.* Austin, TX: Southwest Regional Laboratory.
Sinclair, J. M. and Coulthard, R. M. (1975) *Toward an Analysis of Discourse.* New York: Oxford University Press.

Sutton-Smith, B. (1981) *The Folkstories of Children.* Philadelphia: University of
   Pennsylvania Press.
Umiker-Sebeok, J. D. (1979) Preschool children's intraconversational narratives.
   Journal of Child Language 6 (1), 91–110.
Witkin, H., Faterson, F., Goodenough, R. and Birnbaum, J. (1966) Cognitive pat-
   terning in mildly retarded boys. *Child Development* 37 (2), 301–16.

7 Literacies Among the Panjabis in Southall (Britain)

MUKUL SAXENA

This paper is based on an ethnographic study of the literacy situation that exists among Panjabis,[1] particularly Panjabi Hindus, in Southall, an area of the Borough of Ealing, in the Western part of Greater London. The total population of Southall is about 120,000. The South Asian population is approximately 69,000. Of the total South Asian population, about 77 per cent are Panjabi Sikhs, 20 per cent are Panjabi Hindus, and the rest are a mix of various other South Asian minorities, including Panjabi, Gujarati and Urdu speaking Muslims, and Gujarati and Tamil speaking Hindus. Since Sikh and Hindu Panjabis are in the numerical majority, one is more likely to encounter the use of spoken and written Panjabi, Hindi and Urdu in Southall than that of Gujarati, Bangali or Tamil.

The literacy practices in the Panjabi community in Southall, West London, have changed enormously since the first group of Panjabi men came to Britain in 1950s. The third generation Panjabis are now living and growing up in a much more varied and complex situation of multilingual literacies than the first and second generation Panjabis ever did.

In the first part of this paper I present a case study of a Panjabi Hindu family. It shows how individual members of this family are exposed to and make use of different literacies in Southall. It also draws attention to the values they assign to these literacies. In the second part, I provide an historical account of the literacy situation in the regions of origin of Panjabis. It will be helpful in understanding their current literacy practices in Southall. In the third and final part, I look at the political, economic, social and religious processes that have shaped the multiliteracy situation in Southall since the Panjabis migrated to Britain.

I Multiliteracy Practices in Southall: A Case Study of a Panjabi Hindu Family

This section provides an account of some of the literacy practices of individual members of a Panjabi Hindu family in Southall. It will provide

Panjabi is normally written in Gurmukhi script and associated with Sikhs:

ਨਸਲੀ ਭੇਦਭਾਵ ਦੇ ਵਿਰੁੱਧ ਸਾਲ
ਦੀ ਪਾਲਿਸੀ ਦਾ ਵਿਸਥਾਰ

Hindi is normally written in Devanagari script and associated with Hindus:

नस्ली भेदभाव के विरुद्ध वर्ष
की नीति के बारे में बयान

Urdu is normally written in Perso-Arabic script and associated with Muslims:

نسلی مناہرت کے خلاف سال ۔ پالیسی کا بیان

All three languages can be written in all three scripts. Everyday spoken Hindi and Urdu are very similar, especially in their grammatical structures. However, in certain contexts, users of these languages try to bring in the words of Sanskrit or Perso-Arabic origin in their speech and writing to show their allegiance to Hindus or Muslims.

Figure 1 Script choices and religious identities

examples of how they make use of different literacies in their daily lives and, hopefully, throw some light on the literacy repertoire and literacy practices of the Panjabi Hindu community and the larger Panjabi community in Southall. We shall see, in this section, how individuals in this community are exposed to different print media; how they make literacy choices for different purposes; and how they value different literacies in their repertoire.

This family consists of a 4-year-old boy, his parents and grandparents. I chose this family because its members are fairly representative of the Panjabi Hindu community in Southall. They are brought up and have lived in different cultural and linguistic environments in India, East Africa and Britain. They are of different age groups and sex; they have had their education in different political, religious and cultural climates; and they have different attitudes towards different languages and orthographies.

This is one of the families in Southall with whom I have spent most time. Over the course of five years, I stayed with them on many occasions and observed their literacy practices. Initially, my visits to and stays with this family were a matter of hospitality extended to a student from their country of origin having the same linguistic background. However, over the period, the acquaintance gradually grew into a close relationship. As I was accepted and treated as a member of the family, I could participate in their day-to-day activities. This relationship also provided me with the freedom of questioning and discussing their actions and views, even though they were fully aware of my study and its purpose.

The literacy events presented below all took place but did not necessarily happen in one single day. In order to give the account more cohesion they are presented as if they occurred in a single day.

Grandfather

(educated in the Panjab in pre-liberated India; migrated to East Africa before coming to England):

He takes bus no. 74 signposted in English 'Greenford' to go to the Community Club for the elderly people. There he reads a local newspaper in Urdu[2] about the South Asians in Britain, Southall's local news, and political news from India and Pakistan. He picks up a national newspaper in English, skims through it to get general news about British and international affairs.

He then walks down a few blocks to a publishing house which publishes a fortnightly newspaper to promote Panjabi nationalism in terms of its secular political ideology and Panjabi culture. He exchanges greetings with the editor in Panjabi and shows him a poem he has written in Panjabi/Gurmukhi in praise of Panjab rivers. The editor considers it for publication.

On the way home, he goes to a book store which specializes in print media (newspapers, magazines, children's and literary books, novels, etc.) from India, Pakistan and Britain in various South Asian scripts. He buys a Hindi film magazine from India for his daughter-in-law. He also notices advertising posters in English in the street.

At home, when his grandson comes back from school, he reads him a nursery book written in English.

Grandmother
(brought up in East Africa with little formal education; learnt Hindi at home):

She waits for a bus, at the bus stop, to go to a Hindu temple. She does not read English. One of the buses that go to the temple is No. 36. When buses other than No. 36 come, she checks with the drivers (bus drivers in Southall are mostly Panjabi) if the buses go in the direction of the temple. None does. No. 36 arrives with Hayes sign written in English. Though she does not read English, she recognizes the shape of the word, because she sees it so often. She also recognizes the driver and the adverts on the bus. She boards the bus without feeling a need to check it with the driver. She compensates her lack of knowledge of written English by relying on her memory of certain objects, events, people, etc. and assistance from other people.

On entering the temple, she reads a notice in Hindi about the weekend's events at the temple. Inside the main hall, after offering prayers to each of the Hindu gods, she asks the priest about the date of a particular festival. The priest then checks a yearly magazine from the Panjab, written in Perso-Arabic script, about the Hindu religious calendar.[3] Later, with other women and some elderly men, she listens to a Hindu religious book read out in Hindi by the priest. Then she goes upstairs where there is a Hindu cultural centre and a library. She reads a Hindi newspaper from India there, and borrows a religious book in Hindi.

On the way home, she notices shop names displayed in bilingual signs in Panjabi-English, Hindi-English or Urdu-English. She goes into a *sari* (an Indian women's dress) shop. The shop has English-Hindi bilingual signs outside. The shop owner is the president of the Hindi temple.[4]

Father
(born in East Africa, but brought up and educated in England from an early age):

In the morning he reads an English newspaper for national and international news before leaving for work. At work, he supervises about two hundred and fifty workers of South Asian origin in a factory. As and when required, he also mediates, as an interpreter, between the workers and the factory bosses. He also has the responsibility of making available bilingual materials published by social service agencies on safety, workers' legal rights, medical benefits, etc. in the factory.

After work, in the evening, he goes to a Hindu temple where he is a member of the temple executive committee. With other committee members, he prepares a draft letter in English about the annual general meeting to be sent out to the registered members of the temple. It was agreed that when the temple has enough funds, the committee will send English-Hindi bilingual letters and notices to its members, as one of the roles of the temple is to promote Hindi. At the moment, the temple has only an English typewriter. The committee members also prepare some hand-written notices in Hindi for the temple notice board regarding the agenda of the annual general meeting.

On the way home, he notices some new Sikh nationalistic and communal slogans on street walls written in Panjabi. He discusses these slogans with his family when he comes home. At home, his mother reads to him from a weekly Hindi newspaper published locally about some local news and some news from the Panjab. This newspaper also has a few articles on Indian Hindi films written in English which he reads himself.

Mother
(born, brought up and educated in the Panjab during and after the reorganisation period of the Panjab in India before coming to England for marriage):

In the morning, she takes her son to a nearby nursery. She brings back a note in English from the teacher about some activity which the child and the parents have contributed to. She shows it to her husband in the evening. He reads it and explains it to her in Panjabi.

After finishing the household chores, she gets a little time to read a few pages from a Hindi novel. Later, with her mother-in-law, she writes a letter to a relative in Delhi. They discuss and write the contents of the letter in Panjabi-Hindi mixed code using Devanagari script. She also writes a letter in Panjabi/Gurmukhi to a friend in the Panjab.

In the evening, before putting her son to sleep, she tells him a story in Panjabi.

Son
(born in Southall):

In the morning as he enters the school, he sees bilingual signs. He can distinguish between Gurmukhi, Devanagari and Roman scripts. In the classroom, he is exposed only to the Roman script for teaching and learning purposes.

At home in the afternoon, his grandmother sends him with a small shopping list in Hindi/Devanagari to a corner shop next door. The shopkeeper records the goods sold to the boy in Hindi/Devanagari in his ledger.[5]

During the day, the boy observes his parents and grandparents using different literacies for different purposes.

Dinner time
One of the topics discussed during and after dinner is why the child should learn Hindi or Panjabi.

The grandfather wants his grandson to learn Panjabi in the Gurmukhi script when he goes to school, but not in the Sikh temple. He thinks this way his grandson can learn Panjabi and retain Panjabi culture. He favours Panjabi because it is also the official language of the Panjab states. However, grandmother, mother and father think that the child should learn Hindi/ Devanagari. Grandmother and father take more of a religious stance whereas mother takes the nationalistic/secular stance. Grandmother and father think that it is important to learn Hindi to retain Hindu culture and religion; whereas mother thinks that the child should learn Hindi because it is the national language of India. A further argument put forward in favour of Hindi related to the interpersonal communicative functions of literacy: grandmother, mother and father argue in favour of Hindi by saying that with the knowledge of the Hindi script the child will be able to correspond with the relatives both in Delhi and the Panjab, whereas the knowledge of the written Panjabi would restrict him only to the Panjab. Grandfather is outvoted, and it is decided that the child would go to the Hindi voluntary classes held in the Hindu temple initially and later would also opt for Hindi in school.

In the above section, I have talked about what individual members of this family do with different literacies in different situations, and how they value these literacies. In the following two sections, I will address the question: Why do these people make different literacy choices in their everyday lives the way they do?; and how are these choices shaped by the different social conditions in which they are living or have lived? These questions will help us understand that multiple literacy choices Panjabi individuals of Southall make in their everyday literacy practices reflect their differing ideological way of thinking. Nevertheless, rather than restraining their actions, these choices provide them with multiple identities and freedom to operate in different worlds of literacies to achieve different goals. These questions will also reveal the fact that a decade or so ago one would not have encountered this kind of multiplicity of literacies in Southall as reflected by their literacy practices.

II Literacies in Places of Origin of Southall Panjabis: An Historical Account of Cultural Practices in Different Social Conditions

This section outlines the historical literacy background of the Panjabis who live in Southall. The historical literacy situation presented in this section is reconstructed through in-depth interviews with Panjabi community leaders, elders and other individuals in Southall, and on the basis of various studies of Panjabis in the Panjab and Delhi.

Panjabi Hindus in Southall have migrated from India and East Africa. Those from India are either from Delhi or different rural and urban parts of the Panjab.

Literacies in the Panjab

There are three main phases in which people have been mobilized around language and literacy in the Panjab: from the turn of the century to the Independence of India in 1947; from the Independence to the reorganisation of these Panjab state boundaries in 1966; and from 1966 to the present time. During the first phase, there was a movement to replace Urdu/Perso-Arabic in schools, courts and official institutions with the vernacular mother tongues, Panjabi and Hindi. At the same time, there was competition between those who wished to promote Panjabi/Gurmukhi or Hindi/Devanagari. In the post-independence period, during the second and third phase, the language/literacy cleavage has been exclusively between Hindi and Panjabi (cf. Gopal, 1968; Das Gupta, 1970; Brass, 1974; Jones 1976).

There are Panjabi Hindus in Britain who were brought up and had their education around and before the independence period. At that time, the political and religious situation was such that among Panjabi Hindus a positive feeling towards Hindi-Devanagari-Hinduism and negative feeling towards Panjabi-Gurmukhi-Sikhism were running very high. Panjabi/Gurmukhi did not have any support in the education, administration and mass media. At that time, the languages used as the media of education in schools were Urdu/Perso-Arabic and English/Roman. Hindi and Urdu, written in either the Perso-Arabic or Devanagari scripts, were the language of literate exchange. Panjabi/Gurmukhi was only promoted by schools and voluntary classes run by the Sikh religious and political institutions. Hindi was widely supported and learnt by Hindus and by many Panjab-speaking Hindus through religious and political institutions. Access to Panjabi/Gurmukhi and Hindi/Devanagari depended on religious affiliation, and the knowledge of Urdu/Perso-Arabic and English/Roman depended on whether somebody had had formal education.

Those Panjabi Hindus in Britain brought up in the post-independence period (1947) were socialized into a different socio-literacy environment. At that time, the Muslim population had become established on the Pakistan side of the Panjab and Urdu was no longer the language of administration and education. In the Indian Panjab, the main political and religious rivalry was between Panjabi and Hindi. As the education curricular options provided Panjabi and Hindi, educational choices by Panjabi Hindus and Sikhs reflected the wider religio-political environment prevalent at that time. Panjabi Hindus with strong Hindu tendancies learnt Hindi in Devanagari script.

Another group of Panjabi Hindus I encountered in the Southall context were those brought up in the post-reorganisation (1966) period in the Panjab. At that time, Panjabi had become the Panjab state official language and Panjabi in Gurmukhi Script was the first and main language of education in schools. Hindi and English as subjects of study were introduced in the fourth and sixth years of schooling, respectively. Even those Panjabi Hindus who had very strong Hindu tendencies had to face this practical problem: if they did not encourage their children to be proficient in Panjabi in the Gurmukhi script, then their children would not stand good chances of competing with the Panjabi Sikh children. Therefore, the motivation for the children brought up during this third phase to learn Panjabi/Gurmukhi was of a different kind from the ones who were brought up before the reorganisation period. Hindi in Devanagari script in this situation acquired only a second place in terms of the comparative importance of the language in the lives of these children. This relative importance of Hindi and Panjabi was also evident in the mass media. For instance, as soon as the government started encouraging the Gurmukhi script in the school system there was a concomitant decrease in the publication of books in Hindi and an increase in Panjabi books. The use of Panjabi also increased in radio broadcasting. The sociolinguistic situation in the post 1966 period shows clearly people's, especially, Panjabi Hindus' sensitivity towards the change in the official importance assigned to Panjabi/Gurmukhi, as opposed to the religious importance of the language/script.

To sum up, in response to the domination of Muslim religion, the Urdu language and Perso-Arabic script in the Panjab, there was a growth of Hindu and Sikh religious revival movements and the literature associated with them at the turn of this century. In consequence, Sikhs came to attach increasing significance to the writing of Panjabi in the Gurmukhi script as the language of the Sikhs and of the Sikh religion just as Hindus developed an attachment to Hindi in the Devanagari script. Close symbolic linkages, therefore, were made between Panjabi, Hindi and Urdu with Gurmukhi, Devangari and Perso-Arabic scripts for religious reasons.

However, all the three scripts can be and have been used to write the three languages. Panjabi being the main language for informal discourse, there was incompatibility between the competence in Devanagari/Perso-Arabic scripts and Hindi-Urdu languages if these languages were not learnt formally. As there was more emphasis on learning the scripts to appreciate the religious scriptures written in these languages, many people had passive knowledge of formal Hindi-Urdu. Many of them spoke in Panjabi in their day-to-day lives, but wrote it in Gurmukhi, Devanagari and/or Perso-Arabic scripts. A Hindu might write a letter to a relative in other parts of the Panjab or in Delhi in Panjabi language but in Devanagari script. This choice of script could simply be a matter of mutual convenience for writer and reader or a

matter of symbolizing Hindu solidarity. In the same way, the choice of Gurmukhi script might be made as much for practical as ideological reasons.
Although people in the Panjab have learnt and used different languages and
scripts in different political, religious and educational environments over the
period of three different phases, the symbolic linkage between language and
literacy has been maintained for religious identity since the turn of the century.

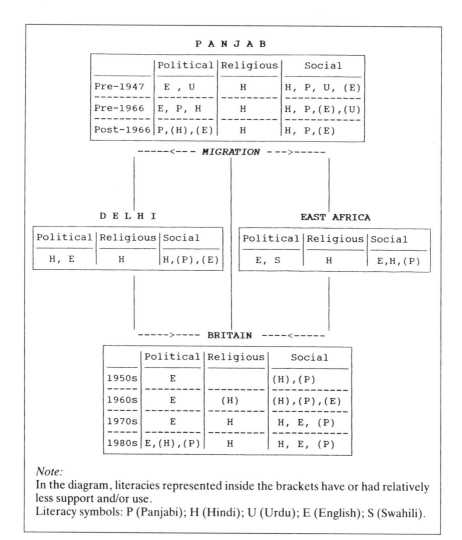

Figure 2 Political, religious, social support to and use of multiliteracies in
the lives of Panjabi Hindus: change and migration

Literacies in Delhi and East Africa

Patterns of literacy of Panjabis who came from Delhi and East Africa are not as complex as those who migrated from the Panjab. Delhi saw the influx of Panjabi refugees after the partition of India who came from communal war stricken Panjab. After independence Hindi/Devanagari became the official language and the language of education in Delhi. Sikhs and even those Panjabi Hindus who had strong loyalty towards Panjabi had little choice but to learn Hindi/Devanagari, and to operate in that literacy environment. The majority of Panjabi Hindus, on the other hand, identified themselves with Hindi-Hindu tradition and, thus, found the language and literacy situation of Delhi in their favour as compared with the Panjabi Hindus in the Panjab who had to fight for it. Pandit's (1974) and Mukherjee's (1980) studies show that the sociolinguistic situation among the Panjabi Hindus in Delhi was generally such that they chose to relegate Panjabi to the status of spoken language of the home, and use Hindi for social and written interaction, either as their religious identity or for practical needs. In contrast, Sikhs maintained the Panjabi language in Gurmukhi script as a symbol of their religious identity.

Panjabi Hindus and Sikhs in East Africa had similar attitudes towards Hindi and Panjabi literacies as did many of their counterparts in Delhi and the Panjab.

III Minority Literacies in the British Context, 1950s– 80s: Differing Cultural Responses to Changing Social Conditions

The functions of literacies in the literacy repertoire of Panjabis have been changed, elaborated and redistributed, since they arrived in Britain. This section looks at the changing social conditions in Britain since the arrival of Panjabis and their differing cultural responses to these conditions in the context of proliferating functions of home/minority literacies (viz. Panjabi, Hindi, Urdu). The information presented in this section is gathered through my interviews with various people in the Panjabi community, (such as businessmen, community leaders, teachers, intellectuals, factory workers, housewives and students); through detailed observations in Southall over the period of five years; and through various multidisciplinary studies of Panjabi communities in Britain.

Literacies in the 1950s

The first South Asian Panjabi-speaking men arrived in Southall in the boom years of the 1950s as a response to Britain's enormous need for an unskilled labor force (Harox & McRedie, 1979; Southall, 1981). Since then

the composition of Southall's South Asian population has changed enormously. Until around 1960, the Southall Asian population consisted of
mainly Panjabi Sikh and Hindu men from India. The main literacy activity
at that time was writing letters in Panjabi and Hindi to their families and
friends in India. If one was illiterate, one could seek help through a friendship network. Since their aim at that time was to earn as much money as
possible and then go back to India, these men usually worked on shifts, and
lived in cheap accommodations shared by many others. They in fact preferred to rent houses with shared rooms, kitchens, bathrooms and toilets in
order to save money to send home (cf. Jung, 1985). Men working on different shifts even shared beds to save the money. Sometimes, in such situations, the only way of communication between these men sharing beds or
houses was to leave notes in Panjabi or Hindi. There were very few who
knew English, those who knew English acted as interpreters and translators
between the managements and the workers.

Literacies in the 1960s

The 1962 Commonwealth Immigration Act changed the demography of
Southall and with that its literacy situation. The widespread belief that the
impending legislation would impose a complete ban on immigration increased
the flow of immigrants from South Asia into Britain. By this time, these men
were well enough established in Southall and were able to bring their wives
and children to join them. Once here, these parents looked for ways in which
they could advance the educational prospects of their children. As children
started going to schools, literacy in English assumed importance. On the one
hand, to survive and to be successful in the British system of schooling, children needed to learn English. On the other hand, once a contact was established between the schools and the linguistic minority community, letters in
English began to arrive from schools. They would be about, for instance,
children's progress or events taking place in the school. In order to communicate with the schools' staff or authorities, parents needed literacy in
English too. In most cases they got help from someone who knew English in
the community/friendship network. It was then for the first time that spoken
and written English, the language of the host community outside home
began to make inroads into the homes in the form of school correspondence
and children's books.

The material ties in Britain were established when Panjabi men bought
houses for their families and sent their children to schools. Socio-economic
obligations in Britain, thus, began to assume greater importance. Other
ways in which English literature made inroads into the homes were various
types of house bills, mortgage and insurance papers, etc. For reasons such as
better living standards, independence, prestige in the community, elimina-
tion of rent payments, or even income from lodgers, Panjabis were becom-

ing owner-occupiers of the properties in Southall. This, inevitably, brought financial pressures on the families and many women had to find some kind of work. However, poor English, cultural barriers and responsibility for rearing children made these women an obvious source of cheap labour for the homeworking industry (cf. Wilson, 1978). For those men and women who were well motivated to climb the socio-economic ladder by securing better jobs and avoiding poor working conditions and shift work in factories, it became imperative for them to learn English. This brought about the need for adult literacy classes in the area. English was no longer just a language of the host society that one could get by using the friendship network, it was becoming a reality of their daily lives for full participation in the wider community. They began to take interest in the social, cultural, economic and political aspects of the host country with which their future was becoming associated. This need was mainly fulfilled by radio, television and English newspapers since there was not much contact with the host community at the social level. The absence of contact between the two communities was mostly because of lack of interest among the host society to let the 'immigrant' minority community participate in their social lives. The basis for this discrimination was racism.

As the settlement grew in size, the social networks of these people began to be confined to immigrants from specific areas, castes or groups of villagers. With the development of social networks, social obligations in Britain became more important than the links with families in India. As a result, written communication in Panjabi and Hindi became less frequent between India and Britain and more frequent within Britain.

Literacies in the 1970s

The period around the 1970s brought further changes in the demographic situation and literacy environment in Southall. There were three reasons for these changes:

(1) decline in the British economy;

(2) increasing cultural and linguistic gap between migrant parents and their children; and

(3) arrival of South Asians from East Africa as political refugees.

South Asians, like other groups of workers, were involved in the industrial conflicts during the recession in the late 1960s and in 1970s. With the realization that they would not be returning to India, and with the blockage of social mobility due to their low earnings or high unemployment conditions during the recession, they found themselves fixed in working class jobs (Westergard & Resler, 1975). Their greater participation in industrial disputes along with their white counterparts brought about a working class consciousness among them (cf. Rimmer, 1972). They became more involved in Trade Union activities at work and took greater interest in politics at community level. This led to a greater reliance on literacy activity among these people to achieve their political goals. English literacy became necessary to maintain and to develop contacts with the national Trade Unions, and to understand and to participate in their activities. Posters in Panjabi and Hindi were also used to inform the local minorities about the Trade Union movement and to encourage greater local participation. The local newspapers in Panjabi and Hindi also played a role in achieving this political goal. The second generation Panjabis, having gone through the British school system, found a new role in contributing towards written communication in English as they had a good command of English.

As the recession deepened, the level of unemployment increased along with discrimination and racism (cf. Rimmer, 1972; Taylor, 1976; Smith, 1977). Some politicians used the 'immigrants' as scapegoats to create the myth that they were in the way of the native labour force in finding jobs. As the racism against these minorities increased in the wider society, the potential employers also discriminated against them. Demonstrations against racial violence in 1970s by British educated South Asian youth in Southall (Southall SWP, 1979) proved that, unlike their parents, they were much more prepared to take direct action in defence of their interests and identity. As the British political and economic environment became instrumental in transforming the Panjabis' immigrant identity into a new British working class identity, it also created a social environment in Britain which made Panjabi youth think about their own cultural identity. The Panjabi and Hindi languages and associated literacies became significant resources for the construction of their distinct cultural identity.

The same period also saw the development of voluntary language classes in Panjabi and Hindi, with emphases on literacy. Also, a greater demand for these languages to be taught in the schools was made by the parents, as the linguistic and cultural gap between first and second generations began to surface.

In the beginning, when the Panjabi families came to this country, the assimilatory forces into the 'host' society were compelling. The political trend of the host country was to assimilate the newly arrived immigrants into the host society through the education system as quickly as possible. A great emphasis was put on learning English. The Panjabi parents themselves saw English as a passport to success in British society and in the education system, but at the cost of home languages. Some people in the education system were convinced and led parents to believe that if children spoke and learnt their home languages, it would hinder their progress in learning English and thus, access to the school curriculum.[6] Gradually English became the main language of communication for children at school and home alike. This led to a communication gap between parents and their children. This was felt more by mothers who were not fluent in English. This further led to a conflict with their cultural beliefs, such as marriage and religion. Having been brought up in a western cultural system, the second generation children saw the arranged marriage system and their parents' religious beliefs as backward (cf. Dhir, 1975). The parents found this situation very threatening to their cultural identity and to repair the situation, the South Asian community made a concerted effort to open temples where children could learn and appreciate their religions, cultures and languages. The arrival of South Asian political refugees in Britain from East Africa around this time was of great assistance and morale boosting in building up of this infrastructure. Unlike the Panjabis from India who came mainly from villages with little or no education, the new immigrants from East Africa were well educated and had had the experience of maintaining their languages and culture through voluntary efforts there.

Literacies in the 1980s

The period of 1980s brought in further changes in the literacy situation in Southall, mainly in the context of home literacies. For the first time since the arrival of these Panjabis, the religious division between the Sikhs and Hindus begin to surface. Their sociolinguistic history provided them with the symbols, i.e. either Gurmukhi or Devanagari script, to emphasize this religious division. This process began to take shape with the politically motivated communal violence between Sikhs and Hindus in the Panjab state in India, which led to the assassination of India's prime minister in 1985. The assassination resulted in communal violence in the Hindi speaking states of India, the worst violence was felt in Delhi. Southall in Britain had by then become the main Sikh militant centre outside India which supported the cause of an independent Panjab as a separate Sikh nation. The self proclaimed president of the perceived Sikh nation, the Khalistan, had his office in Southall. This office issued passports (to those Sikhs who believed in the cause) written in Gurmukhi, symbolizing the Sikh nation. A Sikh temple there became the main centre for promoting the Sikh political cause and engaged in a renewed effort of teaching Panjabi in Gurmukhi script. Those Panjabi Hindus who used to visit the Sikh temple stopped doing so after the temple took this political stance. Some of them started sending their children to learn Hindi in the Hindu temple instead.

The Hindu temple had thus become a main centre for promoting Hindu culture and the Hindi language for those Hindus who dissociated themselves from Śikhs and the Gurmukhi script. These Hindus did not mind their children speaking Panjabi, but considered Devanagari, and not Gurmukhi, to be the fit written medium for a Hindu child to be able to appreciate the

Hindu scriptures. However, there was a small proportion of these Panjabi Hindus who preferred their children to speak Hindi rather than Panjabi, and to learn Devanagari and not Gurmukhi script. Their preference for Hindi-Devanagari over Panjabi-Gurmukhi was not due to the fact that they were Hindus, but because of their positive attitude towards Hindi for different ideological and practical purposes. These Panjabi Hindus think that since Hindi is a national language and a language of wider communication in India, it is the right language for an Indian to learn in order to maintain an Indian cultural identity. In addition, the mastery of it also provides a better chance of keeping business contacts and links with their relatives in India.

Besides these three groups of Panjabis in Southall who are motivated by either the religious or nationalistic ideology, there is a fourth grouping of Panjabis. This group is comprised of both Hindus and Sikhs, and is motivated by a socialist political ideology. Unlike those who support the Khalistan cause, this group believes in an Indian national cause. They see the Panjab as a Sikh-Hindu state within the Indian political system. They also believe in the maintenance of the Panjabi language in the Gurmukhi script as an emblem of Panjabi culture rather than the Sikh religion. Similarly, they are very clear about treating Hindi-Devanagari as a national language of India, in contrast to those Panjabi Hindus who see it as an emblem of their religious identity. They disagree with the adoption of Hindi-Devanagari at the cost of Panjabi-Gurmukhi by the Panjabis. This group, therefore, has added a new symbolic value to Panjabi-Gurmukhi for one cultural identity to all Panjabis, Hindus and Sikhs. It is important to note here that the development of this secular identity among this grouping of Panjabis has come directly in response to the social conditions within the Panjabi community which divided the community on religious grounds.

Educational role of minority literacies

In the context of education, during the 1980s, the Sikh-Hindu religious polarization became prominent. In schools, most Panjabi Hindu children chose to learn Hindi and the Panjabi Sikh children chose Panjabi. By this time, Hindi and Panjabi were offered as part of school curriculum in the secondary schools in Southall. The print environment in the schools at all levels had begun to reflect the multicultural and multilingual nature of the local communities. In the period during which I carried out my fieldwork, multiliteracy posters in Panjabi, Hindi and English were seen on classroom and school corridor walls. They depicted curriculum contents (e.g. science and arts projects) and cultural aspects (e.g. food, religion, dress, etc.) of the school and the community. Doors of head teachers' rooms, staff rooms, classrooms, school offices, toilets, etc. bore labels in multiliteracies. This multiliteracy environment in the schools that the third generation Panjabis are being exposed to was not experienced by the second generation.

Commercial role of minority literacies

Another development that became instrumental in boosting the home literacies was the boom in the British economy during the 1980s. During this period, government enterprise initiative schemes gave encouragement and support to new businesses. Many Panjabis in Southall, who were in low-paid jobs in industry and other institutions, took advantage of these initiatives and set up their own business. Most of their business was in the area of trading consumer goods such as food and clothing, suitable to the ways of life of the Panjabis in Southall and neighbouring areas. Since not many of these items are produced in Britain, the obvious market is India and other South Asian countries. The import of these goods has renewed the link of the Panjabis with their country of origin.

Those businesses that deal with large international exporters from India can communicate in written English, but those importing from small, local industry through friendship and familial network in India have to rely on Hindi and Panjabi literacies. This provided a new role for home literacies as facilitators of international business.

As the purchasing power of the local community increased, more people began to eat out, and the role of home literacies proliferated too. They found the Indian restaurants which offered multiliteracy menus more friendly and authentic and less intimidating. If one visits shops in Southall catering in daily consumer items — food, clothes, utensils, toiletries, jewelry, decoration, books, newspapers, magazines, stationery, etc., one can see bilingual labels in Panjabi, Hindi and/or English on the items and the shelves. This literacy environment in the shops especially facilitates the shopping of housewives, and older men and women as they tend to have little or no command of written English. Also children are often sent with shopping lists in home literacies to corner shops. Many small family businesses make their everyday inventories of their stocks in home literacies. Children from such families learn home literacies informally while working alongside their parents in the shops.

Institutional role of minority literacies

It is only in the past decade that the social service provisions (DHSS, police, immigration, etc.) are made available in minority languages (through interpreters) and literacies (through translations) by the Local Authorities in Britain. This has come about in response to the continuing demand by the linguistic minority communities as citizens of their right to resources provided by the state. One can find in social service agencies (such as hospitals, community relations offices, citizen's advice bureaux) leaflets about health, safety, law, immigration, etc. written in Panjabi, Hindi, Urdu, Chinese, Polish, etc. beside English. Such information provided in home languages has helped many women, particularly housewives who, either due to poor command of English or due to other social and domestic reasons, cannot get independent professional help in areas of health, hygiene, child care, women's rights in marriage, etc. Similarly, for the general linguistic minority communities information regarding law, immigration, housing, etc. is now more accessible. This material, for those who do not want to rely on networks of friends and family, has meant that personal problems need not become public knowledge. They are now, therefore, in a position to achieve personal freedom and independence.

As the minority languages like Panjabi and Hindi have gained official status, they have opened up job opportunities for bilinguals who have good command of English and one (or more) of these languages, especially in the area of literacy skills. Although many of them have had school or college education in these languages in India, they need to pass professional examinations conducted by British language institutions, such as the Institute of Linguists and the Royal Society of Arts, to qualify as interpreters and translators. To obtain jobs as translators and interpreters, it is no longer enough to be able to speak, write or have had an education in these languages.

However, these recognized standards and the job prospects linked to them have given qualified Panjabis and their home literacies a professional status. For the first time, the younger generations of Panjabis born and/or brought up in Britain have seen the role of home literacies extended beyond their own community to an institutional level. This has motivated many of them to learn and improve their knowledge of home languages and literacies to obtain the recognized qualifications. Jobs in 'community' interpreting and translation, especially part-time ones have proved to be very popular among women who cannot get into full-time employment because of their domestic responsibilities. Also these jobs have provided them with a respectable professional status as well as personal independence.

IV Summary and Conclusion

Historically and ideologically Britain has largely remained a monolingual, monocultural and monoliterate state; in this context, however, linguistic minorities exist as multilingual, multicultural and multiliterate subsystems both in terms of their ideologies and practices. The Panjabis in Southall are one such subgroup who, in turn, exist as constellations of differing language and literacy practices and ideologies.

The different kind of responses amongst different Panjabi subgroups to the changing social conditions in Britain are manifested in a variety of changing literacy practices and ideologies in the Panjabi community in Southall. External factors (such as inequality and racism in the wider society) and internal factors (e.g. different religious ideologies, and the need for the transmission of Panjabi cultures and for maintaining cultural ties with the country of origin) have contributed to this manifestation. Until very recently, English literacy had a place in the material market, whereas the home literacies served ideological purposes for these linguistic minorities. However, there has been a struggle to get Panjabi minority literacies a place alongside English literacy in institutional domains. Panjabis are now trying to create a multiliteracy market to serve their own needs and purposes. These multiple literacy resources are associated with multiple identities of Panjabi individuals, and are reflected in the choices that they make in their everyday literacy practices. As compared to the previous generations, the third generation Panjabi children now live in a very different world of literacies.

Hindi literacy, with or without its spoken form, has been firmly associated with the Hindu religion and is maintained by many Panjabi Hindus. Similarly, Panjabi language and Gurmukhi scripts are linked with Sikhs and the Sikh religion. On the other hand, Hindi literacy and Panjabi literacy are in competition on the issue of representating Panjabi secular culture. Urdu literacy has only an informative function (e.g. newspapers) along with Hindi and Panjabi literacies, for those who had their education in Urdu before the partition of India. The constitution of these multiple religious and secular identities as exemplified by different literacy practices of Panjabis have come not only in response to the changing economic, political and social conditions in the wider British context, but also in response to the changing political, religious, economic and social conditions in India as well as within the Panjabi community in Southall itself.

The three distinct literacies and religious communities associated with the Panjabi language provide a particularly useful and important case for the discussion of different worlds of literacies. For instance, it exemplifies that being literate means one thing and being literate in a particular language/ orthography is another. By being literate, a person can be identified with a literate world, whereas being literate in a particular language may imply identification with a particular cultural tradition or a particular ideology.[7] A study of bi/multiliteracy situation like the one among Panjabis discussed in this paper highlights the salient issues of 'identity' and 'ideology'.

In a multiliteracy situation, institutional support given to one particular literacy bestows power in the hands of the users of that literacy over the users of other literacies. People who are literate in a lower status language but illiterate in the higher status language may be subjected to similar negative experiences as would be an illiterate person from the higher status language background. Further, if the lower status language or literacy is associated with a particular ethniç background, people from that group may be subjected to discrimination or racism in the wider society. For example, in Britain, a Panjabi person literate in Panjabi, Hindi or Urdu, but illiterate in English, may find him or herself in this situation, and may be discriminated against in finding a job.

But the same person may have a very different kind of social experience in his or her own community in Britain. Being literate in Panjabi, Hindi or Urdu, s/he may be identified with the Sikh, Hindu or Muslim religions. But being illiterate in English, s/he may be considered to be not westernized enough as English is often associated with westernization, modernity and success in the wider Panjabi community. Therefore, in the British context, being literate in both English and Panjabi, Hindi or Urdu may mean taking on two complementary, rather than, competing identities, viz. western and Indian, either Sikh, Hindu or Muslim. Whereas, being literate in Panjabi, Hindi or Urdu alone may imply taking on different identities, which may become competing and not complementary.

In contrast to a monoliteracy situation, a bi/multiliteracy situation readily identifies the categories such as 'diversity', 'choice', 'identity' and 'ideology' which are essential to the theoretical goal that sets out to look at a literacy situation in terms of a variety of 'literacies' within an 'ideological model' (Street, 1984) or different 'worlds of literacy'.

Acknowledgment

I am grateful to Jane Mace, David Barton, Roz Ivanic, Brian Street, Mary Hamilton and Marilyn Martin-Jones for their helpful comments on earlier drafts of this chapter.

Notes

1. Mother-tongue Panjabi speakers belong to three different religious groups: Sikhs, Hindus and Muslims.
2. Generally, Urdu language is written in Perso-Arabic script, Panjabi language in Gurmukhi script, and Hindi language in Devanagari Script.
3. One would expect a Hindu calender to be written in Devanagari script, rather than in Perso-Arabic script. But people of the priest's generation, as himself, who were educated in the pre-partition period in India, still refer to magazines, etc. written in Perso-Arabic.
4. As I found out in interviews with shop owners, different linguistic signs represented their interest more in terms of their ideological stance and less of their commercial need.
5. Following the business tradition practised in India, some corner shopkeepers have separate accounts for the families living in the vicinity. These customers do not pay the shopkeepers for what they buy on a day-to-day basis, but settle their accounts weekly or monthly.

6. This view was held among some practitioners in education due to the narrow understanding of bilingualism in educational research (cf. Martin-Jones & Romaine, 1985; Romaine, 1989), and the low esteem in which the South Asian minorities and their languages were held.
7. For example, a person may become or aspire to become literate in Gurmukhi to be associated with the Sikh religious tradition and or with the Panjab cultural tradition.

References

Brass, P. L. (1974) *Language, Religion and Politics in North India*. London: CUP.

Cameron, J. (1982) *Unemployment in Southall*. London: Shakti Publications.

Das Gupta, J. (1970) *Language Conflict and Language Development*. London: University of California Press.

Dhanjal, B. (1976) Sikh women in Southall. *New Community* 5 (1–2), 369–70.

Dhir, R. (1975) Emotional and social conflict. In P. Parekh and B. Parekh (eds) *Cultural Conflict and the Asian Family*. Report of the conference organised by the National Association of Indian Youth.

Economic Intelligence Unit Ltd (1964) A report. *The Immigrant Community in Southall*.

— (1967) A report. *Social Characteristics of Commonwealth Immigrants in Southall*.

Gopal, R. (1968) *Linguistic Affairs of India*. Bombay: Asia Publishing House.

Gumperz, J. J. (1964) Hindi-Panjabi code-switching in Delhi. In H. G. Lunt (ed.) *Proceedings of the Ninth International Congress of Linguistics* (pp. 115–34). The Hague: Mouton.

Harox, A. and McRedie (1979) *Our People*. London: Thames Television.

Institute of Race Relations (1981) *Southall: The Birth of Black Community*.

Jones, K. W. (1976) *Arya Dharm: Hindu Consciousness in 19th Century Punjab*. New Delhi: Manohar Publications.

Jung, G. (1985) The impact of Indian video films on an Indian community in London. Unpublished BA dissertation. University of Essex.

Khubchandani, L. M. (1979) A demographic typology for Hindi, Urdu, Punjabi speakers in South Asia. In W. C. McCormack and S. A. Wurm (eds) *Language and Society* (Anthropological issue). The Hague: Mouton.

Kirwan, P. (1965) *Southall: A Brief History*. London: Shakti Publ.

Lee, G. L. and Wrench, K. J. (1977) *Accidents are Colour-Blind: Industrial Accidents and the Immigrant Workers*. London: CRE.

Luthra, M. (1982) *Black Minorities and Housing in Ealing*. London: Snalt Publications.

Martin-Jones, M. and Romain, S. (1985) Semilingualism: A half-baked theory of communicative competence. *Applied Linguistics* 6, 105–17.

Morrison, L. (1976) *As They See It*. London: CRE.

Mukherjee, M. (1980) Language maintenance and language shift among Panjabis and Bengalis in Delhi: A sociolinguistic perspective. Unpublished PhD thesis. Delhi University.

Parekh, B. C. (1978) *Asians in Britain: Problem or Opportunity*. London: CRE.

Pandit, P. B. (1978) Language and identity: The Panjabi language in Delhi. *International Journal of Sociology of Language* 16, 93–108.

Peggie, A. C. W. (1979) Minority youth politics in Southall. *New Community* III, 2, 170–7.

Rimmer, M. (1972) *Race and Racial Conflict*. London: Heinemann.

Romaine, S. (1989) *Bilingualism*. Oxford: Basil Blackwell.

Smith, D. J. (1977) *Racial Disadvantage in Britain*. London: Penguin.
Street, B. (1984) *Literacy in Theory and Practice*. New York: CUP.
SWP, Southall (1979) The fight for our future. *Socialist Worker*. A report. London.
Taylor, J. H. (1976) *The Half-Way Generation*. Slough: NFER.
Westgard, J. and Resler, H. (1975) *Class in Capitalist Society*. London: Penguin.
Wilson, A. (1978) *Finding a Voice*. London: Virgo.

8 The Struggle for Voice: Narrative, Literacy and Consciousness in an East Harlem School[1]

MICHELE SOLA and ADRIAN BENNETT

In her illuminating discussion of the printed book and popular culture in 16th-century France, Natalie Zemon Davis considers 'the printed book not merely as a source for ideas and images, but as a carrier of relationships'. Davis shows how 'social structure and values' channeled 'the uses of literacy and printing' in 16th-century France, and how printing helped to establish 'new relations . . . among people and among hitherto isolated cultural traditions' (Davis, 1975: 192). Similarly, we would argue, the written texts children are taught to produce in US schools today are used to carry certain kinds of social relationships and to construct certain kinds of cultural knowledge. Schools use writing instruction not only to inculcate certain skills, but to shape their students into particular kinds of social beings.

A number of studies of the writing done in schools have focused on the internal organization of information in the written texts, emphasizing the linguistic, textual and cognitive structures that, as all the 'crisis in education' reports agree, every student must learn (Frawley, 1982; Michaels, 1981; Tannen, 1982). In the crisis reports themselves we often find statements to the effect that 'Clear writing leads to clear thinking; clear thinking is the basis of clear writing' (Boyer, 1983: 90). Such statements reify both the kind of thinking and the kind of writing that schools teach, without questioning the nature of the cultural and social relationships that written texts in school are made to carry.

Rather than approach school writing from this point of view, we will consider how particular forms of written texts produced in classrooms are made to carry certain kinds of relationships by the participants involved in producing them. This approach will take the focus away from 'skills' considered as value-neutral entities whose influence on the social and cultural reality of those who are supposed to acquire them can be considered negligible, to direct our attention to how writing instruction in school is used to establish 'relations . . . among people and . . . cultural traditions'. In particular, we will explore how the relationships carried by written texts produced in East Harlem junior high school classrooms by working-class Puerto Rican students can be understood as pieces of a more encompassing relationship between schooling and an ethnic minority community whose students have traditionally not been well served by the public schools.

Our interest in the social production of these written texts is stimulated in part by a number of recent studies that indicate an important role played by narratives in the verbal life of the East Harlem community in New York City. Alvarez (1983), Bennett (1984), Bennett & Pedraza (1984), and Sola (1984) have begun to show that in oral discourse, personal narratives are crucial to establishing relationships between speakers and in carrying on the daily social and cultural life of the community. These studies also suggest that the specific ways in which narratives are used to construct social relationships may reflect members' experience and history in the Puerto Rican community. The way people use narratives and the more performative features of their discourse may be related to how much contact they have maintained with Puerto Rico itself, the age at which they migrated to the mainland, and how successfully they have negotiated the limiting economic conditions that confront them (see Bonilla & Campos, 1981, for a discussion of these conditions). Literacy, interpreted in the broad sense as a collection of cultural and communicative practices associated with the particular uses of both written and spoken forms among specific social groups (Cook-Gumperz & Gumperz, 1981; Heath, 1981) is clearly central to the Puerto Rican community, as it is for all those living in modern urban environments. Hence our interest in looking more closely at the relationship between literacy instruction in the school — an institution which enlists virtually all members of the community for an extended period of social participation — and the social and cultural environments within which the school is embedded.

The 'crisis' facing the Puerto Rican child in the schools is rather more drastic than that described in the most publicized of the crisis reports, which complain, for example, that our high school graduates cannot produce a simple, clearly written paragraph, or read anything as 'complex' as the *New York Times* (e.g. NCEE, 1983). The most dramatic statistic is the 79.2% dropout rate of Puerto Ricans in New York who begin high school (ASPIRA, 1983). Although scores on standardized tests which are administered every year in New York City to the third, sixth and eighth grades, have improved recently for the district in which the junior high school of our study is situated, they are still well below the norm for the city as a whole, and even further below those achieved in school with predominantly middle-class populations. In our study, Bennett was present the day the eighth graders received their responses to their applications to high school. Many of them had applied to alternative high schools, which require high performance in school and, in some cases, on standardized tests. Not one was admitted. There were many looks of morose disappointment and anger on the students' faces that day, and many tears. One girl, considered by the students to be the most intelligent in the class, could be heard sobbing uncontrollably for a good part of that afternoon in the stairwell that led to the fifth-floor classrooms of the junior high grades.

The study on which our discussion will be based was conducted in the winter of 1984 by Bennett using ethnographic methods and an anthropological perspective informed by recent work in discourse analysis (Gumperz, 1982), classroom ethnography (Spindler, 1982), and language philosophy (Bakhtin, 1968, 1981; Volosinov/Bakhtin, 1973), as well as by anthropological studies of literacy in its social contexts (Goody, 1968; Heath 1983). The junior high school program which was the focus of the study was a small, alternative program designed to serve children living in the neighborhood of the school and who had attended the same school in the primary grades. About 80% of these students were Puerto Rican, the rest black. They were all of working-class origin. The program was limited to one seventh and one eighth grade group in order to provide more individualized attention and to allow students to maintain contact with the cohesive peer groups they had formed in the earlier years. The program was not limited to 'high achieving' students, as is the case with so many alternative programs in the New York City schools, but purposely included a range of academic achievers. The principal, who had instituted the program in 1978 out of an awareness of the special needs of these students, noted that he looked for students who needed to remain in close association with their friends, who could use the special attention that the program could give them (unlike the large junior high school of several hundred students most of them would otherwise have gone to), and who could themselves contribute to the development of a vibrant school program that all could take pride in. He placed a special emphasis on writing in the program, encouraging all his junior high teachers to incorporate as much writing as possible into their curricula. He had created a special class in composition as well, a rare feature in city junior high schools, seeing to it that one of his experienced teachers received the special training offered to school districts by the New York City Writing Project. Observations soon showed that all of the teachers in the three classrooms which were observed over a three-month period — composition, social studies, and language arts — were taking their mandate very seriously. Selection of these classrooms for intensive study was in fact based on the fact that considerable writing and discussion of writing was taking place in them.

Dialogue and Dissonance

As Todorov notes in his study of Bakhtin, culture can be thought of as consisting of 'the discourses retained by collective memory . . . discourse in relation to which every uttering subject must situate himself' (1984: x). For Bakhtin, though, culture was not simply a set of acquired discourse patterns, communicative rules, or language games (Wittgenstein, 1953), although this is the way ethnographers of communication and sociolinguists have in fact tended to portray both culture and communication. For Bakhtin the discourses which social groups construct and reify to achieve particular ends are in constant flux and tension between the homogeneous and the heterogeneous, between that which makes people uniform and that which separates them and pulls them apart, sometimes to create new forms, sometimes to destroy:

> Such is the fleeting language of a day, of an epoch, a social group, a genre, a school and so forth. It is possible to give a concrete and detailed analysis of any utterance as a contradiction-ridden, tension-filled unity of two embattled tendences in the life of language. (Bakhtin, 1981: 272)

Unlike that other post-revolutionary Russian who has so captured the attention of American students of language, L. S. Vygotsky, Bakhtin was not a specialist in child language development. However, one can infer from the many statements he made regarding individuals' consciousness that he saw growing up in any society, encountering its many different 'ways with words' (Heath, 1983) in which people conduct their daily business, as less akin to learning a set of rules than to feeling one's way through a forest with tracks veering off in every direction. In this forest, all ways are equally obscure or equally clear:

> Language is not a neutral medium that passes freely and easily into the private property of the speaker's intentions; it is populated — over-populated — with the intentions of others. Expropriating it, forcing it to submit to one's own intentions and accents, is a difficult and complicated process. (Bakhtin, 1981: 294)

Dialogue and community are always possible, given a certain sharing of knowledge, ways, and purposes. But conflict is also always possible, and always present, at least implicitly:

> Our ideological development is . . . an intense struggle within us for hegemony among various available verbal and ideological points of view, approaches, directions and values. (Bakhtin, 1981: 346)

Nowhere in this rough and tumble of exchange and conflict so evident as when cultures come into contact with each other, which is why Bakhtin chose to produce one of his most ambitious works on Rabelais, who marked for him the beginning of the end of the common people's culture, or at least of its legitimate public expression (Bakhtin, 1968).

The Play of Discourses in the School

Although it is something of a simplification, a convenient way to think about the discourse in the school to be discussed here is to see it as divided between two 'streams' of communication, an official and an unofficial stream, an overt discourse governed by teachers and administrators and a more covert form constructed by the students. Gilmore refers to the latter as 'sub rosa' discourse (1983: 236). In the classrooms in the East Harlem school, sub rosa discourse could take many forms and could involve non-verbal (winks, grimaces, stares, gestures, body postures, and orientation) as well as verbal channels. It could involve oral as well as written messages, very loud speech as well as whispering. It could also include students passing each other, often surreptitiously, a variety of materials that anthropologists would call 'cultural artifacts': comic books, teen magazines, combs, 'walk-man' radios, white gloves in the style affected by Michael Jackson, hand-held computers games, and the like. These objects were sometimes confiscated by teachers, with or without comment.

Meanwhile, 'above' this rich, multilayered, and shifting stream of sub rosa discourse, teachers conducted their own models of classroom inter-action. In fact, it became clear during the observations that one of the attri-butes of a skilled teacher is the ability to deal satisfactorily with the inevita-ble undercurrents of sub rosa discourse while at the same time maintaining instructional discourse and personal composure.

Some ethnographers of schools, notably Willis (1977) and Everhart (1983) have characterized peer discourse in terms of resistance to the authoritative discourse of the school. This is a useful way to think of it, if only to counter the influence of the school's view that it is illegitimate. In our own research, there was clearly a continuous interplay between the two streams of official and sub rosa discourse, such that it might almost be said that they mutually defined and constrained each other. Their relationship was more subtle, more of a mixture, than either Willis's or Everhart's analysis implies.

Gilmore suggests that certain aspects of the sub rosa discourse of the stu-dent peer groups she observed not only violated certain norms, but operated on rather different principles, values, and genre expectations. They repre-sented different ways with words, different ways of constructing meanings, and were the medium for qualitatively different kinds of social relationships.

The studies of Puerto Rican adults' discourse cited above suggest the further implication that sub rosa discourse is created out of different needs than those defined by the school — and the social groups that govern schooling in this country — as legitimate. In looking at both the oral and written discourse produced in the three classrooms in our study, we asked these questions: What social conditions is the students' discourse responding to? How does the inter-play of official and sub rosa discourse affect the students' acquisition of writing, literacy, information gathering, and thinking skills? How does this play of discourses define their understanding of the uses to which these skills can be put, and shape their developing awareness of who they are, or might be, in relation to community, school, and society?

Discourse in the Composition Class

'Mr C,' the composition teacher, was schooled through New York City Writing Project workshops on the 'writing as a process' model and uses some of the procedures associated with this method in his teaching (Emig, 1983; Graves, 1983; Moffett, 1968). In addition, the pattern of *elicitation/student response/teacher evaluation* that Mehan (1979) and Sinclair & Coulthard (1975) have found to be a basic pattern of classroom discourse is a familiar one in his classroom. Very often, he begins a class with a review of some points covered in the previous class and follows up with a discussion of some new aspect of writing. This discussion begins with his dictating some rules which the students copy down. One day in the eighth grade he focused on rules for revision and the discussion proceeded as follows:

Mr C: I'm going to dictate to you a specific list of things to look for. Copy it down. Number one: 'When you have finished your draft comma allow some time comma preferably.'

Student: (Interrupting) What?

Mr C: 'Preferably at least a day comma before you start revision.' Ricardo read it back please?

Ricardo: When you have finished your draft comma allow some time preferably at least a day comma before you start revision.

Mr C: Very good, Richard.

Mr C goes on dictating and in between each rule conducts a short discussion of what the rule means, what the technical terms mean, and why these rules are helpful to the writer.

While this interaction could be thought of as belonging to the official discourse stream, and both teacher and the student appear to be engaged in it, the description is deceivingly simple. For instance, as Mr C reads the fourth rule, the discourse goes as follows:

Mr C: Number four: 'Read through again looking particularly for unity and organization.'

Student: Can you repeat that?

Mr C: Sure. 'Read through again looking particularly for unity and organization.' I would venture to say that most of us after we fix the spelling, and the punctuation and change a *word* or two, leave it at that. What is organization?

Student: Order

Mr C: Okay — outline — what else?

Student: The ideas tied together

Mr C: Very good. Arcadio, you hear that?

Arcadio: Can he say it again?

Mr C: He can but he wouldn't have to if you listened the first time.

From this and other transcripts and field notes we can see that students in Mr C's classroom have learned how to engage in the kind of oral interactions that are generally supported in school. They show evidence of this by copying rules down when directed to do so, by requesting clarification of something they did not catch the first time through, by repeating back the rules so exactly that they include Mr C's dictated punctuation marks, and by answering content questions. But some of the students are talking to each other in the back of the room. Mr C singles out Arcadio in this example, and chastises him for being engaged in some kind of interaction with his peers. This does not necessarily mean that the interaction in question is unconnected to the official discourse stream, as Arcadio could just as easily have been asking a classmate for clarification as engaging in sub rosa discourse meant to subvert the official lesson. In this classroom there is a great deal of interplay between the two streams of discourse, and it is impossible to separate the streams on the basis of the forms of the language. This becomes apparent in Arcadio's response to the teacher's query. Arcadio's 'Can he say that again?' is not so unlike a previous question addressed to the teacher by another student, 'Can you repeat that?' Yet the teacher's responses to these two questions are entirely different. In the context of Arcadio's interaction with another student, his question is treated as what Gilmore calls an 'interference' with official discourse and is subsequently 'thwarted, suppressed and punished'.

At this point, Mr C goes on dictating a few more rules for revision. When he has completed the list he asks a student to repeat back the whole set of seven rules, appears satisfied with the result, and suggests the following exercise:

Mr C: Okay . . . I think the most likely follow-up for this is to look over your work and revise it . . . Do you have any suggestions?

Not getting any, he directs the students to go to their writing folders, pick out a piece of writing, and revise it using the rules he has just dictated. Another possibility he suggests is revising someone else's writing. Most of the students go to their folders and read either their own or someone else's composition. Some start rewriting and others do not. Ricardo, who complied so precisely with the discourse rules in the dictation earlier, gets up and walks over to three girls and plays a game over whether he will keep a pen he has borrowed from one of them, then walks over to Jack and talks for quite a long time. Mr C finally looks up from his desk where he is working with two girls on their papers and asks, 'What is the matter, Ricardo?' Ricardo says, 'Nothing', and sits down. He continues to talk to the girls across the room and eventually shifts his attention to Juan, who is sitting next to him. A couple of other boys in the front are lobbing wadded pieces of paper into a wastebasket, glancing over their shoulders at Mr C, who does not see them. Many students talk among themselves, at first quietly, but gradually louder. Half of them seem to be talking about the assignment, and half do not. Some kind of resistance to the writing assignment seems to be taking place, but it is not particularly organized and does not involve the entire class as it has on other occasions. And even Ricardo, who seems to be engaging in resistance, is minimally complying with the assignment. As the class is nearing a close Ricardo hands Juan his corrected paper and comments: 'Instead of 'everyone' you should have wrote 'anyone'. Mr C ends the class by saying: 'The paper you're correcting is your revision — put it in your folder.'

This attempt to connect the oral discourse with a written assignment was quite typical of the classes conducted by Mr C. In an interview, he stated that he sees himself, not as teaching specific writing skills, but as trying to get students to connect writing with something that interests and excites them, to make it fun somehow. He also stated that he occasionally likes to give free writing, as sometimes the students produce interesting texts. While Mr C may have the eventual goal of making writing meaningful and interesting for students, he knew that there is considerable pressure from the district office to teach the so-called basic skills of writing and that he is chiefly responsible for seeing that the students master such skills. During the time his class was being observed, Mr C had the students produce quite a variety of writing genres, including speeches, composition, and plays. Each of these exercises was preceded by a discussion of rules for constructing these genres. Yet there always seemed to be some sort of tension between the official assignment and the students' rendition of it.

Perhaps the most graphic example of a conflict between official and unofficial discourse in the composition class was revealed when the seventh-grade students worked in small groups writing plays. From Mr C's point of view, or from the point of view of the official discourse, the assignment was an exercise in producing dramatic scripts in which characters disagreed with each other and argued their opposing positions in 'a convincing way'. Several days of class time were devoted to this project and Mr C continually told the students to make their characters' arguments as convincing as possible. He seemed to be looking for dialogue in which characters used formal logic to be convincing. The students showed a great deal of enthusiasm for the assignment. They devised their own dramatic subjects and wrote out the dialogue in a script format. While one or two students in each group usually ended up with the major responsibility for writing down the scripts, everyone participated actively in the discussion about what actions to portray and what the characters should say. For the students, one of the most important elements in producing the play was how the performance of it would look. They engaged in much acting out of parts, banter, laughing, mimicry, teasing, and joking in the process of the collaborative writing. The other element that seemed to be of utmost importance to the students was a focus on a conflict that has meaning for them in their own lives. The three groups produced plays which focused on teenage pregnancy, a young girl getting caught sneaking out of the house to attend a party, and an involved set of social relationships that is set up at a weekend party in a lakeside cabin.

Mr C had each group perform its play for the class and the students took a great deal of pleasure in performing for each other. The performers exuberantly took on their roles, and the audience was totally engrossed in the plays. They showed their appreciation by laughing, pounding on the desks, and offering comments to the actors and to other members of the audience throughout the performance. While Mr C obviously enjoyed the students' performances he was still dissatisfied with the students' attempts to resolve the central conflict of the play via a 'persuasive argument'. He also remarked to the researcher that he was tired of themes like teenage pregnancy that come up every year. His two concerns obscure the fact that the students demonstrated obvious skills with dramatic form, particularly in the economical use of dialogue and other dramatic devices to set the scene, portray character, and move the action along. They were also skilled in using humor and irony to manipulate their audience's reactions to the dialogue. Bennett & Sola (1984) suggest that much of the students' awareness of how to construct such plays may have their roots in television soap operas, situation comedies, and other popular dramatic forms.

This play-writing event raises the question of how students who are so involved in the writing process can produce texts so unsatisfactory to Mr C, whose expressed objective is for students to enjoy writing. If we think of these students as using the play scripts and performances as a vehicle for establishing relationships with other students in the class, we may have part of the answer. The students' enthusiasm for and involvement in writing these plays may have stemmed from the opportunities that plays provide to establish relationships to each other through performance. Earlier studies have shown that performance is an important element of discourse in the Puerto Rican community, and in this play-writing event students tried to legitimately bring performance into the classroom. Through the performance, the selection of themes relevant to adolescent lives, and the expropriation of discourses from widely popular soap operas and situation comedies, these students were perhaps creating a community within the classroom. Mr C did not seem to value these elements of the students' plays, and was never able to get the students to engage the skill lesson he was trying to teach them. The struggle that ensued as Mr C attempted to make the official assignment the primary focus of the students' attention is one that occurred over and over again in this classroom.

Discourse in the Social Studies Class

'Ms S', the social studies teacher, teaches both American History and Civics, which includes some discussion of current events. She is a competent, intelligent and committed teacher. Her comments in interviews on the history and status of the working-class Puerto Rican community showed much awareness and sensitivity. She seems to recognize that the community is politically and economically oppressed and wants to help students understand this. During some of the civics lessons she often tries to bring these understandings into the content of the lessons and this sometimes resulted in the sub rosa stream of discourse 'taking over' the classroom interaction. One discussion where this complex process became obvious involved a lesson on neighborhood vandalism. Ms S handed out xeroxed copies of pages from a text developed by the New York City Board of Education. The text moved from defining vandalism to a consideration of its illegality and the threat of arrest, and then to the property damage and harm that vandalism can cause. The technique was to interpolate questions and pictures, leaving room for students to fill in blank spaces with answers.

Ms S followed the format of the text, but rephrased and repeated questions and topics for oral discussion, gradually eliciting more and more student opinion, and moving thereby away from the constraints of the test into more open discussion. Most of the students paid attention and tried to answer her questions when called on. When Ms S asked the following question the discussion quickly became more and more animated:

Ms S: When would you break a law for your friends? What do you really owe them?

In asking this question, Ms S is building on prior responses of students who had said they might (or might not) commit acts of vandalism if their friends urged them to, but they wouldn't tell on their friends in any case. Several students give answers to her question. Then David says:

David: I expect my friends to be loyal like if my friend said he'd be there, I'd
expect him to be there. I might help him cheat on a test.

Ms S: Okay, that's a common thing. How many of you would do that?

Several students raise their hands. When they put them down in this
'hand vote' several are still holding them up, waving frantically to get Ms S's
attention. Robert, for example, like several other students, is leaning across
his desk, half standing, making loud sounds with his mouth closed, moving
his hand, arm, and upper body in rapid back-and-forth motions. Ms S calls
on Ellie:

Ellie: I don't owe them anything. Like I didn't ask my mother to bring me
into this world. It depends on the situation.

At this point, the discussion gets very animated and proceeds much
faster. Several students are talking at once. The teacher is trying to call on
those with hands raised, and for a while she tries to summarize, and mediate
between, points made by different students. For example, she says more
than once, 'Wait a minute, wait a minute! There's not as much difference
between what Ellie is saying and the rest of you as you think,' following this
(when the students allow her) with an explanation and summary of points
different students have offered. But more and more students shout out short
responses to Ellie, who sticks to her original point (which may not be well
understood by everyone, but it is an open question of how much the precise
argument mattered to each of the students). Students confer with each other
in loud overtones, giving each other their own viewpoints. They give the
impression that they are too eager to say something to wait to be called on.
Some bang hands or books on desks when someone else makes a particularly
funny joke or a salient or controversial point. They sometimes mimic disgust
with someone's expressed view, sometimes support it with a nod and a 'right
on!'

The students are clearly excited about the argument and are very eager to
participate. But this is no longer a performance *for* the teacher, but a real
exchange of views between the students. Ms S finally stops attempting to
intervene (it is difficult to get the floor in all the uproar), and lets the students compete freely for turns at talk, which results in a lot of simultaneous
turntaking and use of both verbal and nonverbal strategies for getting a
chance to be heard by others. When the bell signals the end of the period, the
students continue to argue, shout, and laugh as they file out of the room, still
focused on the issue of what one owes one's friends.

The teacher's reaction to this session was revealing of her own sense of
being caught between two poles of peer and school discourse. The students
had been genuinely interested in the topic and had actively participated in
their own ways. However, Ms S felt that it was all right to 'let them go' like

that only once in a while — allow them to let off steam, but not too often. She said she used to encourage students to do this more in her first couple of years of teaching, but then she became concerned that they were not learning enough of the 'skills' they would need later. It was fine to let them express themselves, but to do it all the time was, in her words, too 'touchy-feely'. We assume that the 'skills' she referred to were those related to essayist or school literacy in the broad sense. When the researcher asked her how one can make a connection between what the students could get excited about and these 'skills', she pointed to the writing assignment on the board: 'What responsibilities does the President have?' She said, 'I will probably get them to talk about who the President is responsible to, his immediate acquaintances, his friends, people he doesn't know, and so forth.' This raises an interesting question about how Ms S actually brings her understanding of the Puerto Rican community to bear in the classroom. On the one hand, she is sometimes open to straying from the official discourse embodied in the civics text on vandalism, and students obviously enjoy these opportunities to express their own opinion. On the other hand, Ms S's distinction between 'touchy-feely' and skills lessons raises a question about how legitimate she actually feels their opinions to be, or how she feels their opinions and experiences are related to the economic and political status of their community she explicates so well. The writing assignment she has given provides a partial answer, and points out something about the way information is organized in official discourse as well. Students are asked to draw analogies between their own and someone else's experience; they are supposed to become aware of the general nature of one person's responsibility to another, and in this way arrive at an understanding of vandalism in the abstract.

A similar process took place in the oral discussion we just described. It provides an implicit comment on Ms S's expressed views. As she summarized students' arguments she changed their form. The Puerto Rican students usually provided a hypothetical narrative to support their points, and made these more and more personalized as the argument grew more and more heated. For example, they might say something like, 'If a friend of mine got in a fight, and asked me to help, I would do it. But if he didn't ask me, I might not.' Later, in the more heated part of the argument, they might personalize by referring directly to people they knew — such as their friends and relatives — or to people everyone in the class knew, such as specific students in the class. 'If Robert got in a fight, and he asked me to help . . .' Ms S, on the other hand, would paraphrase the logic and generalize the point: 'Okay, you believe in helping your friends when they ask you to, but you wouldn't volunteer to get in trouble with them.' Although she used this pattern several times to show students that they did not disagree as much as they thought, they did not follow her example in formulating their own arguments. Two hypotheses suggest themselves here, which future research might consider. One is that the students simply did not understand the form of her paraphrases, or that she intended them as an example of how to develop an argument in a discussion. Another is that, although they may have understood what she was doing, they chose not to follow her lead because they wanted to 'play out' the open debate. Their reliance on hypothetical narrative to make points, and their dramatizations of their attitudes through body movements and shouting of approval and disapproval shows an interesting parallel with previously mentioned studies of adult Puerto Rican discourse. Bennett & Pedraza (1984) and Bennett & Sola (1984) suggest that using such narratives and performative forms may tell us something about the ways community members construct particular forms of consciousness through their ongoing daily communications with each other. Further, they suggest that such forms can help us understand how that consciousness, in its variability, provides members with responses to particular socio-historical conditions as they experience them. What we may be seeing here, then are students in this East Harlem junior high school in the process of creating a sense of a Puerto Rican community within the classroom. They may be using the resources available to them in the larger community to make some statement about who they are vis-a-vis the official institution of schooling.

Discourse in the Language Arts Class

'Ms L,' the language arts teacher, is a black woman who grew up in East Harlem, though she does not live there at present. Her ethnicity is an important part of her background. She manages to incorporate certain aspects of black culture and communicative practices into her teaching and these are an essential ingredient in her success in eliciting oral participation of students. In particular, she shows a genuine appreciation of performance before an audience as a value in itself and as a source for achieving rapport and solidarity with students. She is an able performer herself and encourages students to 'take the floor' and perform as well. This includes having students perform pantomimes of scenes demonstrating dramatic irony; having students read about their own written work, creating situations where students have to 'think on their feet', as she expresses it; and performing (not merely reading) written works of literature herself. Her style of 'dialoguing' with the class also often has elements of drama built into it, as we will explain below.

Closely related to her implicit valuing of dramatic aspects of oral discourse is Ms L's use of personal narrative. She consistently attempts to get students to see the relevance of assigned reading to their own lives by eliciting narratives of personal experience from them in both oral and written forms. Most importantly, she reciprocates by providing personal narratives of her own, making them relevant to readings and topics current in the class.

Although during the three-month period in which this study took place, Ms L exposed the seventh- and eighth-grade students to classical myths, fables, short stories, and poems, our discussion will focus on the material presented in February, which had been designated Black History Month.

Ms L took the opportunity to augment the regular texts with selections of literature written by Langston Hughes, Richard Wright, Nikki Giovanni, and Gwendolyn Brooks, among others. She clearly enjoyed making dramatic presentations of these works, yet did not confine herself to oral presentation and discussion of them. Through various skillful means she converted them into writing exercises of various kinds. We have chosen to present an example of the oral and written discourse that took place around a chapter of Langston Hughes's autobiography, *The Big Sea* (1940), but it should be made clear that the kinds of things we are about to describe also happened when Ms L presented authors and genres that were much more remote from these students' personal experiences. Ms L's overall philosophy of teaching is one of making literature in all of its forms in some way relevant to the students' lives and we will try to show how she went about doing so.

The Big Sea is the first installment of Hughes's autobiography and provides the reader with a series of glimpses of his first three decades of life, during which he decided to make writing his profession. Many of the chapters read like closed narratives, more or less complete within themselves. This is the case with the chapter entitled 'Salvation', which tells of his experience in being 'saved' when he was 12. The opening paragraph sets the scene:

> I was saved from sin when I was going on thirteen. But not really saved. It happened like this. There was a big revival at my Auntie Reed's church. Every night for weeks there had been much preaching, singing, praying, and shouting, and some very hardened sinners had been brought to Christ, and the membership of the Church had grown by leaps and bounds. Then just before the revival ended, they held a special meeting for children, 'to bring the young lambs to the fold.' My aunt spoke of it for days ahead. That night I was escorted to the front row and placed on the mourners' bench with all the other young sinners, who had not yet been brought to Jesus. (p. 18)

From Ms L's reading of this passage, her students may get an impression of a stronger and blacker voice speaking than most readers would. Yet, in many ways, Hughes's style is constituted by a matter-of-fact restraint and understatement. These qualities are manifest particularly in his presentation of conflict and of contradictions to which that conflict is a response. In church in 'Salvation' the twelve-year-old boy is the last one still sitting on the mourners' bench. All the other children have joined the 'saved' and are all standing by the altar. Even Langston's friend Westley has finally given in, saying, '"God damn! I'm tired o' sitting here. Let's get up and be saved."' So he got up and was saved.' Langston presents the conflicts in his mind in this way:

> Now it was really getting late. I began to be ashamed of myself, holding everything up so long. I began to wonder what God thought about Westley, who certainly hadn't seen Jesus either, but who was sitting proudly on the platform, swinging his knickerbockered legs and grinning down at me, surrounded by deacons and old women on their knees praying. God had not struck Westley dead for taking his name in vain or for lying in the temple. So I decided that maybe to save further trouble, I'd better lie too, and say that Jesus had come, and get up and be saved. So I got up. (p. 20)

Focus here is not on the emotional response to the conflict, nor on the pain that conflict is inflicting on Langston except the one mention of being 'ashamed'. Instead our attention is focused on his observations and his reasoning that finally led to resolution of the conflict, if not of the contradiction. Nor is the contradiction analyzed, or even discussed. It is only implied when later that night Langston is crying in bed. His aunt wakes up and tells his

> uncle I was crying because the Holy Ghost had come into my life, and because I had seen Jesus. But I was really crying because I couldn't bear to tell her that I had lied, that I had deceived everybody in the church, that I hadn't seen Jesus, and that now I didn't believe there was a Jesus any more, since he didn't come to help me. (p. 21)

The same church that has been an important historical force for unity, solidarity and resistance for Afro-Americans, at the very same time can act as a force dividing a family, and challenging a boy's allegiance *to* that family. This is the kind of analysis that Hughes shuns. We get the point, but we may not recognize the power of the voice that presents it.

Ms L picks up on the black language that is embedded or sometimes only hinted at in Hughes's language. While Hughes may be read, and has certainly read his own works for recording, as 'almost white', with very moderate inflections of pitch, rhythm and tempo, Ms L turns the reading into an effective evocation of the revival meeting and thereby conveys much of the intensity of the experience that casual readers might well miss if left to their own devices. Ms L creates an 'evangelical' tone in her reading. She uses sharp contrasts of stress, pitch, tempo, vowel length, and pitch contours which are clearly modeled on black preaching styles, as described by Gumperz (1982), Kochman (1980) and others.

About a third of the way through the three-page narrative the students begin to shout out responses, as the elders that Hughes describes do. Truman, a Puerto Rican student, was a leader in this, the first to shout out an appropriate 'revival-style' response: 'Hallelujah!' Some students laugh, Ms L interrupts her reading to respond, 'Hallelujah!', and she then goes on with the reading. When Ms L reads, 'Then he said: "Won't you come? Won't you come to Jesus? Young lambs, won't you come?"' Truman responds with, 'Yeess, come to the Lord, Come to Jesus!' Other students are chiming in, so that by the middle of the story, when Ms L reads the following passage, several of the students are calling out similar responses: 'Langston, why don't you come? Why don't you come and be saved? Oh, Lamb of God! Why don't you come?' Ms L reads this with great drama. The students are calling out: 'Come to Jesus.' 'Hallelujah!' 'Come and be saved!' 'Why don't you come?'

After reading there is a brief discussion about revival metings, what they are for, when they happen and where, and Ms L tells of her own personal experience of them. She asks them the meaning of 'salvation', its denotation and connotation. After some discussion, she gives them an impromptu writing assignment. They are to write a poem on the theme of 'salvation'. This is an in-class assignment and they will get to read them aloud to the class. Truman is so excited he can hardly sit still in his seat. He gets up to check the door, near where his table stands, shuffles his books and papers, sends sudden grins to people, raises and waves his arms frantically, and meanwhile produces odd excited utterances. Truman's excitement becomes more irrepressible when Ms L says they can read their poems aloud to the class. He begins to say things like 'Oh boy! I wanna read mine, I wanna read mine', as he gets down to work. Less than five minutes later he is waving his hand and muttering to attract Ms L's attention. He has two poems ready of about ten or twelve lines each.

Ms L can hardly ignore him. Even before he finishes she promises him he can read his poem aloud first and, yes, he can come up to the front of the room. Once he gets there, Truman doesn't simply stand there and read his poem in a soft monotone. He spreads his legs wide apart to get a solid footing, he arches his body backward, thrusts his chest out, raises his chin ready to expostulate. He swings stiffly back and forth, swaggers, adusts his thick glasses, and stares wide-eyed out over his audience, his 'congregation'. A grin flicks over this face repeatedly, and he sometimes glances down when he smiles in an 'Aw shucks' pose. He seems very aware of and appreciative of his own performance. Ms L always conveys a sense of her own enjoyment when she performs her readings, but Truman is almost ecstatic. He never stops moving, gyrating, swinging an arm, or even raising both arms straight out to either side, hands opened palm outward toward his 'congregation' in a Martin Luther King-style 'embrace'. He delivers his reading in a deep, loud tone, exaggerating the evangelical preaching style. This is his first poem:

Lord help me in this time of need
I need your salvation quick,
Help me Lord in the sins of the
past, I need your salvation quick,
Lord help Lord help me. We
know you're all mighty but Lord
help me in the time of need.

After reading this poem, Truman begs to be allowed to read his second, promising it will be short: 'See, see, Ms L' he cried, holding out his paper, 'it's only, let's see, um' (and he counts the lines), 'only nine lines short.'

Although not all the students show Truman's excitement, many of them volunteer to read their poems aloud. Ms L asks as many as she can, trying to give everyone a chance. This reflects her goal of creating opportunities for the students to express themselves, to be spontaneous, and to 'think on their feet'. Their creations show they have caught and can reproduce in their own writing certain characteristic features of black preaching styles and genres. Truman's performance of course brought out many features having to do with the use of body and vocal modulations. Many of the written poems show a sensitivity to certain characteristic images (e.g. light/dark, good/evil, sin/holiness, damnation/redemption, suffering/salvation, devil/angel). They make sharp contrasts of theme, idea, image, and setting, and use structural repetition to link themes or make contrasts. They use invocations to 'the Lord' and 'Jesus', and they position the poem's speaker in the role of supplicant. Consider, for example, a poem produced by Francine, a Puerto Rican girl:

Come! Come! Come oh Lord!
Come and save me.
I have lived my life as a
sinner.
I have been put through
sin and misery.
I need your salvation!
I need the light!
O Lord come save me!

Francine has produced a highly articulated structure, built on contrast, repetition, and parallelism. In her poem, the speaker invokes the 'Lord', relying on repetition ('Come! Come! Come oh Lord!'), and on sharp, simple contrasts ('sin' and 'misery' vs. 'salvation' and 'light'). The speaker is cast in the role of supplicant, confessing to sinfulness and begging for 'salvation' and 'light'. The last line is a repetition, with variation, of the opening invocation in lines 1 and 2. This shows a certain subtlety of technique. The poem is framed by the vocative plea ('oh Lord, come save me') found in the opening and closing lines. Sandwiched in between is a middle section which divides neatly into two parts: lines 3–6 use two sentences to foreground the 'my life as a sinner' theme, lines 7–8 use two sentences to foreground the speaker's 'need'. Each of these two parts also divides neatly into two sub-parts. For example, 'I have lived my life as a sinner' implies someone making choices, an active agent. But 'I have been put through sin and misery' implies conditions not chosen but given. Contrasts of this nature capture the sense of Langston Hughes's 'Salvation' in poetic verse.

We make no claim that Francine is aware of this structure, or even that she could reproduce it at will. That she can *produce* it, however, is evident. It would be interesting to know more about how she learned these ways with words, and about how Ms L's reading, and general presentation of literature selections, influence Francine's writing and understanding of particular genres of both writing and speaking.

Conclusion

The students in these classrooms used written texts and spoken language to carry relationships in varied, complex, and subtle ways. The discourses they constructed were 'channeled', though not totally determined, by the 'social structure and values' of their cultural milieu. They began, as everyone must, with the discourse that surrounded them, discourses 'over-populated with the intentions of others'. They sometimes managed, as we have seen, to make these discourses submit to their own intentions, and in doing so created a voice that was neither wholly of the school nor of the community, but a *bricolage* of their own creation that met particular needs in specific situations. Ricardo handled a piece of school discourse — Mr C's dictation of rules for revision — with such facility that his performance bordered on parody. The seventh graders' plays gave them an opportunity to comment on, through performance, situations and issues of interest to them but not to the official discourse of the composition class. The eighth graders, in their dramatization of a heated debate in the social studies class, took a piece of school discourse — the 'discussion' — and turned it into an opportunity to take all control of topic-comment, evaluation, questioning, and turntaking into their own hands. At the same time, their discussion was more serious and concerned than any other witnessed in that class. In the language arts class the students and teacher worked together to construct a discourse in which a communal voice became strongly resonant, accomplishing along the way some of the teacher's instructional objectives.

Thus, sometimes the students' discourse was at odds with the purposes of school discourse, sometimes peer and school discourse seemed to merge, and sometimes the students expanded a piece of school discourse beyond its usual limits to accomplish their own ends. As we have seen, the responses of the three teachers to the ebb and flow of language and intentions were rather varied. Mr C struggled hard to bring the students around to the ways of school discourse, but encountered considerable frustration along the way. Ms S had a good understanding of the oppressive social conditions under which the Puerto Rican community struggles, but was baffled by the discourse in her classroom that so clearly erupted out of that struggle. Ms L, on the other hand, having considerable facility herself with some of the key features of the community discourse — narrative, performance, dramatization — was often (though not always) able to accommodate the school official discourse to the peer-community ways with words. In so doing, she legitimated the discourse of the community and the students, and elicited a quite different mode of participation than they were able to offer in the other two classes.

But we would not want to suggest that the answer to the struggles of these students (who are members of a social group rejecting schooling in impressive numbers) is simply to tolerate, or even to utilize, their own ways with words. Partial legitimation of their peer discourse is clearly possible, as in Ms L's classroom, but that does not mean that schools could let peer discourse dominate the school environment. If they did, their structure, their policy, their purpose, their whole cultural milieu would have to be drastically changed. The solution to the dropout problem — if it is a problem — does not lie merely in training more teachers to be like Ms L, or teaching prospective teachers more about the 'cultural ways' of Puerto Ricans and blacks. Not that this would be a bad thing to do — in fact, it ought to be considered a minimum of teacher training, at least for teachers who will teach these students. But to train teachers in this way, useful as it might be, would not change the basic organizational structure of schooling in US society which puts all teachers of these populations of students into positions of major conflict and contradiction.

No matter how well teachers are trained, no matter how much knowledge researchers gather about the variable cultural ways of different subgroups in our society, the fact remains that ethnic minority communities like East Harlem have historically been politically and economically marginalized. The symptoms of this marginalization are well known: high unemployment, low income, high disease rates, low educational attainments. These are the social conditions in which schools like the one discussed here are embedded. At least in practice, for most community members the schools remain major progenitors of unequal opportunity. And failure in school is used to justify rejection in the job market later on. As long as such conditions exist, schools remain in a contradictory position, covertly undermining what they overtly intend.

What is almost amazing is the ingenuity with which students like those in our study created solutions to this contradiction as they experienced it in school. They readily seized opportunities to create their own voice in response to the conditions they found themselves in. Their spontaneous ability to accomplish this testifies to the viability of their community's culture. But to the extent that the schools — and other key institutions — fail to listen to that voice, or attempt to transform that voice into something alien, 'failure' is almost predetermined.

There are many ways to reject schooling, dropping out being only one. But schools cannot easily offer ethnic minority students something meaningful, because that would require those who govern the schools to acknowledge the marginality of minority communities, as well as the political and economic reasons for that marginality. The answer does not lie in formulating ever new versions of policy. Rather, we suggest that the processes of schooling need to be examined on a very specific and concrete level, as we have tried to do here, and interpreted in the light of the social, political and economic realities which form their context.

We have tried to adumbrate in our examples the pull and push of various discourses that inhabit a particular environment, the struggle for voice. What we believe we have seen is an important piece of a larger struggle between a minority community and the classes that rest on the labor of the community. This is the struggle for hegemony over the productive processes of consciousness formation — or ideology in Bakhtin's terminology. Against this backdrop, the concern with so-called basic skills becomes only one more piece of the struggle for consciousness. Questions remain: Who will define these 'skills'? Who is to say what is 'basic'? Whose purposes will it serve that particular 'skills' be learned, not by everyone, but by a select few? Whatever policy makers decide, students like those in this study will go on constructing their own voices in response to the conditions they find in community, school and the rest of the world. If we learn to understand and acknowledge these cultural processes, we might even learn to facilitate them instead of frustrating them.

Note

1. Funding for this research was provided under a contract with the National Institute of Education and the National Center for Bilingual Research.

References

Alvarez, C. (1983, October) *Narrative Performance in Conversational Interaction.* Paper presented in Spanish in the US Conference, Hunter College, New York City.

ASPIRA (1983) *Racial and Ethnic High School Dropout Rates in New York City: A Summary Report.* New York: ASPIRA of New York.

Bakhtin, M. M. (1968) *Rabelais and his World*. H. Iswolsky, trans. Bloomington: Indiana University Press.

— (1981) *The Dialogic Imagination*. C. Emerson and M. Holquist, trans. Austin: University of Texas Press.

Bennett, A. T. (1984) *Literate Discourse and the Puerto Rican Child*. Report to the National Center for Bilingual Research.

Bennett, A. T. and Pedraza, P. (1984) Political dimensions of discourse, consciousness and literacy in a Puerto Rican neighborhood in East Harlem. In M. O'Barr, C. Kramara and M. Schultz (eds) *Language and Power: Linguistic Resources Against Discrimination*. Beverly Hills, CA: Sage.

Bennett, A. T. and Sola, M. (1984, October) Writing, voice and school: Literacy and consciousness in an East Harlem junior school. Paper presented at Fourth Annual Bilingual/ESL Conference. William Paterson College, Wayne, NJ.

Bonilla, F. and Campos, R. (1981) A wealth of poor: Puerto Ricans in the new economic order. *Daedalus* 110 (2), 133–76.

Boyer, E. L. (1983) *High School: A Report on Secondary Education in America*. New York: Harper and Row.

Cook-Gumperz, J. and Gumperz, J. (1981) From oral to written discourse: The transition to literacy. In M. F. Whiteman (ed.) *Variation in Writing*. Hillsdale, NJ: Lawrence Erlbaum.

Davis, N. Z. (1975) *Society and Culture in Early Modern France*. Cambridge: Harvard University Press.

Emig, J. (1983) *The Web of Meaning: Essays on Writing, Teaching, Learning, and Thinking*. Upper Montclair, NJ: Boynton/Cook.

Everhart, R. (1983) *Reading, Writing and Resistance: Adolescence and Labor in a Junior High School*. Boston: Routledge and Kegan Paul.

Frawley, W. (ed.) (1982) *Linguistics and Literacy*. New York: Plenum.

Gilmore, P. (1983) Spelling 'Mississippi': Recontextualizing a literacy-related speech event. *Anthropology and Education Quarterly* 14, 235–55.

Goody, J. (ed.) (1968) *Literacy in Traditional Societies*. Cambridge: Cambridge University Press.

Graves, D. (1983) *Writing: Teachers and Children at Work*. Exeter, NH: Heinemann.

Gumperz, J. (ed.) (1982) *Language and Social Identity*. London: Cambridge University Press.

Heath, S. B. (1981) Toward an ethnohistory of writing in American education. In M. F. Whiteman (ed.) *Variation in Writing*. Hillsdale, NJ: Lawrence Erlbaum.

— (1983) *Ways with Words: Language, Life and Work in Communities and Classrooms*. London: Cambridge University Press.

Hughes, L. (1940) *The Big Sea*. NY: Hill and Wang.

Kochman, T. (1981) *Black and White Styles in Conflict*. Chicago: University of Chicago Press.

Mehan, H. (1979) *Learning Lessons*. Cambridge: Harvard University Press.

Michaels, S. (1981) 'Sharing time'. Children's narrative styles and differential access to literacy. *Language in Society* 10, 423, 442.

Moffett, J. (1968) *Teaching the Universe of Discourse*. Boston: Houghton Mifflin.

NCEE (National Commission on Excellence in Education) (1983, April) *A Nation at Risk: The Imperative for Educational Reform*. Washington, DC: Government Printing Office.

Sinclair, J. and Coulthard, R. M. (1975) *Towards an Analysis of Discourse*. Oxford: Oxford University Press.

Sola, M. (1984, May) *Coherence, Contradiction and Resistance in Child Discourse*. Paper presented at New York Child Language Group, New York City.

Spindler, G. (ed.) (1982) *Doing the Ethnography of Schooling.* New York: Holt, Rinehart & Winston.

Tannen, D. (1982) The oral/literate continuum in discourse. In D. Tannen (ed.) *Spoken and Written Language.* Norwood, NJ: Ablex.

Todorov, T. (1984) *Mikhail Bakhtin: The Dialogical Principle.* Minneapolis: University of Minnesota Press.

Volosinov, V. N. (M. Bahktin) (1973) *Marxism and the Philosophy of Language.* New York: Seminar Press.

Willis, P. (1977) *Learning to Labour.* Farnborough, England: Saxon House.

Wittgenstein, L. (1953) *Philosophical Investigations.* New York: Macmillan.

9 Cross-Cultural Perspectives on Literacy

BRIAN V. STREET

I would like to put discussion about contemporary literacy into broader perspective through accounts of the uses and meanings of literacy in other places and times. By considering literacy practices in such varied contexts as South East Asia in the 15th century, a contemporary South Pacific atoll, and recent accounts of New Guinea and Philadelphia, I hope to demonstrate the variety and complexity of literacies and to challenge some dominant assumptions about literacy in our own culture. I want to consider literacy, firstly, outside the framework of education in which it is often embedded in discussions in Britain and the USA; to provide qualitative rather than quantitative analysis; and to locate literacy practices in the context of power and ideology rather than as a neutral, technical skill.

We need to begin, I think, by trying to be self-conscious about the language we use and the questions we ask. The power to define and to name is itself one of the essential aspects of the uses of literacy so we need to be even more careful about terms when addressing literacy itself. Accordingly, I put forward some key concepts as a kind of framework on which to hang descriptions of literacy in practice. I prefer, firstly, to talk about 'literacy practices' than about 'literacy as such'. There are many different ways in which we act out our uses and meanings of reading and writing in different social contexts and the evidence from different societies and eras demonstrates that it is misleading to think of one single, unified thing called literacy . The notion that the acquisition of a single, autonomous literacy will have pre-defined consequences for individuals and societies has been shown to be a myth, often premised on narrow culturally specific values about what is proper literacy (Graff, 1979; Grant, 1986; Street, 1990). I prefer to work from what I term an 'ideological' model of literacy, that recognises a multiplicity of literacies; that the meaning and uses of literacy practices are related to specific cultural contexts; and that these practices are always associated with relations of power and ideology, they are not simply neutral technologies (Street, 1984; 1993).

I would like to extend some of these propositions to argue that literacy practices are constitutive of identity and of personhood. What I mean by this is that whichever forms of reading and writing we learn and use have associated with them certain social identities, expectations about behaviour and role models. For instance, Kate Rockhill's (1987) work on gender and literacy in the USA has shown that Hispanic women attempting to break out of poverty and out of the stranglehold of dominating and often violent men, construct an image of an alternative identity for themselves that they associate with the acquisition of a new literacy. They in fact already practise considerable literacy skills in managing the household and in relations with government agencies and schools, but this domestic literacy is marginalised and is associated with low status. The kind of literacy offered by college courses, on the other hand, is associated with higher status and with the jobs and identities to which they aspire: the kinds of images put forward in cinema and magazine representations of the 'professional' woman, the secretary, the woman who is 'SOMEBODY' (Rockhill, 1987b).

Horsman, (1989) writing about women in the Maritime areas of Canada, similarly notes how those providing courses for them assume that literacy is associated with specific female identities: where the women themselves see literacy as a way out of the home and of domestic constraints, the programmes often take literacy lessons back to the home, reinscribing women in their domestic identity. The kinds of literacy skills provided are those associated with the jobs it is assumed are appropriate for women: domestic related, 'caring', often child focussed, a quite different identity than that for which women have come to a literacy programme in the first place.

There is an anthropological literature on the notion of 'personhood' in different cultures that can be helpful in this context. Kirkpatrick, for instance, suggests that 'personhood is best viewed as a field that is ideologically structured in any society.' (1983). By this he means, not that the person is determined by dominant or top-down institutions, but that it is 'a site of articulation of dominant and subordinate ideological components'. There is a struggle over the appropriate definitions of the person, rather than a single, 'totalizing concept such as the individual' with which many western societies (and theorists) operate. Different cultural understandings are called upon in different contexts regarding the nature and potentialities of the person. In many western societies, the person is linked with the idea of a single, persistent and whole individual as though this persona operated across all contexts. In Polynesia, in contrast, the varied meanings of personhood in different contexts is more evident. The cross-cultural data, then, suggest that the 'notion of the person held in society is inevitably complex and ambiguous' and different facets of the person are called upon for different purposes and contexts. Despite this variation, however, in a given social milieu 'the person constructs retain a core of values and meaning for social participants'. In particular, the judgements of people and events as 'moral' is frequently focussed upon notions of personhood: what is proper behaviour, what is human/not human; how 'we' and 'they' are classified in some universal world order; all of these ordering procedures make central use of the concept of person.

I would like to develop this analysis in two ways for purposes of the account of literacy. Firstly, the uses and meanings of literacy in different societies are similar to the uses and meanings of the concept of person, in that both represent what Kirkpartick calls 'fields' in which dominant and other ideological structures are visible' (p. 12). Secondly, there is frequently a crucial relationship between the ideological fields of personhood and of literacy. What it is to be a person, to be moral and to be human in specific cultural contexts is frequently signified by the kind of literacy practices in which a person is engaged. This is highlighted by the ways in which agencies including Unesco came to associate literacy with the idea of a fully human person, with enlightenment in contrast to the dark space of 'illiteracy'. This, I would like to suggest, is characteristic of the ways in which literacy and personhood are intertwined in many cultural discourses and serve to remind us that the acquisition of literacy involves more than simply technical skills.

These general principles are applied by Niko Besnier to a specific account of 'Literacy and the notion of person' on the Pacific Atoll of Nukulaelae where he conducted anthropological fieldwork. 'The person on Nukulaelae', he says, 'is perceived as a complex system of more or less autonomous uiga "meanings"' which appear in different contexts and may be in conflict with each other. 'Each aspect of the person is related in complex ways to particular emotional experiences, interactional dynamics and emotional roles. In Nukulaelae ethnopsychology, the notion of self as locus of psychological experience and that of person as social performer are interrelated' (1991: 19). The relevance of this to our present concerns is that in Nukulaelae 'literacy itself is viewed as an important element in the very definition of person in that being able to read and write is presupposed in the characterisation of a socially competent person. Literacy is thus constitutively related to personhood'. In this context there are two different literacies, that associated with giving sermons and that associated with letter writing, and each involves different aspects of personhood and identity. Personal letters are associated with affect and locate the individual in a socioeconomic system of generosity, sociability and concern for younger kin (which generates admonitions and moral advice). The person as represented in letters is a vulnerable entity at the mercy of emotional experience and the circumstances of life. Sermons, on the other hand, bring out 'authoritarianism and assertiveness and highlight assymetries in power, knowledge and morality between the writer-performer and the audience' (p. 20). Sermon givers harangue their audience, letter writers express empathy.

Different literacies are, then, associated with different personhood and identities. Similar sets of associations can be seen in western culture, once the significance of literacy for these processes is recognised. Whether we attend a course or school, or become involved in a new institutional set of literacy practices, through work, political activism, personal relationships, we are doing more than simply decoding script, producing essays or writing a proper hand: we are taking on — or resisting — the identities associated with those practices. The idea that literacy practices are constitutive of identities provides us with a different — and I would argue more constructive — basis for understanding and comparing literacy practices in different cultures than the current emphasis on a simple literacy/illiteracy dichotomy, on educational needs as inevitably endemic to literacy and on the type of literacy associated with a small academic sub-culture, with its emphasis on the essay text and the typical identity associated with it.

However, whilst I appear to be arguing that literacy practices may position us, I would also want to consider how literacies may be sites of negotiation and of transformation. It was popular in social science until recently to envisage society as mainly a top-down process of domination, with ideology serving the purposes of a ruling group and the rest passive or unwilling victims. Recently this viewpoint has shifted to one which gives more recognition to 'agency', to the way in which people in different positions may resist and negotiate the positions to which they are apparently ascribed. The implications of this for Literacy Studies are considerable: the acquisition of a particular set of literacy practices, whilst clearly associated with particular cultural identities, may actually be a focus for transformation and challenge. Rockhill's Hispanic women were not simply passive victims of the media stereotypes of women and literacy — they used their ideas about new forms of literacy to resist the dominance of husbands and sons who had different stereotypes again, ones which women had to struggle hard to resist. The outcome of such struggles between different versions of identity and of literacy remains to be analysed in each case: it cannot be read off as a direct product of the acquisition of literacy as such. This recognition leads to a further perspective on the kind of literacy that is dominant in our own society, although from within the society the question of why this should be so is seldom on the agenda.

The fact that one cultural form is dominant is more often disguised behind public discourses of neutrality and technology in which the dominant literacy is presented as the only literacy. Where other literacies are recognised, as for instance in the literacy practices associated with young children or with different class and ethnic groups, these are presented as inadequate or failed attempts to match the proper literacy of the dominant culture: remedial attention is therefore required and those who practise these alternative literacies are conceived of as culturally deprived. Within the field of linguistics it is now clearly recognised that there are a great variety of language forms — dialects, registers, creoles — and that the standard is itself only another 'variety'. How a standard achieves this status has been further emphasised by the coining of the term 'dominant language' (Grillo, 1989), which makes explicit that the issue is one of power and of struggle for dominance, rather than a natural process of the emergence of the 'best' as standard. I would like to suggest that we similarly adopt the notion of 'dominant literacies' in order to highlight the extent to which the literacy that is treated as standard is only one variety amongst many and that the question of how it became the standard is likewise a power issue. This, then, involves us referring to 'literacy varieties' just as we have now become accustomed to talk of 'language varieties'. How the dominant literacy marginalises other varieties, asserts its own proper dominance and disguises its own class and cultural basis are questions that have scarcely been asked in the field of literacy: the development of some of the concepts I am proposing here will, I hope, help to bring such questions to the fore and to facilitate research and enquiry in these neglected areas.

John Ogbu, a well known educational researcher, recently suggested an even narrower definition of literacy than I have been criticising so far, but which probably represents the dominant view, at least in educational circles: 'I define literacy as the ability to read and write and compute in the form taught and expected in formal education . . . [literacy then is] synonomous with academic performance' (Ogbu, 1990). Up against this educationally-based and academic account of literacy I would like to pose a description of a form of literacy in SE Asia that provides a different basis from which to begin our consideration of literacy practices: 'The old Indonesian ka-ga-nga alphabet was taught in no school and had no value either vocationally or in reading any established religious or secular literature. The explanation given for its persistence was the local custom of manjan, a courting game whereby young men and women would gather in the evenings and the youths would fling suggestive quatrains [pantun] written in the old script to the young women they fancied' (Reid, 1988: 218). There is more to literacy practices than is dreamt of in the westerner's philosophy.

Literacy in Non-European Contexts

The evidence from SE Asia provides further material to challenge the narrow view of literacy. Literacy practices, it appears, were widespread in the era preceding western impact. This was a matter neither of elite nor of commercial interests but of a variety of local customs and practices. Writing in the Phillipines in the 16th century, for instance, served no religious, judicial or historical purposes, but was used only to write notes and letters. Elsewhere women used writing actively for exchanging notes and recording debts, whilst in southern Sumatra as late as 1930 high proportions of the population employed literacy for poetic courting contests (Reid, 1988). The arrival of Islam and Christianity had the effect of reducing the literacy rates, particularly amongst women, by restricting writing to the male, sacral, and monastic domains. In the Philippines knowledge of the traditional scripts had gone within a century of Christianisation and a similar fate befell pre-Islamic scripts in Malaya and parts of Sumatra. These examples raise novel questions about relative gender participation in and uses of literacy. Since literacy was not taught in any formal institution and had no vocational or religious value, its transmission tended to be mainly the responsibility of mothers and older siblings. The social context of literacy learning, then, facilitated the uses of literacy by women, who themselves employed literacy skills in the context not only of the 'poetic courting contests' mentioned above but also for exchanging notes, recording debts and other commercial matters which were in the female domain (Reid, 1988). As a result, literacy rates for women were at least as high as those for men and some travellers found it even higher (Reid, 1988: 219). The advent of westerners, with their male-oriented religious institutions shifted the balance towards male literacy and formal schooling. Such imbalance characterises many accounts of gendered literacy practices in the contemporary world: it is often modernisation and the assumptions embedded in western educational theory, not traditional culture or 'backwardness', that lie behind the inequalities we observe.

During the last century a number of societies that previously had little or no acquaintance with literacy have come to use reading and writing as part of their communicative repertoire. Questions about the 'impact' of literacy on such peoples, or its 'consequences' for cognition and social development have tended to assume a single literacy — that of the imparters — and a single predictable process — that of transformation of passive 'illiterates' into literates. Kulick and Stroud found, in reading the literature on literacy transfer, that 'it is often difficult to escape the conclusion that human beings are basically passive objects who become affected by literacy in ways they are not fully aware of or can control' (Kulick & Stroud, 1990). Those responsible for imparting literacy have tended to treat indigenous peoples as they would school pupils, debating whether they are 'ready' for literacy, whether they should have access to it and what problems are associated with its 'impact'. From a pedagogic point of view, the process is seen as the acquisition of specific technical skills and the learning of those conventions and assumptions about literacy held by the teachers.

I would suggest that we need to take a less paternalistic and less narrowly pedagogic view of the process: Kulick & Stroud, for instance, state: 'rather than stress how literacy affects people, we want to take the opposite tack and examine how people affect literacy'. They want to demonstrate 'how individuals in a newly literate society, far from being passively transformed by literacy, instead actively and creatively apply literate skills to suit their own purposes and needs': how they 'take hold' of literacy rather than what is its 'impact' on them. A new literacy is incorporated into the receiving culture's already existing conventions and concepts regarding communication — the 'subjects' are not 'tabula rasa' as many development literacy campaigns appear to assume (Street, 1987). It also reveals how literacy processes cannot be understood simply in terms of schooling and pedagogy: they are part of more-embracing social institutions and conceptions.

Kulick and Stroud analyse the adaptations to literacy they observed in a rural, newly literate Papua New Guinea village. They demonstrate how local ideas of the self and others are articulated and reinforced through an emphasis on particular dimensions of oral language use. Many of the conventions employed in oral discourse, particularly in speech making, carry over into written forms: the avoidance of 'hed' — of appearing pushy and self-oriented — and the emphasis on 'save' — a complex concept indicating both openness to knowledge and sensitivity to others' interests. Some of the new written forms that emerged under missionary influence were obliged to come to terms with these values and conventions, leading to outcomes not necessarily envisioned by the missionaries themselves.

The example cited above from the South Pacific atoll of Nukulaelae also demonstrates how new literacies may be assimilated to pre-existing communicative conventions, as in the New Guinea case, and also the ways in which the repertoire may expand and alter local forms of communication (Besnier, 1988). Again, the introduction of literacy by missionaries involved the adaptation of their purposes to those of the islanders. The primary purpose of literacy production on Nukulaelae is to write letters. Nukulaelae letters are sent to relatives on neighbouring atolls, and serve a variety of functions: monitoring economic reciprocity; informing kin of family events; and admonishing younger people. Permeating every aspect of letters is a heavy emphasis on the overt expression of affect, of a nature not generally found in other arenas of Nukulaelae social life. The new literacy, then, facilitated an expansion of the communicative repertoire in this social context. The overt expression of certain types of affect in letters, whilst in oral communication islanders normally express affect through covert means, suggests that traditional assumptions about the association of the medium of communication with particular expressions of emotion or detachment cannot be generalised: the ways in which affect is encoded in the communicative repertoire varies across cultures and across media and we cannot assume that as people acquire literacy so they will acquire the conventions for using the repertoire expected in the imparting culture. Besnier's detailed ethnography of the particular uses and meanings of literacy on Nukulaelae pro-

vides a challenge to traditional western assumptions regarding the use of
writing for detached and unemotional purposes rather than to convey
feeling.

Literacies in Urban America

Nor is this kind of evidence restricted to non-European, rural societies:
recent anthropological studies of the uses and meanings of literacy in urban
contexts in the USA suggest that here too literacy is best understood in
broader terms than those employed within much educational writing.
Miriam Camitta (1993), for instance, describes the kinds of texts produced
by adolescents outside of school in urban Philadelphia, and draws a contrast
with schooled texts: 'the kinds of written texts I wish to study are not essays,
the officially designated discourse genre of academia, but rather those that
adolescents choose to write within the framework of adolescent culture and
social organisation. These texts I shall call "vernacular" in the sense that
they are most closely associated with culture which is neither elite nor
institutional. By vernacular writing I mean writing which is traditional and
indigenous to the diverse cultural processes of communities as distinguished
from the uniform, inflexible standards of institutions'. In the school context,
however, such writing has been treated mainly in moral terms, as rebellious,
as inadequate attempts at proper literacy, along with graffiti and other literate forms that differ from the essay text model.

Camitta worked for three years with adolescents at Community High
School, Philadelphia, talking about their writing and sharing the intimacies
this involved. The experience forced her to revise assumptions and beliefs
about writing that she had held as a teacher at the school and which she
suggests are dominant in educational circles in America. She gradually
became aware of the texts and contexts for unofficial or self-sponsored writing, practised by adolescents: writing, she discovered, was an important and
varied activity and identified major areas that 'organised' adolescent culture.
The written material included rap verses and rehearsal notes, letters, entries
in journals, diaries, poems, rhymes and parodies and texts copied into
notebooks. The young people were 'taking hold' of literacy. The interest
generated in writing when it was free of school constraints also led to much
oral sharing amongst students, including a great deal of verbal interaction
around the texts: they might read texts aloud to each other, offer feedback
or take it in turns reading texts silently and then commenting on them.
Camitta concludes that 'collaboration, both oral and written, as it takes
place in the writing process, is a kind of performance in which an audience
for the text is actualised, as opposed to fictionalised'. Further, 'we saw writing take place in what has traditionally been characterised as a condition of

oral literature and performance, that is, in the context of face-to-face communication'. Thirdly she noted the recursive nature of this kind of writing: 'performance of texts took place at any point in the drafting process and revision, as a result of audience feedback, was during not after drafting. This aspect of composition can be compared with the improvisation that takes place during oral performance of traditional texts'. These findings have considerable implications for the analysis of oral and literate practices, in modern and traditional contexts, for our definitions of 'literacy' and for our methods of studying it. The literacy practices of different generations may be as different as those of different cultures. Individuals may pass through different stages of literacy as they grow older or they may, as in Camitta's example, switch between one form and another according to context.

Amy Shuman (1986) also worked with adolescents at an inner-city Junior High School, in the eastern USA. Whilst her interest, like Camitta's was in oral and written narratives, her particular focus was on storytelling rights: in standard written form these involve questions of legal copyright, in the context of vernacular literacies, rights are embedded in everyday social relationships and interactions. These Shuman investigated through a variety of methods: she lived among groups of adolescents at the school for three years, tape-recorded many conversations especially naturally occurring narrative performance, conducted interviews and designed a questionnaire with the help of the students themselves. She also obtained copies of written material, often on lined notebook paper, she photocopied diaries and kept a 'Daily Diary' herself and allowed students access to the parts that concerned them.

Again the relationship of written to oral conventions is crucial: 'oral storytelling rights differ among cultures and groups, and therefore are subject to constant misunderstanding among people who operate according to different systems'. Rights in written stories amongst urban adolescents are equally complex, conventionalised and subject to misconception. Indeed, the stories Shuman examines are themselves about rights: she describes them as 'junior high school fight stories, that is narrative accounts of quarrels about who has the right to say what to whom'. In the communities from which these adolescents come, it is they rather than older or younger people who are assigned the task of managing written documents: they mediate the community to the state through documentation, filling in forms, writing letters. The young people also, however, keep their own narratives and diaries that record fight stories and provide discourses on storytelling rights within their community. And they use both speaking and writing to categorise their experience. General theory regarding the respective roles and associations of written and oral communication do not hold in such contexts: 'in contrast to conventional models that assume the use of speaking for face-to-face communication and writing for absent-author communication, the adolescents often used oral narratives to convey messages to absent third parties (through he-said-she-said rumours) and used writing as part of face-to-face exchanges in which documents were collaboratively produced and read aloud or as solitary communication with oneself in diaries'. The difference between proximity and distance, and the standardisation frequently created by distance, was more consequential than writing itself. This, then, underlines the point that not all writing belongs to the genre of the essay and not only literacy but also genre can be an important way of distributing knowledge and attitudes towards texts in a community.

Shuman does not evaluate the students' texts by standard school criteria of competence, but rather as part of a single community's repertoire: from this perspective they represent choices among channels and genres of communication, rather than examples of greater or lesser deficiency, as the current debate in the US about 'standards' would appear to require. The practices described by Shuman do not represent anomolies, rather they demonstrate 'a need to reevaluate the current models used for categorising writing and speaking'. Labov (1972) and others have demonstrated that there is much more of interest in the language practices of the inner city than is elicited by standardised tests and by folk judgements: the work of Shuman, Camitta and others is now revealing the rich repertoire of written as well as oral practices to be found there.

Gail Weinstein-Shr (1993) lived and worked with Hmong refugees in Philadelphia and brings to attention aspects of the linguistic repertoire of such new immigrant groups that have likewise gone unrecognised in much previous literature. The shift in focus in literacy studies led her to ask new questions: 'how does life in a literate environment affect or change social relationships?', 'how do social relationships influence the way that literacy is acquired and used?'. Literacy is a relatively recent innovation for the Hmong, so it is possible to observe rapid changes as it is introduced 'into their repertoire of communicative resources'. Over a period of six years Weinstein-Shr conducted household surveys and developed several in-depth 'portraits' of Hmong adults in the city as well as meeting a number of them in the English language classes that she ran. She examines the ways in which kinship and literacy existed for the Hmong historically and how they now operate in their new lives in urban Philadelphia. She describes two men's lives in detail and brings out contrasts in their ways of using literacy and their ways of making/maintaining relationships, in the context of Philadelphia's wider community and of a general discussion of literacy and social process. Whilst one man, Chou Chang, uses the standard literacy learnt in classes to mediate between his community and the agencies of the state, in a classic 'broker' role; another Pao Youa, seems to 'fail' in the formal classes and yet uses literacy with considerable skill to reinforce aspects of traditional Hmong culture and his own authority in relation to it. Chou spends a great deal of time writing letters to welfare offices: Pao keeps cuttings from newspapers in scrapbooks, collects reference materials and maintains personal journals that together take on the authority of chronicles, making him the history and news keeper for his community. Like Shuman and Camitta's adolescents, he extends the range of literacy practices well beyond the narrow definitions of the school and the classroom. Both men have adapted the new literacy to current needs, one via new relationships with the host authorities, the other through building on traditional forms of authority. Both are active and creative mediators of this addition to their community's communicative repertoire, not simply passive recipients of a new technology.

Weinstein-Shr's conclusions provide also an apt summary of the arguments presented here: (1) that the study of the meanings and uses of literacy in specific people's lives can provide general insights into human organisation and social process; and (2) that anthropological insights can contribute to informing literacy instruction and educational practice as contemporary society becomes increasingly culturally diverse. This approach might force us to rethink the question of how standards of functional literacy can be established in varying contexts and instead ask how local requests for different literacies can be met by national and international providers. The answers that emerge from the kind of analysis and data cited above are also the three themes which underlie this paper:

(1) we need first to clarify and refine concepts of literacy, to abandon the great divide between 'literacy' and 'illiteracy' and to study instead 'literacy practices' in diverse cultural and ideological contexts,

(2) we have to start where people are at, to understand the cultural meanings and uses of literacy practices and to build programmes and campaigns on these rather than on our own cultural assumptions about literacy,

(3) we need to link theory of the kind being developed in the 'New Literacy Studies' with the experience and insights of practitioners — the teachers, facilitators, animators who have been working in the field of literacy for many years and who have much to teach us about people's needs and desires in this area and the problems encountered in meeting them.

These three approaches provide, I would suggest, a richer and more sustainable approach to policy in the field of literacy than the aim of establishing 'standards of functional literacy'. Research and practice in the next decade will tell whether this is a valid claim.

References

Besnier, N. (1989) Literacy and feelings: The encoding of affect in Nukulaelae letters. *Text* Vol. 9, No. 1.
— (1990) Literacy and the notion of person on Nukulaelae Atoll. *American Anthropologist* 93.

Bloch, M. (ed.) (1975) *Political Language and Oratory*. New York: Academic Press.
— (1989) Literacy and enlightenment. In K. Scousboe and M. T. Larsen (eds) *Literacy and Society*. Akademsig Gorlag, Centre for Research in the Humanities, Copenhagen University.
Camitta, M. (1993) Vernacular writing: Varieties of literacy among Philadelphia high school students. In B. Street (ed.) *Cross-Cultural Approaches to Literacy*. Cambridge University Press.
Graff, H. (1979) *The Literacy Myth*. New York: Academic Press.
Grant, A. (1986) Defining literacy: Common myths and alternative readings. *Australian Review of Applied Linguistics*.
Grillo, R. (1989) *Dominant Languages: Language and Hierarchy in Britain and France*. Cambridge: Cambridge University Press.
Horsman, J. (1989) From the learner's voice: Women's experience of IL/Literacy. In M. Taylor and J. Draper (eds) *Adult Literacy Perspectives*. Ontario: Culture Concepts Inc.
Kirkpatrick, J. (1983) *The Marquesan Notion of the Person*. Ann Arbor, Michigan: UMI Research Press.
Kulick, D. and Stroud, C. (1990) Conceptions and uses of literacy in a Papua New Guinean village. *Man.*, n.s.
Labov, W. (1972) *Language in the Inner City*. Pennsylvania: Pennsylvania University Press.
Ogbu, J. (1990) Defining literacy. In J. W. Stigler (ed.) *Cultural Psychology: The Chicago Symposia on Human Development*. Cambridge: Cambridge University Press.
Reid, A. (1988) *South East Asia in the Age of Commerce: 1450–1680* Vol. 1. *The Lands Below the Winds*. New Haven and London: Yale University Press.
Rockhill, K. (1987a) Gender, language and the politics of literacy. *British Journal of the Sociology of Education* Vol. 8., No. 2.
— (1987b) Literacy as threat/desire: Longing to be somebody. In J. S. Gaskell and A. McLaren (eds) *Women and Education: A Canadian Perspective*. Calgary: Detselig.
Shuman, A. (1986) *Storytelling Rights: The Uses of Oral and Written Texts by Urban Adolescents*. Cambridge: Cambridge University Press.
Street, B. (1984) *Literacy in Theory and Practice*. Cambridge: Cambridge University Press.
— (1987) Literacy and social change: The significance of social context in the development of literacy programmes. In D. Wagner (ed.) *The Future of Literacy*. Oxford: Pergamon Press.
— (1990) Putting literacies on the political agenda. Open letter. *Australian Journal for Adult Literacy Research and Practice* Vol. 1., No. 1. Deakin University.
— (1993) *Cross-Cultural Approaches to Literacy*. Cambridge: Cambridge University Press.
Weinstein-Shr, G. (1993) Literacy and social process: A community in transition. In B. Street (ed.) *Ibid*.

10 The Legacies of Literacy

HARVEY GRAFF[1]

Until quite recently, scholarly and popular conceptions of the value of literacy have followed normative assumptions about the changes wrought by its *diffusion*. Furthermore, literacy has been intimately tied to post-Enlightenment, 'liberal' social theories and expectations of the role of literacy and schooling in socioeconomic development, social order, and individual progress. This set of conjectures constitutes what I have come to call 'the literacy myth'. Along with other tenets of a worldview dominant in the West for the greatest part of the past two centuries, the 'literacy myth' no longer suffices as a satisfactory explanation for the place of literacy in society, polity, culture, or economy (see 7, 24, 26, 27, 42, 47, 48, 58).

The past misconstrual of the meanings and contributions of literacy are rooted in the ideological origins of Western society. Expectations and assumptions of the primacy and priority of literacy and print for society and individual, the necessity of 'functional' skills for survival (whatever they might be), or the mass condition of literacy as an index of the condition of civilization — all have been guiding assumptions that have obscured a deeper, more grounded understanding of the complexities of literacy.

A more adequate conceptualization of literacy must consider three things. First, a definition of literacy must be made explicit so that it can then be used comparatively over time and across space. If, for example, what is meant by literacy are the basic abilities to read and write, then the evidence of changes in such measures as Scholastic Aptitude Tests, undergraduate composition abilities, and Armed Forces Qualifying Tests as appropriate representations of literacy become problematic. The evidence of such measures should not be ignored but their application to understanding literacy should be made cautiously, if at all.

In my view, basic or primary levels of reading and writing constitute the only flexible and reasonable indications or signs that meet the essential criterion of comparability: a number of historical and contemporary sources, while not wholly satisfactory in themselves, may be employed (see Table 1). Included here are measures ranging from the evidence of written documents, sources that reveal proportions of signatures and marks, the

Table 1 Sources for the historical study of literacy in North America and Europe

Source	Measure of literacy	Population	Country of availability	Years of availability	Additional variables
Census	Questions: read and write, read/write Signature/mark (Canada 1851, 1861 only)	Entire 'adult' population (in theory): ages variable, e.g. over 20 years, 15 years, 10 years	Canada, United States	Manuscripts: nineteenth century	Age, sex, occupation, birthplace, religion, marital status, family size and structure, residence, economic data
Wills	Signature/mark	20–50 percent of adult males dying; 2–5 percent of adult females dying	Canada, United States, England, France, etc.	Canada, eighteenth century on, US 1660 on, others from sixteenth–seventeenth century on	Occupation, charity, family size, residence, estate, sex
Deeds	Signature/mark	5–85 percent of living landowning adult males; 1 percent or less of females	Canada, United States	Eighteenth century on	Occupation, residence, value of land, type of sale
Inventories	Book ownership	25–60 percent of adult males dying; 3–10 percent of adult females dying	Canada, United States, England, France, etc.	Seventeenth–eighteenth century on (quantity varies by country and date)	Same as wills
Depositions	Signature/Mark	Uncertain: potentially more select than wills, potentially wider. Women sometimes included	Canada, United States, England, Europe	Seventeenth–eighteenth century on (use and survival varies)	Potentially, age, occupation, sex, birthplace, residence
Marriage records	Signature/Mark	Nearly all (80 percent +) young men and women marrying (in England)	England, France, North America	From 1754 in England; 1650 in France	Occupation, age, sex, parents' name and occupation, residence (religion – North America)

Catechetical examination records	Reading, memorization, comprehension, writing examinations	Unclear, but seems very wide	Sweded, Finland	After 1620	Occupation, age, tax status, residence, parents' name and status, family size, migration, periodic improvement
Petitions	Signature/mark	Uncertain, potentially very select, males only in most cases	Canada, United States, England, Europe	Eighteenth century on	Occupation or status, sex, residence, political or social views
Military recruit records	Signature/mark or question on reading and writing	Conscripts or recruits (males only)	Europe, esp. France	Nineteenth century	Occupation, health, age, residence, education
Criminal records	Questions: read, read well, etc.	All arrested	Canada, United States, England	Nineteenth century	Occupation, age, sex, religion, birthplace, marital status, moral habits criminal data
Business records	Signature/mark	1. All employees 2. Customers	Canada, United States, England, Europe	Nineteenth, twentieth century	1. Occupation, wages 2. Consumption level, residence, credit
Library/ mechanics Institute records	Books borrowed	Members or borrowers	Canada, United States, England	Late eighteenth– early nineteenth century	Names of volumes borrowed, society membership
Applications (land, job, pensions, etc.)	Signature/mark	All applicants	Canada, United States, England, Europe	Nineteenth– twentieth century	Occupation, residence, family, career history, etc.
Aggregate data sources*	Questions or direct tests	Varies greatly	Canada, United States, England, Europe	Nineteenth– twentieth century	Any or all of the above

* Censuses, educational surveys, statistical society reports, social surveys, government commissions, prison and jail records, etc.
Source: (48, Appendix A, pp. 325–7). This is a modified and greatly expanded version of Table A in (76).

evidence of self-reporting (surprisingly reliable, in fact), responses to surveys and questionnaires, test results, and the like (see Table 1; see also 16, 21, 37, 48 [introduction and appendixes], 57, 76, 100). Such basic but systematic and direct indications meet the canons of accuracy, utility, *and* comparability.

Some may question the quality of such data, or argue that tests of basic skills are too low a standard to employ. To account for such objections is a second component of a definition of literacy. Literacy, above all, is concerned with the human capability to use a set of techniques for decoding and reproducing written or printed materials. Writing and printing are separate, mechanical techniques. Neither writing nor printing per se are 'agents of change'; their impacts are determined by the manner in which human beings exploit them. Literacy is a learned skill, usually acquired in a way in which oral ability or nonverbal, nonliterate communicative modes are not.[2]

Writings about the imputed 'consequences', 'implications', or 'concomitants' of literacy have assigned to literacy's acquisition a truly daunting number of cognitive, affective, behavioral, and attitudinal effects. These characteristics usually include attitudes ranging from empathy, innovativeness, achievement-orientation, 'cosmopoliteness', information- and media-awareness, national identification, technological acceptance, rationality, and commitment to democracy, to opportunism, linearity of thought and behavior, or urban residence. Literacy is sometimes conceived of as a skill, but more often as symbolic or representative of attitudes and mentalities. On other levels, literacy 'thresholds' are seen as requirements for economic development, 'take-offs', 'modernization', political development and stability, standards of living, fertility control, and so on. But empirical investigations of these purported consequences and correlations are infrequent. Further, the results of macro-level, aggregative, or ecological studies are usually much less impressive either statistically or substantively than are the normative theories and assumptions.

Viewing literacy in the abstract as a foundation in skills that can be developed, lost, or stagnated is meaningless without connection to the possessors of those skills. Hence, understanding literacy requires a third specification — its use in and application to precise, historically specific material and cultural contexts. The major problem is that of reconstructing the contexts of reading and writing — how, when, where, why, and to whom literacy was transmitted, the meanings that were assigned to it, the uses to which it was put, the demands placed on literate abilities and the degrees to which they were met, the changing extent of social restrictedness in the distribution and diffusion of literacy, and the real and symbolic differences that emanated from the social condition of literacy among the population.

The context in which literacy is taught or acquired is one significant area of research. The work of Cole and Scribner with the Vai people in Liberia and elsewhere suggests that the environment in which students acquire their literacy has a major impact on the cognitive consequences of their possession of the skill and the uses to which it can be put. Children who were formally educated in schools designed for that purpose acquired a rather diferent set of skills as part of their training than those who learned more informally. Whereas previous empirical studies had confounded literacy with schooling, Scribner and Cole attempted to distinguish the roles and contributions of the two. In contrast with other researchers, they found that 'the tendency of schooled populations to generalize across a wide range of problems occurred because schooling provides people with a great deal of practice in treating individual learning problems as instants of general classes of problems. Moreover, we did not assume that the skills promoted by schooling would necessarily be applied in contexts unrelated to school experience' (104, p. 453, see also 42, 43, 44, 102, 103). These findings of the restricted impacts of literacy have wide implications, especially regarding the time and place in which literacy is acquired and transmitted in circumstances outside the environment of the schoolroom and formal institutional settings (see 57, 67, 68, 69, 105, 106, 116). Such research must also limit the assumptions and expectations that students carry to studies of literacy — such as presupposing literacy to be 'liberating' or 'revolutionary' in its consequences.

A second focus of research on literacy involves the tyranny of conceptual dichotomies in its study and interpretation. Consider the common phrases: literate and illiterate, written and oral, print and script, and so on. None of these polar opposites usefully describes actual circumstances; all of them, in fact, preclude contextual understanding.

The oral-literate dichotomy is the best example. The proclained decline in the pervasiveness and power of the 'traditional' oral culture dating from the advent of moveable type obscures the persisting power of oral modes of communication. The work of Havelock on classical Greek literacy (52, 53, 54) or that of Clanchy on medieval English literacy (16) richly illustrates the concurrent and complementary oral and literate communicative processes. Clanchy reveals the struggle that writing and written documents waged for their acceptance from the eleventh through the thirteenth centuries — a time of rising lay literacy. Early written documents, impelled by the state and the interests of private property, faithfully reproduced the 'words' of oral ceremonies and the rituals that traditionally had accompanied formal agreements; they were also adorned with the traditonal badges of sealed bargains (see 4, 14, 16, 22, 33, 34, 39, 41, 48, 53, 54, 73, 81). According to Havelock, Western literacy, from its 'invention' in the Greek alphabet and first popular diffusion in the city-states of classical times, was formed, shaped, and conditioned by the oral world that it penetrated. Then literacy was highly restricted and a relatively unprestigious craft; it carried relatively little of the association with wealth, power, status, and knowledge that it would later acquire. Even with the encroachment of literacy, the ancient world remained an oral world, whether on street corners or in marketplaces, assemblies, theaters, villas, or intellectural gatherings. The word as spoken was most common and most powerful. This tradition continued from the classical era through the 1000 years of the Middle Ages and may well be reinforced today by the impact of the newer electronic media.

The oral and the literate thus complement and augment each other. The poetic and dramatic word of the ancients was supplanted, though not replaced, by a religion rooted in the Book, but propagated primarily by oral preaching and teaching. Classical and other forms of education long remained oral activities, with literacy by oral instruction. The written and then printed word were spread to many semiliterates and illiterates via oral processes; information, news, literature, and religion were thereby spread far more widely than purely literate means could have allowed. For many centuries, reading itself was an oral, often collective activity, not the private, silent one we now consider it to be.

Thus, it is not surprising that the history of literacy is also commonly a truncated one, ignoring, as irrelevant or inaccessible, the first 2000 years of Western literacy before the advent of moveable type. This linear perspective, with its emphasis on changes wrought by literacy, obscures the continuities and contradictions in the historical role of literacy. The role of tradition is a case in point. The use of elementary schooling and learning one's letters, for example, for political and civic functions such as moral conduct, respect for social order, and participant citizenship, was prominent in the Greek city-states during the fifth century before Christ. This use of literacy is a classical legacy that was regularly rediscovered by persons in the West during each age or reform movement (for a summary of key points in the history of literacy, see Table 2). Recognizing this continuity or legacy of literacy allows us to consider the similarities and differences in rates of literacy, schooling configurations, practical and symbolic uses of literacy, and the like that accompany renewed recognition of the positive value of expanded popular literacy within the differing social or economic contexts.

Similarly, the strength of the idea of the oral-literate dichotomy, as discussed earlier, also was due in part to the exaggerated emphasis on change and discontinuity. Finally, the primary users of literacy — the state, the church, and commerce — have remained in effect, regardless of the degree of social restrictiveness that regulated the supply curve of popular diffusion of literacy. Although the balance among these institutions has shifted, this triumvirate has retained its cultural and political hegemony over the social functions of literacy. The development of these three institutions and their uses of literacy illustrates the continuities and contradictions of literacy itself.

Table 2 Key points in the history of literacy in the West

ca. 3100 BC	Invention of writing
3100–1500 BC	Development of writing systems
650–550 BC	'Invention' of Greek alphabet
500–400 BC	First school developments, Greek city-states, tradition of literacy for civic purposes
200 BC–200 AD	Roman public schools
0–1200	Origins and spread of Christianity
800–900	Carolingian language, writing, and bureaucratic developments
1200 and onward	Commercial, urban 'revolutions', expanded administration and other uses of literacy and especially writing, development of lay education, rise of vernaculars, 'practical' literacy, Protestant heresies
1300 and onward	Rediscovery of classical legacies
1450s	Advent of printing, consolidation of states, Christian humanism
1500s	Reformation, spread of printing, growth of vernacular literatures, expanded schooling (mass literacy in radical Protestant areas)
1600s	Swedish literacy campaign
1700s	Enlightenment and its consolidation of traditions, 'liberal' legacies
1800s	School developments, institutionalization, mass literacy, 'mass' print media, education for social and economic development: public and compulsory
1900s	Nonprint, electronic media
late 1900s	Crisis of literacy

The significant link between literacy and religion is perhaps the best example. The sixteenth-century reformations, both Protestant and Catholic, are of course the most striking examples of this phenomenon. But the religious impulse to use reading for the propagation of piety and faith predates that time. Within the history of Western Christianity the dialectic between the oral and the written has resulted in different balances being struck in different periods, places, and sects. Literacy served to record for time immemorial the Word, but its influence and diffusion came, for centuries, overwhelmingly through oral means of teaching and preaching.

The Reformation constituted the first great literacy campaign in the history of the West, with its social legacies of individual literacy as a powerful social and moral force. One of the great innovations of the Reformation was the recognition that literacy, a potentially dangerous or subversive skill, could be employed (if controlled) as a medium for popular schooling and training on a truly unprecedented scale. The reform was hardly an unambiguous success in its time, but it may well have contributed more to the cause of popular literacy than to that of piety and religious practice (see, e.g. 4, 15, 41, 48, 57, 72, 76, 83, 84, 108).

Literacy's relationship with the processes of economic development provides another striking example of the patterns of contradictions. In general, commerce and its social and geographical organization stimulated rising levels of literacy from the twelfth century onwards in advanced regions of the West (see 13, 15, 16, 43, 110). However, major steps forward in trade, commerce, and even industry took place in some periods and places with remarkably low levels of literacy; conversely, higher levels of literacy have not been proved to be stimulants or springboards for 'modern' economic developments. More important to economic development than high rates or 'threshold levels' of literacy (see, e.g. 1, 11, 12, 117, 118, 119) have been the educational levels and power relations of key persons, rather than of the many. Major 'take-offs', from the commercial revolution of the Middle Ages to eighteenth-century proto-industrialization in rural areas and even factory industry in towns and cities, owed relatively and perhaps surprisingly little to popular literacy abilities or schooling. In fact, industrialization often reduced opportunities for schooling and, consequently, rates of literacy fell as it took its toll on the 'human capital' on which it fed. In much of Europe, and certainly in England — the paradigmatic case — industrial development (the 'first industrial revolution') was neither built on the shoulders of a literate society nor served to increase popular levels of literacy, at least in the short run. In other places, typically later in time, however, the fact of higher levels of popular education *prior* to the advent of factory capitalism may well have made the process a different one, with different needs and results. Literacy, by the nineteenth century, became vital in the process of 'training in being trained'. It may also be the case that the 'literacy' required for the technological inventiveness and innovations that made the process possible was not a literacy of the alphabetic sort at all, but rather a more visual, experimental one.[3]

In the history of the Western world, one may distinguish the roles of private and public schooling in the attainment of high rates of popular literacy, as well as the operation of informal and formal, voluntary and compulsory education. High rates of literacy have followed from all of these approaches in different cases and contexts. The developmental consequences are equally varied.

Historical experiences thus furnish a guide to such crucial questions as how and to what degree basic literacy contributes to the economic and individual well-being of persons in different socioeconomics contexts, and under what circumstances universal literacy can be achieved. History provides a basis for evaluating and formulating social policy. The costs and benefits of the alternative paths can be discerned too. Thus, the connections and disconnections between literacy and commercial development, a favorable relationship, and literacy and industrial development, often an unfavourable linkage at least in the short run of decades and half-centuries, offer important case studies and analogs for analysis. If nothing else, the data of the past strongly suggest that a simple, linear, modernization model of literacy as a prerequisite for development, and development as a stimulant to increased levels of schooling, will not suffice.

The example of Sweden is perhaps the most important in this respect. Near-universal levels of literacy were achieved rapidly and permanently in Sweden in the wake of the Reformation (see 57, 58, 71). Under the joint efforts of the Lutheran church and the state, reading literacy was required for all persons under law, from the seventeenth century. Within a century, remarkably high levels of literacy among the population existed — without any concomitant development of formal schooling or economic or cultural development that demanded functional or practical employment of literacy, and in a manner that led to a literacy defined by reading and not writing. Urbanization, commercialization, and industrialization had nothing to do with the process of making the Swedish people perhaps the most literate in the West before the eighteenth century. Contrary to the paths of literacy taken elsewhere, this campaign, begun by King Charles XI, was sponsored by the state church. By legal requirement and vigilant supervision that included regular personal examination by parish clergy, the church stood above a system rooted in home education. The rationale of the literacy campaign, one of the most successful in Western history before the last two decades, was conservative; piety, civility, orderliness, and military preparedness were the major goals (see 120).

The home and church education model fashioned by the Swedes not only succeeded in training a literate population, but it also placed a special priority on the literacy of women and mothers. This led to Sweden's anomalous achievement of female literacy rates as high or higher than male rates, a very rare result in the Western transitions to mass literacy. Sweden also marched to its impressive levels of reading diffusion without writing; it was not until the mid-nineteenth century and the erection of a state-supported public school system that writing, in addition to reading, became a part of a popular literacy and a concern of teachers in this Scandinavian land. The only other areas that so fully and quickly achieved near-universal levels of literacy before the end of the eighteenth century were places of intensely pious religion, usually but not always Protestant: Scotland, New England, Huguenot French centers, and places within Germany and Switzerland.

From the classical period, leaders of polities and churches, reformers as well as conservers, have recognized the uses of literacy and schooling. Often they have perceived unbridled, untempered literacy as potentially dangerous, a threat to social order, political integration, economic productivity, and patterns of authority. But, increasingly, they also concluded that literacy, if provided in carefully controlled formal institutions created expressly for the purposes of education and supervised closely, could be a powerful and useful force in achieving a variety of important ends. Precedents long predated the first systematic efforts to put this conception of literacy into practice, in Rome, for example, and in the visionary proposals of the fifteenth- and sixteenth-century Christian humanists. With the Enlightenment and its heritage came the final ideological underpinnings for the 'modern' and 'liberal' reforms of popular schooling and institutional building that established the network of educational-social-political-economic relationships central to the dominant ideologies and their social theoretical expressions for the past century and a half.

Although these crucial topics are not within my main focus here, the significance of literacy to individuals and groups throughout history is undoubted. There is already a large if uneven volume of studies with this emphasis, highlighting the value of literacy to individual success, the acquisition of opportunities and knowledge, and collective consciousness and action. The writings of Robert K. Webb, Richard Altick, Thomas Laqueur, and Michael Clanchy, among many others, make this case with force and evidence. The role of class- and group-specific demands for literacy's skills, the impact of motivation, and the growing perceptions of its values and benefits are among the major factors that explain the historical contours of changing rates of popular literacy. Any complete understanding and appreciation of literacy's history must incorporate the large, if sometimes exaggerated and decontextualized, role of demand (in dialectical relationship to supply) and the very real benefits that literacy may bring. Literacy's limits must also be appreciated, but cannot be if they are not specifically discussed.

It is important to stress the integrating and hegemony-creating functions of literacy provision through formal schooling. Especially with the transition from pre-industrial social orders based in rank and deference to the class societies of commercial and then factory capitalism, schooling became more and more a vital aspect of the maintenance of social stability, particularly during periods of massive, but often poorly understood, social and economic change. Many persons, most prominently social and economic leaders and social reformers, grasped the uses of schooling and the vehicle of literacy for the promotion of the values, attitudes, and habits considered essential to the maintenance of social order and the persistence of integration and cohesion.[4]

Because of the nature of the evidence, virtually all historical studies have concentrated on the measurement of the extent and distributions of reading and writing; issues involving the level of the skills themselves and the abilities to use those skills have not attracted a great deal of attention. What research has been conducted, however, comes to the common conclusion that qualitative abilities cannot be deduced *simply* or *directly* from the quantative levels of literacy's diffusion. Studies of early modern England, eighteenth- and nineteenth-century Sweden, and urban areas in the nineteenth century all suggest that there is a significant disparity between high levels of the possession of literacy and the usefulness of those skills. In Sweden, for example, where systematic evidence exists, a great many persons who had attained high levels of *oral* reading skill did not have comparable abilities in *comprehension* of what they read. This means that the measurement of the distribution of literacy in a population may in fact reveal relatively little about the uses to which such skills could be put and the degree to which different demands on personal literacy could be satisfied with the skills commonly held. Second, it is also possible that with increasing rates of popular literacy did not come ever-rising capabilities, or qualititive abilities — or, for that matter, declining capabilities.

Such evidence places the often-asserted contemporary decline of literacy in a new and distinctive context, leading to a fresher and historical perspective. Mass levels of ability to use literacy may have, over the long term, typically lagged behind the near universality of literacy rates. Perhaps we should pay more attention to longer term trends than a decade or two and to changes in popular communicative abilities and compositional effects among students, than to 'competency examinations' and SAT test scores (see 7, 21, 24, 26, 42, 47, 48, 58). In the words of Galtung:

> What would happen if the whole world became literate? Answer: not so very much, for the world is by and large structured in such a way that it is capable of absorbing the impact. But if the world consisted of literate, automonous, critical, constructive people, capable of translating ideas into action, individually or collectively — the world would change (38, p. 93).

Notes

1. Harvey J. Graff teaches comparative social history in the History and Humanities Programs at the University of Texas, Dallas. This essay derives from his general history of literacy in progress, entitled *The Legacies of Literacy: Continuities and Contradictions in Western Society and Culture,* to be published by Academic Press. The author wishes to acknowledge the assistance of the American Council of Learned Societies, the National Endowment for the Humanities, the Spencer Foundation, and the Newberry Library.
2. For more on literacy as a learned skill, see (6, 16, 17, 18, 20, 21, 25, 37, 42, 43, 44, 45, 46, 48, 49, 50, 76, 77, 79, 80, 88, 89, 90, 91, 92, 95, 102, 103, 104).

3. Among a large literature on these issues, see (8, 9, 10, 23, 29, 30, 31, 32, 35, 36, 48, 51, 59, 61, 62, 63, 66, 74, 75, 78, 94, 96, 97, 98, 101, 109, 111, 112); for an opposing view, see (1, 11, 12, 18, 55, 117, 118). On inventiveness, see (28, 56, 115).
4. For more on this notion, see (2, 3, 5, 19, 20, 37, 40, 48, 49, 57, 60, 64, 65, 70, 71, 76, 82, 83, 85, 86, 87, 93, 99, 113, 114).

References

1. Anderson, C. A. (1965) Literacy and schooling on the development threshold. In C. A. Anderson and M. J. Bowman (eds) *Education and Economic Development* (pp. 247–63). Chicago: Aldine.
2. Appleby, Joyce (1978) Modernization theory and the formation of modern social theories in England and America. *Comparative Studies in Society and History* 20, 259–85.
3. Applewaite, H. B. and Levy, D. G. (1971) The concept of modernization and the French enlightenment. *Studies on Voltaire and the Eighteenth Century* 84, 53–98.
4. Aston, Margaret (1977) Lollardy and literacy. *History* 62, 347–71.
5. Ballinger, Stanley E. (1959) The idea of progress through education in the French enlightenment. *History of Education Journal* 10, 88–99.
6. Bantock, G. H. (1966) *The Implications of Literacy*. Leicester University Press.
7. Bataille, Léon (ed.) (1976) *A Turning Point for Literacy*. New York and Oxford: Pergamon Press.
8. Blaug, Mark (1966) Literacy and economic development. *School Review* 74, 393–417.
9. Bowen, W. G. (1968) Assessing the economic contribution of education. In Mark Blaug (ed.) *The Economics of Education* Vol. 1. (pp. 67–100). Harmondsworth: Penguin.
10. Bowles, Samuel and Gintis, Herbert (1976) *Schooling in Capitalist America*. New York: Basic Books.
11. Bowman, M. J. and Anderson, C. A. (1963) Concerning the role of education in development. In Clifford C. Geertz (ed.) *Old Societies and New States* (pp. 247–79). New York: Free Press.
12. Bowman, M. J. and Anderson, C. A. (1976) Education and economic modernization in historical perspective. In Lawrence Stone (ed.) *Schooling and Society* (pp. 3–9). Baltimore, MD: Johns Hopkins University Press.
13. Bruneau, William A. (1973) Literacy, urbanization and education in three ancient cultures. *Journal of Education* (British Columbia) 19, 9–22.
14. Burke, Peter (1978) *Popular Culture in Early Modern Europe*. New York: Harper and Row.
15. Cipolla, Carlo (1969) *Literacy and Development in the West*. Harmondsworth: Penguin.
16. Clanchy, Michael T. (1979) *From Memory to Written Record: England, 1066–1307*. Cambridge, MA: Harvard University Press.
17. Cole, Michael (April 1978) How education affects the mind. *Human Nature* 51–8.
18. Cole, Michael *et al.* (1971) *The Cultural Context of Learning and Thinking*. New York: Basic Books.
19. Commager, H. S. (1977) *The Empire of Reason*. Garden City, NY: Doubleday/Anchor.
20. Cremin, Lawrence (1970) *American Education: The Colonial Experience*. New York: Harper and Row.

21. Cressy, David (1980) *Literacy and the Social Order.* Cambridge: Cambridge University Press.
22. Davis, Natalie Z. (1975) Printing and the people. In *Society and Culture in Early Modern France* (pp. 189–226). Stanford, CA: Stanford University Press.
23. Dore, Ronald (1967) *Education in Tokugawa Japan.* London: Routledge and Kegan Paul.
24. Douglas, G. H. (1977) Is literacy really declining? *Educational Records* 57, 140–8.
25. Eisenstein, Elizabeth L. (1979) *The Printing Press as an Agent of Change.* Cambridge: Cambridge University Press.
26. Farr, Roger, Fay, Leo and Negley, Harold H. (1974) *Then and Now: Reading Achievement in the U.S.* Bloomington, IN: University of Indiana School of Education.
27. Farr, Roger, Fay, Leo and Negley, Harold H. (1978) *Then and Now: Reading Achievement in Indiana (1944–45 and 1976).* Bloomington, IN: University of Indiana School of Education.
28. Ferguson, Eugene (1977) The mind's eye: Nonverbal thought in technology. *Science* 197, 827–36.
29. Field, Alexander J. (1974) Educational reform and manufacturing development in mid-nineteenth century Massachusetts. Unpublished PhD dissertation, University of California, Berkeley.
30. Field, Alexander J. (1976) Educational expansion in mid-nineteenth century Massachusetts. *Harvard Educational Review* 46, 521–52.
31. Field, Alexander J. (1979) Economic and demographic determinants of educational commitment: Massachusetts, 1855. *Journal of Economic History* 39, 439–59.
32. Field, Alexander J. (1979) Occupational structure, dissent, and educational commitment: Lancashire, 1841. *Research in Economic History* 4, 235–87.
33. Finnegan, Ruth (1970) *Oral Literature in Africa.* Oxford: Oxford University Press.
34. Finnegan, Ruth (1979) *Oral Poetry.* Cambridge: Cambridge University Press.
35. Flora, Peter (1973) Historical processes of social mobilization. In S. N. Eisenstadt and S. Rokkan (eds) *Building States and Nations* Vol. 1 (pp. 213–58). Beverly Hills, CA: Sage.
36. Furet, François and Jacques Ozouf (1976) Literacy and industrialization. *Journal of European Economic History* 5, 5–44.
37. Furet, François and Jacques Ozouf (1977) *Lire et Ecrire.* Paris: Les éditions de Minuit.
38. Galtung, Johan (1976) Literacy, education, and schooling — For what? In Léon Bataille (ed.) *A Turning Point for Literacy* (pp. 93–105). New York and Oxford: Pergamon Press.
39. Ganshof, F. L. (1971) *The Carolingians and the Frankish Monarchy.* Ithaca, NY: Cornell University Press.
40. Gay, Peter (1969) *The Enlightenment: The Science of Freedom.* New York: Knopf.
41. Gerhardsson, Birger (1961) *Memory and Manuscript: Oral Tradition and Written Transmission in Rabbinic Judaism and Early Christianity.* Uppsala, Lund, and Copenhagen: Acta Seminarii Neotestamentici Upsaliensis, XII.
42. Goody, Jack (1977) *The Domestication of the Savage Mind.* Cambridge: Cambridge University Press.
43. Goody, Jack (1968) *Literacy in Traditional Societies.* Cambridge University Press.
44. Goody, Jack, Cole, Michael and Scribner, Sylvia (1977) Writing and formal operations: A case study among the Vai. *Africa* 47, 289–304.

45. Goody, Jack and Watt, Ian (1968) The consequences of literacy. In Jack Goody (ed.) *Literacy in Traditional Societies*. Cambridge: Cambridge University Press.
46. Graff, Harvey (1976, 1979 rev. ed.) *Literacy in History: An Interdisciplinary Research Bibliography*. Chicago: The Newberry Library. York: Garland Press (1981).
47. Graff, Harvey (1978) Literacy past and present: Critical approaches to the literacy-society relationship. *Interchange* 9, 1–21.
48. Graff, Harvey (1979) *The Literacy Myth: Literacy and Social Structure in the Nineteenth-Century City*. New York and London: Academic Press.
49. Graff, Harvey (manuscript in process) The legacies of literacy: Continuities and contradictions in Western society and culture.
50. Graff, Harvey (ed.) (1982) *Literacy and Social Development in the West*. Cambridge: Cambridge University Press.
51. Gutman, Herbert (1973) Work, culture, and society in industrializing America, 1815–1919. *American Historical Review* 78, 531–88.
52. Havelock, Eric (1963) *Preface to Plato*. Cambridge, MA: Harvard University Press.
53. Havelock, Eric (1976) *Origins of Western Literacy*. Toronto: Ontario Institute for Studies in Education.
54. Havelock, Eric (1977) The preliteracy of the Greeks. *New Literary History* 8, 369–92.
55. Inkeles, Alex and Smith, David H. (1974) *Becoming Modern*. Cambridge, MA: Harvard University Press.
56. Ivins, William M. Jr. (1953) *Prints and Visual Communications*. Cambridge, MA: MIT Press.
57. Johansson, Egil (1977) *The History of Literacy in Sweden, in Comparison with Some Other Countries*. *Educational Reports*, no. 12. Umeå, Sweden: Umeå University and School of Education.
58. Johansson, Egil (1979) The postliteracy problem — Illusion or reality in modern Sweden? In Jan Sundin and Erik Söderlund (eds) *Time, Space and Man* (pp. 199–212). Stockholm: Almqvist and Wiksell.
59. Johnson, Richard (1976) Notes on the schooling of the English Working Class, 1780–1850. In R. Dale, G. Esland and M. MacDonald (eds) *Schooling and Capitalism* (pp. 44–54). London: Routledge and Kegan Paul.
60. Kaestle, Carl (1976) 'Between the scylla of brutal ignorance and the charybdis of a literary education': Elite attitudes toward mass schooling in early industrial England and America. In Lawrence Stone (ed.) *Schooling and Society* (pp. 177–191). Baltimore, MD: Johns Hopkins University Press.
61. Kaestle, Carl and Vinovskis, Maris (1980) *Education and Social Change in Nineteenth-Century Massachusetts*. Cambridge: Cambridge University Press.
62. Katz, Michael B. (1976) The origins of public education: A reassessment. *History of Education Quarterly* 14, 381–407.
63. Katz, Michael B. (1978) Origins of the institutional state. *Marxist Perspective*, 6–22.
64. Kerber, Linda K. (1974) Daughters of Columbia: Educating women for the republic. In Stanley M. Elkins and Eric L. McKitrick (eds) *The Hofstadter Aegis* (pp. 36–60). New York: Knopf.
65. Kuritz, Hyman (1967) Benjamin Rush: His theory of Republican education. *History of Education Quarterly* 7, 432–51.
66. Laqueur, Thomas (1974) Critique of Sanderson's literacy and social mobility in the Industrial Revolution. *Past and Present* 64, 96–108.
67. Laqueur, Thomas (1976) The cultural origins of popular literacy in England, 1500–1800. *Oxford Review of Education* 2, 255–75.

68. Laqueur, Thomas (1976) *Religion and Respectability*. New Haven: Yale University Press.
69. Laqueur, Thomas (1976) Working-class demand and the growth of English elementary education, 1750–1850. In Lawrence Stone (ed.) *Schooling and Society* (pp. 192–205). Baltimore, MD: Johns Hopkins University Press.
70. Leith, James A. (1973) Modernisation, mass education and social mobility in French thought, 1750–1789. In R. F. Brissenden (ed.) *Studies in the Eighteenth Century*, Vol. 2 (pp. 223–38). Canberra: Australian National University Press.
71. Leith, James A. (ed.) (1977) *Facets of Education in the Eighteenth Century. Studies on Voltaire and the Eighteenth Century* 167.
72. LeRoy Ladurie, E. (1975) *Montaillou, The Peasants of Languedoc*. Urbana, IL: University of Illinois Press.
73. LeRoy Ladurie, E. (1978) *Montaillou: Promised Land of Error*. New York: Braziller.
74. Levine, David (1977) *Family Formation in an Age of Nascent Capitalism*. New York and London: Academic Press.
75. Levine, David (1979) Education and family life in early industrial England. *Journal of Family History* 4, 368–80.
76. Lockridge, Kenneth A. (1974) *Literacy in Colonial New England*. New York: Norton.
77. Lockridge, Kenneth A. (1977) L'alphabétisation en Amèrique. *Annales, e, s, c* 30, 503–18.
78. McClelland, David C. (1966) Does education accelerate economic growth? *Economic Development and Cultural Change* 14, 257–78.
79. McLuhan, Marshall (1962) *The Gutenberg Galaxy*. Toronto: University of Toronto Press.
80. McLuhan, Marshall (1964) *Understanding Media*. New York: McGraw-Hill.
81. Martin, H.-J. (1975) Culture écrite et culture oral, culture savante et culture populaire dans la France d'Ancien Régime. *Journale des Savants* 225–82.
82. May, Henry (1976) *The Enlightenment in America*. New York: Oxford University Press.
83. Maynes, Mary Jo (1977) Schooling the masses. Unpublished PhD dissertation, University of Michigan.
84. Maynes, Mary Jo (1979) The virtues of anachronism: The poltical economy of schooling in Europe, 1750–1850. *Comparative Studies in Society and History* 21, 611–25.
85. Meyer, Donald H. (1976) *The Democratic Enlightenment*. New York: Putnam's Sons.
86. Mortier, Roland (1968) The 'philosophies' and public education. *Yale French Studies* 40, 62–76.
87. Nipperday, Thomas (1977) Mass education and modernization — The case of Germany. *Transactions, Royal Historical Society* 27, 155–72.
88. Olson, David (1975–76) Review: *Toward a Literate Society. Proceedings*. National Academy of Education, 109–78.
89. Olson, David (1977) From utterance to text: The bias of language in speech and writing. *Harvard Educational Review* 47, 257–86.
90. Ong, Walter (1970) *The Presence of the Word*. New York: Simon and Schuster.
91. Ong, Walter (1971) *Interfaces of the Word*. Ithaca, NY: Cornell University Press.
92. Ong, Walter (1971) *Rhetoric, Romance, and Technology*. Ithaca, NY: Cornell University Press.

93. Palmer, Robert R. (n.d.) The old regime origins of the Napoleonic educational structure. In Albert Crèmer (ed.) *De L'Ancien Régime à la Révolution Française* (pp. 318–33). Gottingen, West Germany: Vandenhoeck and Rupprecht.
94. Pollard, Sidney (1968) *The Genesis of Modern Management.* Harmondsworth: Penguin.
95. Resnick, Daniel P. and Resnick, Lauren B. (1977) The nature of literacy: An historical exploration. *Harvard Educational Review* 47, 370–85.
96. Sanderson, Michael (1967) Education and the factory in industrial Lancashire. *Economic History Review* 20, 266–79.
97. Sanderson, Michael (1968) Social change and elementary education in industrial Lancashire. *Northern History* 3, 131–54.
98. Sanderson, Michael. Literacy and social mobility in the Industrial Revolution. *Past and Present* (1972) 56, 75–105; reply to Laqueur (1974) 64, 109–12.
99. Schleunnes, Karl A. (1977) The French Revolution and the schooling of European society. *Proceedings,* Consortium on revolutionary Europe, 140–50.
100. Schofield, Roger S. (1968) The measurement of literacy in pre-industrial England. In J. Goody (ed.) *Literacy in Traditional Societies* (pp. 311–25). Cambridge: Cambridge University Press.
101. Schofield, Roger S. (1973) The dimensions of illiteracy in England, 1750–1850. *Explorations in Economic History* 10, 437–54.
102. Scribner, Sylvia and Cole, Michael (1973) Cognitive consequences of formal and informal education. *Science* 182, 553–9.
103. Scribner, Sylvia and Cole, Michael (1976) Studying cognitive consequences of literacy. Unpublished manuscript.
104. Scribner, Sylvia and Cole, Michael (1978) Literacy without schooling: Testing for intellectual effects. *Havard Educational Review* 48, 448–61.
105. Spufford, Margaret (1974) *Contrasting Communities.* Cambridge: Cambridge University Press.
106. Spufford, Margaret (1979) First steps in literacy: The reading and writing experiences of the humblest seventeenth-century spiritual autobiographers. *Social History* 4, 407–35.
107. Stephens, W. B. (1977) Illiteracy and schooling in the provincial towns, 1640–1870. In David Reeder (ed.) *Urban Education in the 19th Century* (pp. 27–48). London: Taylor and Francis.
108. Strauss, Gerald (1975) *Luther's House of Learning.* Baltimore, MD: Johns Hopkins University Press.
109. Thompson, E. P. (1967) Time, work-discipline, and industrial capitalism. *Past and Present* 38, 56–97.
110. Trigger, Bruce G. (1976) Inequality and communication in early civilization. *Anthropologica* 18.
111. Verne, E. (1976) Literacy and industrialization — The dispossession of speech. In Léon Bataille (ed.) *A Turning Point for Literacy* (pp. 211–28). New York and Oxford: Pergamon Press.
112. Vinovskis, Maris (1970) Horace Mann on the economic productivity of education. *New England Quarterly* 43, 550–71.
113. Vovelle, Michel (1972) Maggiolo en Provence. Colloque sur le XVIIIème siècle et l'éducation. *Revue de Marseille* 88, 55–62.
114. Vovelle, Michel (1975) Y a-t-il une révolution au XVIIIe siècle? *Revue d'histoire moderne et contemporaine* 22, 89–141.
115. Wallace, A. F. C. (1978) *Rockdale.* New York: Knopf.
116. Webb, R. K. (1955) *The British Working Class Reader.* London: Allen and Unwin.

117. West, E. G. (1964) The role of education in 19th century — doctrines of political economy. *British Journal of Educational Studies* 12, 161–74.
118. West, E. G. (1975) *Education and the Industrial Revolution.* London: Batsford.
119. West, E. G. (1977) Literacy and the Industrial Revolution. *Economic History Review* 31, 369–83.
120. Winchester, Ian. How many ways to universal literacy? Unpublished manuscript presented to the Ninth World Congress of Sociology, Uppsala (1978); and the University of Leicester Seminar on the History of Literacy in Post-Reformation Europe (1980).

11 Orality and Literacy: From *The Savage Mind* to *Ways With Words*

JAMES PAUL GEE

It is now a common claim that there is a 'literacy crisis' in the United States (Gee, 1986; Gumperz, 1986; Kozol, 1985). This claim is based on two social facts: (a) An unacceptably large number of children, a disproportionate number of whom are from low-income and minority homes, fail to gain functional literacy in school; and (b) partly as a result, an unacceptably large number of adults are functionally illiterate or only marginally literate (about one third of the nation). At first sight, it seems obvious what this has to do with the English teachers, after all, literacy is what English teachers teach. But what is literacy? Once we answer this question, the English teacher's role becomes even more crucial and yet at the same time much more problematic.

This article demonstrates how in anthropological studies the term *literate* in the dichotomy *literate/nonliterate* came to replace the term *civilised* in the older dichotomy *civilized/primitive* and then how a distinction between different cultures (nonliterate versus literate ones) came to be applied to different social groups within modern, technological societies like ours, characterizing some as having 'restricted literacy' and others as having 'full literacy'. The importance of these developments is the link often assumed to exist between literacy and higher order mental skills, such as analytic, logical, or abstract thinking.

But a contrary current has developed, a current which sees literacy as necessarily plural: Different societies and social subgroups have different types of literacy, and literacy has different social and mental effects in different social and cultural contexts. Literacy is seen as a set of discourse practices, that is, as ways of using language and making sense both in speech and writing. These discourse practices are tied to the particular world views (beliefs and values) of particular social or cultural groups. Such discourse practices are integrally connected with the identity or sense of self of the

168

people who practice them; a change of discourse practices is a change of identity.

The discourse practices associated with our schools represent the world view of mainstream and powerful institutions in our society; these discourse practices and their concomitant world view are necessary for social and economic success in our society. But they are also tied to the failure of non-mainstream children in our schools and are rapidly destroying alternative practices and world views in less technologically advanced cultures throughout the world. The English teacher is not teaching grammar or even literacy, but rather these mainstream discourse practices, practices which may be at variance with the practices and values, with the identity and sense of self, of nonmainstream students, practices which are related to global political issues and to the literacy crisis in the United States, which is construed as a social crisis. If all this makes the English teacher sound central, that is all to the good — for that is my point.

This article surveys recent work on orality (nonliteracy) and literacy, not by dealing in depth with this now massive literature, but rather by discussing a few key works. These are treated as forming a particular progression, leading to a point of view I advocate. The major texts to be dealt with are Levi-Strauss's *The Savage Mind* (1966), Havelock's *Preface to Plato* (1963), Goody's *The Domestication of the Savage Mind* (1977), Ong's *Orality and Literacy* (1982), Scribner & Cole's *The Psychology of Literacy* (1981), Street's *Literacy in Theory and Practice* (1984), Scollon & Scollon's *Narrative, Literacy and Face in Interethnic Communication* (1981), and finally Heath's *Ways with Words* (1983).

The Primitive and the Civilized

Humans tend to think in dichotomies, and no dichotomy has played on the popular and the academic mind more insidiously than the contrast between 'the primitive' ('the savage') and 'the civilized'. This contrast has often been used to trace an evolutionary process with modern man at its pinnacle or to romanticize the primitive as an Eden from which Civilization represents a Fall.

Societies labeled primitive were usually small, homogeneous, nonliterate, highly personal, regulated by face-to-face encounters rather than by abstract rules, and had a strong sense of group solidarity (Douglas, 1973; Evans-Pritchard, 1951; Musgrove, 1982). They were sometimes said to be 'mystical and prelogical' (Levi-Bruhl, 1910), incapable of abstract thought, irrational, child-like ('half-devil and half-child' in Kipling's phrase), and inferior to modern man. (*Man* is used advisedly — modern women were often seen as intermediate between savages/children and modern man; see Gould, 1977: 126–35.)

On the other hand, modern urban societies — our best current exemplars of 'civilization' — are typified by their large and diverse groupings of people, widespread literacy and technology, and a supposed sense of science and history. Cities are places where many social relations tend to be impersonal and life is lived within 'grids of impersonal forces and rules' (Douglas, 1973: 88; see also Musgrove, 1982).

The primitive/civilized dichotomy has broken down nearly completely at the hands of modern social anthropology (Street, 1984). So-called primitive societies are not primitive in thought, word, or deed, or in any evolutionary sense. A large amount of anthropological and linguistic work has shown that such cultures often had classification systems as complex as that of the modern biologist (Levi-Strauss, 1966); that once we accept their initial premises, their thought processes about such matters as witchcraft were the same as those involved in scientific thought (Evans-Pritchard, 1937; Horton, 1967); and that their languages were often among the world's most complex (Sapir, 1921).

Where there had been a tendency to carry over something like the primitive/civilized contrast to the distinction between lower status socioeconomic groups and mainstream groups in modern urban societies, this was put to rest by the work of Labov (1972). He showed that working-class black youths speak a rule-governed and elegant dialect of English and that their speech has all of the qualities generally associated with logical thought. At the same time Labov showed that much middle-class speech is overly verbose and disorganized.

Levi-Strauss and *The Savage Mind*

The primitive/civilized distinction has repeatedly resurfaced in other guises, even in work that ostensibly put it to rest. Levi-Strauss, the founder of Structuralism in anthropology, demonstrated that there was nothing primitive about thought in so-called primitive cultures; he showed that for primitive humankind, as well as modern, the natural world is good not just to eat, but good to know and admire. (Citations below are from *The Savage Mind*, 1966; see also Levi-Strauss, 1963.) Nonetheless, he reintroduced a dichotomy beween primitive and modern cultures in terms of two distinct ways of knowing, 'two distinct modes of scientific thought'. These were not a function of different stages of development, but rather two different levels at which nature is accessible to scientific inquiry:

> Certainly the properties to which the savage mind has access are not those which have commanded the attention of scientists. The physical

world is approached from opposite ends in the two cases: one is supremely concrete, the other supremely abstract; one proceeds from the angle of sensible qualities and the other from that of formal properties. (p. 269)

Primitive cultures use events from the natural world, ordered in myths and totem systems, for instance, to create structures by means of which they can think about and explain the world of experience. For example, in a 'pure totemic structure' (p. 115), a certain clan associated with a particular species, such as the bear, may be viewed to differ from another clan associated with a different species, such as the eagle, as the bear differs from the eagle in the natural world, thus creating a type of homology between culture and nature. Modern science, on the other hand, manipulates not objects and images from the natural world, but abstract systems, whether numerical, logical, or linguistic, and through these systems seeks to change the world.

In an influential insight, Levi-Strauss characterized the systems of stories that make up mythical thought as a kind of intellectual 'bricolage'. The *bricoleur* (a term which has no real English equivalent but translates roughly as a 'handyman') is adept at performing a large number of tasks. Unlike the modern engineer, he does not design tools for the specific task at hand; rather, his universe of instruments is closed, and the rules of the game are always to make do with 'whatever is at hand'. What is at hand is always a contingent result of all the occasions there have been to renew or enrich the stock or to maintain it with the remains of previous constructions or destructions (p. 17). Mythical thought is 'imprisoned in the events and experiences which it never tires of ordering and reordering in its search to find meaning' (p. 22).

Havelock and the *Preface to Plato*

Levi-Strauss's work raises, without answering, the question as to how cultures move from the science of the concrete to the science of the abstract, and through which stages. Two influential pieces of work have suggested that the answer is literacy: Havelock's *Preface to Plato* (1963) and Goody's *The Domestication of the Savage Mind* (1977). Havelock argues that Homeric Greek culture was an oral (nonliterate) culture. (Citations below are from *Preface to Plato;* see also Havelock, 1982). His characterization of that culture has been taken to typify oral cultures generally and used as a cornerstone in the argument that it is literacy that makes for a 'great divide' between human cultures and their ways of thinking.

The oral epic — such as the *Iliad* and the *Odyssey* in their original forms — was a form of contrived and memorized speech through which the culture passed down its values and knowledge. Havelock argues that the form and functioning of the epic were determined by the demands of human memory in the absence of writing. It was a dramatic story recited with a heavy, metrical rhythm and constructed out of a large set of memorized formulas (short phrases that fit the meter), as well as a large set of memorized motifs (stereotypical characters, actions, and events) and wider themes which recurred throughout the epic (see also Lord, 1960; Parry, 1971). The creativity of the reciter lay in how he arranged and ordered these pre-given building blocks on any given occasion of recitation. This characterization reminds one of Levi-Strauss's view of bricolage in mythic thought (which indeed is what the Homeric epics were).

The values and knowledge which the epic story encapsulated could only be preserved from generation to generation if the teller of tales and his audience fully identified with the story. In fact, Havelock argues, as did Plato, that the teller and his audience were under a 'spell' cast by the epic rhythm (created by the meter and recurrent themes, much like dance or music); the hearer acted out and identified with the values and beliefs of the society in actively participating in the telling of the tale. Under such conditions, innovation in values and ideas was difficult.

Plato, the first great writer of Greek civilization, sought to reorder Greek society, to relocate power. To do so, he had to break the power of the epic poet (Homer) because in his care resided the moral and intellectual heritage of the society. What woke the Greeks from the epic spell? Havelock's answer is 'alphabetic-script literacy', a changed technology of communication. Refreshment of memory through written signs enabled a reader to dispense with most of that emotional identification by which alone the acoustic record was sure of recall. What had been written could be seen as an object (a 'text') and not just heard and felt. You cannot stop and review what you are listening to, especially if you are 'caught up' in its rhythm, but writing allows one to take a second look and thereby to notice contradictions and inconsistencies. Knowledge need no longer be dramatic and compelling (a story) to ensure its preservation; it can now be encoded in abstract language.

Goody and *The Domestication of the Savage Mind*

Goody's *The Domestication of the Savage Mind* (1977) moves beyond ancient Greek culture to modern nonliterate and semiliterate societies. He sees the development and spread of literacy as a crucial factor in explaining how modes of thought and cultural organization change over time. Goody & Watt (1963) laid out some of the outcomes that they saw as linked to the advent of writing and in particular to the invention of the alphabetic system that made widespread literacy possible. They suggested that logic, in the restricted sense of an instrument of analytic procedures, seemed to be a function of writing, since the setting down of speech enabled humans clearly to separate words, to manipulate their order, to develop syllogistic forms of reasoning, and to perceive contradictions. (With writing, one could arrest the flow of speech and compare, side by side, utterances that had been made at different times and places.)

Essentially, Goody takes certain characteristics regarded by Levi-Strauss and others as marking the distinction between primitive and advanced cultures and suggests that many of the valid aspects of these somewhat vague dichotomies can be related to changes in the mode of communication, especially to the introduction of various forms of writing. Goody relates the development of writing to the growth of individualism, the growth of bureaucracy and of more depersonalized and more abstract systems of government, as well as the development of abstract thought and syllogistic reasoning, culminating in modern science. When characteristics which he attributes to orality persist in a society with literacy — and would thus seem to undermine the case for the intrinsic effects of literacy — Goody appeals to a notion of 'restricted literacy' as against 'full literacy'. In fact, Goody comes close to suggesting that restricted literacy is the norm in almost all nontechnological societies and perhaps in large pockets of modern technological societies as well.

Ong and *Orality and Literacy*

The work of Havelock and of Goody is translated into a sweeping statement about orality and literacy as a great divide in human culture, thought, and history in Ong's influential book *Orality and Literacy* (1982). He argues that work on oral and literate cultures calls for a revision of our understanding of human identity. Commitment of the word to space through writing enlarges the potentiality of language 'almost beyond measure' and 'restructures thought'. While oral cultures produce powerful verbal performances which may in fact no longer be possible once writing has become entrenched in a culture, human consciousness cannot achieve its full potential without writing. Literacy is necessary for the development of science, history, and philosophy and for the explicative understanding of literature, art, and language, including speech itself.

Ong offers a set of features that characterize thought and expression in a primary oral culture. The first of these (expanding on Havelock, 1963) is 'formulaic thought and expression', defined as 'more or less exactly repeated set phrases or set expressions (such as proverbs)' (p. 26). Beyond formulaicness, Ong argues that thought and expression in oral cultures are (a) *additive* (strung together by additive relations like simple adjunction or terms/concepts like *and*) rather than subordinative; (b) *aggregative* (clustered elements of thought or expression, e.g. not *the princess* but the *beautiful princess*) rather than analytic; (c) *redundant or* 'copious'; (d) *conservative* or traditionalist, inhibiting experimentation; (e) *close to the human life world*; (f) *agonistically toned*; (g) *empathetic* and participatory rather than objectively distanced; (h) *situational* rather than abstract.

The relevance of this characterization is greatly expanded, however, when Ong argues that 'to varying degrees many cultures and subcultures, even in a high-technology ambience, preserve much of the mind-set of primary orality' (p. 11). He refers to these groups as having 'residual orality', using as examples Arabic and certain other Mediterranean cultures. He also points out that oral habits of thought and expression, including massive use of formulaic elements of a type similar to those in Homer, still marked prose style of almost every sort in Tudor England some 2,000 years after Plato's campaign against Homer.

Furthermore, Ong is aware that many of the features he cites have also been claimed to characterize lower socioeconomic levels of black culture, a culture that has historic ties to a rich oral culture, both from the days of slavery in the United States and from African cultures, and one that arguably is less influenced than mainstream middle-class culture by school-based literacy (Abrahams, 1964, 1970, 1976; Erickson, 1984; Gee, 1985; Kochman, 1981; Labov, 1972; Smitherman, 1977). More generally, it is striking how similar Ong's features are to characterizations that linguists have offered of the differences between speech and writing, educators of the differences between 'good' and 'bad' writers, and sociolinguists of the differences between the way black children of lower socioeconomic status and white middle-class children tell stories (these analogies are discussed in the next section).

Thus, we get to one of the main implications of the Havelock-Goody-Ong line of work: In modern technological societies like the United States, something akin to the oral/literate distinction may apply to groups (usually of lower socioeconomic status) with 'residual orality' or 'restricted literacy' and groups (usually middle and upper middle class) with full access to the literacy taught in the schools. Levi-Strauss's recasting of the primitive/civilized distinction in terms of a contrast between concrete and abstract thought, now explained by literacy, comes then to roost in our 'modern' society.

The Oral/Literate Distinction within Modern 'Literate' Societies

Chafe (1982), in contrasting writing (essays) and speech (spontaneous conversation), suggests that differences in the processes of speaking and writing have led to specific differences in the products. The fact that writing is much slower than speech, while reading is much faster, allows written language to be less fragmented, more syntactically integrated, than speech. The writer has the time to mold ideas into a more complex, coherent, integrated whole, making use of complicated lexical and syntactic devices seldom used in speech (such as heavy use of nominalizations, participles, attributive adjectives, and various subordinating devices). In addition to its integrated quality, Chafe calls attention to the fact that written language fosters more detachment than speech, which is face-to-face and usually more highly socially involved than writing. Thus, writing is integrated and detached, while speech is fragmented and involved.

Chafe is aware that these are in reality poles of a continuum and that there are uses of spoken and written language that do not fit these characterizations (e.g. lectures as a form of integrated and detached speech; letters as a form of fragmented and involved writing; literature, in which involvement features are used for aesthetic effects). However, integration and detachment are part of the potential that writing offers, thanks to the processes by which it is produced. (It is interesting that Richardson, Risk & Okun, 1983, argue that in many US junior colleges, where there is a prevalence of multiple-choice tests, note taking, and forms to fill out, but a lack of essay writing or discursive exams, literacy has become fragmented and socially detached, thus partaking of features of both writing and speech in Chafe's terms.)

The distinction between writing and speech that Chafe draws bears some similarity to Michaels's (1981) distinction between different ways that black and white children tell 'sharing time' stories in the early years of school. Many black children of lower socioeconomic status told what Michaels calls 'topic-associating' stories, while white and black middle-class children tended to tell 'topic-centered' stories. Topic-centered stories are tightly structured around a single topic and lexically explicit, have a high degree of thematic coherence and a clear thematic progression, and feature intonational cues used by the child to mark out syntactically complete, independent clauses. The stories tend to be short and concise. Topic-associating stories associate a series of segments through an implicit link to a particular topical event or theme, rely heavily on inferences to be drawn by the listener on the basis of shared knowledge, and use intonational cues to make out episodic shifts in the story rather than to make syntactic structure clear.

Gee (1985, in press) has shown that the black children in Michaels's study also used a number of devices reminiscent of Havelock's and Ong's characterizations of orality, for example, the creation of a rhythmical structure through formulaic devices, repetition, and syntactic parallelism. These differences, which are ultimately founded on practices in the home, lead eventually to the middle-class children having control over forms of speech that in their integration and detachment resemble essay-text writing, while the black children retain speech that in its fragmentation and social involvement contrasts with the canons of essay-text literacy.

There has, however, been confusion in much of the linguistics and educational literature about what *orality* actually means. Chafe's work (and much of that of Hymes, e.g. 1981) can set us on the right track here. Chafe points out that in many oral cultures the formal ritual-traditional language or forms of language often referred to as 'high rhetoric' are analogous to the integration and detachment of essayist writing. These forms of language, used on sacred, ritual, or otherwise socially important occasions, involve some degree (often a great deal) of memorization or sorts of special learning. They very often involve the formulaic, rhythmical, patterned use of language Havelock and Ong call attention to in Homer, but they may also involve a good deal of lexical and syntactic complexity and explicit reference that relies little on hearer inference.

Thus, the formulaic and rhythmic features of orality are by no means in opposition to the linguistic formality, explicitness, and complexity we associate with writing. Looked at in this way, the speech/writing, or orality/literacy, distinction begins to become problematic: What seems to be involved are different cultural practices that in certain contexts call for certain uses of language, language patterned in certain ways and trading on features like fragmentation and involvement to various degrees.

Literacy and Higher Order Cognitive Skills

The previous section suggests the need for a new approach to the oral/literate divide, one that would study different uses of language, spoken and written, in their cultural contexts. But one major factor keeps literacy, apart from any cultural context, in focus: the claim that literacy leads to higher order cognitive skills. This claim is founded on a large number of empirical studies that go back to the famous work of Vygotsky (see Wertsch, 1985) and Luria (1976) in Soviet Central Asia in the 1930s, when this area was in the midst of collectivization. Many previously nonliterate populations were rapidly introduced to literacy and other practices of modern technological society. Vygotsky and Luria compared nonliterate and recently literate subjects on a series of reasoning tasks.

The tasks consisted of categorizing familiar objects or deducing the conclusion that follows from the premises of a syllogism. For example, in one task subjects were given pictures of a hammer, a saw, a log, and a hatchet and asked to say which three went together. Literate subjects were generally willing to say that the hammer, hatchet, and saw went together because they were all tools, thus grouping the objects on the basis of abstract word meanings. In contrast, the answers of nonliterate subjects indicated a strong tendency to group items on the basis of concrete settings with which they were familiar. Thus, they said things like 'the log has to be here too' and resisted the experimenter's suggestions, based on decontextualized word meanings, that the hammer, hatchet, and saw could be grouped together. Performance on syllogistic reasoning tasks yielded analogous results.

It was concluded that major differences exist between literate and nonliterate subjects in their use of abstract reasoning processes. The responses of nonliterates were dominated by their immediate practical experience, and they resisted using language in a decontextualized manner. These results, of course, fit well with the claims of Havelock, Goody, and Ong, as well as with claims made about semiliterate groups on the United States and Britain.

However, there is a major empirical problem in the Vygotsky-Luria work. It is unclear whether the results were caused by literacy, by schooling, or even by the new social institutions that the Russian Revolution exposed these subjects to. It is extremely difficult to separate the influence of literacy from that of formal schooling, since in most parts of the world the two go together. But school involves much more than becoming literate: 'A student is involved in learning a set of complex role relationships, general cognitive techniques, ways of approaching problems, different genres of talk and interaction, and an intricate set of values concerned with communication, interaction, and society as a whole' (Wertsch, 1985: 35–36).

Scribner and Cole and *The Psychology of Literacy*

The whole question of the cognitive effects of literacy was redefined by the groundbreaking work on the Vai in Liberia by Scribner and Cole in *The Psychology of Literacy* (1981). (All citations below are from this work.) They examine two crucial questions: 'Is it literacy or formal schooling that affects mental functioning?' and: 'Can one distinguish among the effects of different forms of literacy used for different functions in the life of an individual or a society?'

Among the Vai, literacy and schooling are not always coterminous. In addition to literacy in English acquired in formal school settings, the Vai have an indigenous (syllabic, not alphabetic) script transmitted outside an institutional setting and with no connection with Western-style schooling, as well as a form of literacy in Arabic. Each of these literacies is tied to a particular set of uses: English literacy is associated with government and education; Vai literacy is used primarily for keeping records and for letters, many of them involving commercial matters; Arabic literacy is used for reading, writing, and memorizing the Koran (many Arabic literates do not know Arabic but have memorized and can recite large sections of the

Koran). Since some Vai are versed in only one of these forms of literacy, others in two or more, and still others are nonliterate altogether, Scribner and Cole could disentangle various effects of literacy from effects of formal schooling (which affected only the English literates).

Scribner and Cole examined subjects' performance on categorization and syllogistic reasoning tasks similar to those used by Vygotsky (see Wertsch, 1985) and Luria (1976). Their results call into question much work on the cognitive consequences of literacy. Neither syllabic Vai script nor Arabic alphabetic literacy was associated with what have been considered higher order intellectual skills. Neither form of literacy enhanced the use of taxonomic skills, nor did either contribute to a shift toward syllogistic reasoning. In contrast, literacy in English, the only form associated with formal schooling, was associated with some types of decontextualization and abstract reasoning. However, all the tasks on which schooling was the highest ranking determinant of performance were 'talking about' tasks. Schooled subjects showed no such superiority on tasks which did not involve verbal exposition, leading Scribner and Cole to conclude that 'school fosters abilities in expository talk in contrived situations' (pp. 242–3; see also Scribner & Cole, 1973).

Furthermore, Scribner and Cole did not find that schooled, English-literate subjects, many of whom had been out of school a number of years, differed from other groups in their actual performance on categorization and abstract reasoning tasks. They simply talked about them better, providing informative verbal descriptions and justifications of their task activity. However, those who had recently been in school actually did do better on the tasks, suggesting that both task performance and verbal description of task performance improved as a result of schooled literacy but that the former was transient, unless practised in the years following school.

Another very important finding in the Scribner and Cole work is that each form of literacy was associated with some quite specific skills. For example, Vai script literacy was associated with specific skills in synthesizing spoken Vai in an auditory integration task (repeating back Vai sentences decomposed, by pauses between syllables, into their constituent syllables), in using graphic symbols to represent language, in using language as a means of instruction, and in talking about correct Vai speech.

All of these skills are closely related to everyday practices involved in Vai script literacy. For instance, the ability to synthesize spoken Vai appears to follow from the large amount of practice in synthesizing language that one gets in trying to decode a syllabic script that does not mark word divisions. (To construct meaning out of a chain of syllables, the Vai script reader must often hold a sequence of syllables in working memory until the unit of meaning, what words they belong to, is determined.) Or, to take another example, the Vai, in writing letters, often discuss the quality of the letters and whether they are written in 'good Vai'. This practice appears to enhance their ability to talk about correct speech on a grammar task.

Scribner and Cole, on the basis of such evidence, opt for what they call 'a practice account of literacy'. A type of literacy enhances quite specific skills that are practised in carrying out that literacy. Grandoise claims for large and global cognitive skills resulting from literacy are not, in fact, indicated. One can also point out that the effect of formal schooling — being able to engage in expository talk in contrived situations — is itself a fairly specific skill practiced a good deal in school. Thus, we might extend Scribner and Cole's practice account to schooling as well as literacy.

Street and *Literacy in Theory and Practice*

The work of Scribner and Cole (1981) calls into question what Street, in his book *Literacy in Theory and Practice* (1984), calls 'the autonomous model' of literacy: the claim that literacy (or schooling for that matter) has cognitive effects apart from the context in which it exists and the uses to which it is put in a given culture. Street criticizes this model through a discussion of Olson's (1977) work, some recent work by Hildyard & Olson (1978), as well as Greenfield's (1972) study of the Wolof of Senegal.

Olson's (1977) claims for the cognitive effects of literacy — that, for example, it 'unambiguously represents meanings' (p. 264) — refer only to one type of literacy, the essay-text form of writing prevalent in Western culture and supported by our schools. In fact, his claims rest on descriptions of the 'British essayists' of the 17th and 18th centuries, who were:

> among the first to exploit writing for the purpose of formulating original theoretical knowledge . . . Knowledge was taken to be the product of an extended logical essay — the output of the repeated application in a single coherent text of the technique of examining an assertion to determine all of its implications. (pp. 268–9)

This form of literacy is the basis, ideologically, if not always in practice, of our schools and universities. Claims for literacy per se are often in fact tacit claims for essay-text literacy, a form of literacy that is neither natural nor universal, but one cultural way of making sense among many others. Of course, this way of making sense is associated with mainstream middle-class and upper middle-class groups and is, in fact, best represented by the ideology and sometimes the practice of academics, the people who most often make claims for it.

One can go further in showing how claims for literacy are often tacit ways to privilege one social group's ways of doing things as if they were natural and universal. Many of the tasks used to measure such things as cognitive flexibility, logical reasoning, or abstractness, tasks like those used by Vygotsky (see Wertsch, 1985) and Luria (1976), Greenfield (1972), Scribner & Cole (1981), and many others, are, in fact, tests of the ability to use language in a certain way. In particular, they are tests of what we might call explicitness.

Explicitness in language use can be placed on a continuum between two poles that we might label, following Givon (1979), 'the pragmatic mode' and 'the syntactic mode'. At the syntactic-mode end of the continuum, speakers encode what they want to say using precise and varied lexical items and explicit syntactic structures (e.g. subordinating devices), leaving as little as possible to be signaled by prosody or inferred by the listener. The grammar takes on most of the burden for communication, and social interaction is downplayed. At the pragmatic-mode end of the continuum, speakers chain strings of clauses together fairly loosely through adjunction or coordination, use prosodic devices to signal meaning, and rely on the hearer to draw inferences on the basis of mutual knowledge. Social interactions and the participation of the hearer in a mutual negotiation of meaning are paramount.

Givon's distinction is, in fact, a recoding of Ong's (1982) distinction between features characteristic of oral and literate cultures and Chafe's (1982) distinction between speech (conversation) and writing (essays). All speakers of all languages have control over the pragmatic mode and some portion of the continuum toward the syntactic-mode end. Which mode or mixture of modes is appropriate in a given context varies across cultures; how far a speaker can go toward an extreme use of the syntactic mode (in speech or writing) varies with uses a culture has for this sort of language and with access speakers have to the institutions (schools) where it is fostered and practised. How explicit one is in using language is a matter of convention.

For example, in our culture there is a convention that in certain contrived situations, one does not take it for granted that the listener or audience can see or is aware, through shared knowledge, of what is being referred to (even when they indeed are); thus, one is explicit in referring to it (as children are encouraged to do, for instance, at sharing time). Certain other cultures, as well as nonschooled people in our culture, simply do not have, and thus do not use, this convention. In fact, such explicitness may be seen as crude because it is either distancing, blunt, or condescending to the hearer's intelligence or relation to the speaker.

Claims for literacy, in particular for essay-text literacy values, whether in speech or writing, are thus 'ideological'. They are part of 'an armoury of concepts, conventions and practices' (Street, 1984: 38) that privilege one social formation as if it were natural, universal, or at least, the end point of a normal developmental progression of cognitive skills (achieved only by some cultures, thanks either to their intelligence or their technology).

Street proposes, in opposition to the autonomous model of literacy, an 'ideological model', in which literacy is viewed in terms of concrete social practices and the various ideologies in which different cultural expressions of literacies are embedded. Literacy — of whatever type — only has consequences as it acts together with a large number of other social factors, including a culture's or a social group's political and economic conditions, social structure, and local ideologies. Any technology, including writing, is a cultural form, a social product whose shape and influence depend upon prior political and ideological factors.

Despite Havelock's (1963; 1982) brilliant characterization of the transition from orality to literacy in ancient Greece, it now appears that the Greek situation has rarely if ever been replicated. The particular social, political, economic, and ideological circumstances in which literacy (of a particular sort) was embedded in Greece explain what happened there — the flowering of Greek classical civilization. Abstracting literacy from its social setting in order to make claims for literacy as an autonomous force in shaping the mind or a culture simply leads to a dead end.

There is, however, a last refuge for someone who wants to see literacy as an autonomous force. One could claim that essay-text literacy and the uses of language connected with it, such as explicitness and the syntactic mode, lead, if not to general cognitive consequences, then to social mobility and success in the society. While this argument may be true, there is precious little evidence that literacy in history or across cultures has had this effect either. Street discusses, in some detail, Graff's (1979) study of the role of literacy in 19th century Canada.

While some individuals did gain through the acquisition of literacy, Graff demonstrates that this effect was not statistically significant and that deprived classes and ethnic groups as a whole were, if anything, further oppressed through literacy. Greater literacy did not correlate with increased equality and democracy nor with better conditions for the working class, but in fact with continuing social stratification. The teaching of literacy involved a contradiction: Illiterates were considered dangerous to the social order; thus, they must be made literate; yet the potentialities of reading and writing for an underclass could well be radical and inflammatory. So the framework for the teaching of literacy had to be severely controlled, and this involved specific forms of control of the pedagogic process and specific ideological associations of the literacy being purveyed.

Although the workers were led to believe that acquiring literacy was to their benefit, Graff produces statistics that show that in reality this literacy was not advantageous to the poorer groups in terms of either income or power. The extent to which literacy was an advantage or not in relation to job opportunities depended on ethnicity. It was not because you were 'illiterate' that you finished up in the worst jobs but because of your background (e.g. being black or an Irish Catholic rendered literacy much less efficacious than it was for English Protestants).

The story Graff tells can be repeated for many other societies, including Britain and the United States (see Street, 1984, as well as Cook-Gumperz, 1986; Donald, 1983; Gilmore, 1985). In all these societies literacy served as a socializing tool for the poor, was seen as a possible threat if misused by the poor (for an analysis of their oppression and to make demands for power), and served as a means for maintaining the continued selection of members of one class for the best positions in the society.

Scollon and Scollon and *Narrative, Literacy and Face in Interethnic Communication*

Literacy has no effects — indeed, no meaning — apart from particular cultural contexts in which it is used, and it has different effects in different contexts. Two recent works make an excellent beginning at the process of looking at orality and literacy in the context of the social practices and world views of particular social groups: Scollon and Scollon's *Narrative, Literacy and Face in Interethnic Communication* (1981) and Heath's *Ways With Words* (1983). Both of these works realize that what is at issue in the use of language is different ways of knowing, different ways of making sense of the world of human experience, that is, different social epistemologies.

Scollon and Scollon believe that discourse patterns (ways of using language to communicate, whether in speech or writing) in different cultures reflect a particular reality set or world view and are among the strongest expressions of personal and cultural identity. They argue that changes in a person's discourse patterns — for example, in acquiring a new form of literacy — may involve change in identity. Scollon and Scollon provide a detailed study of the discourse practices and world view of Athabaskans in Alaska and northern Canada and contrast these with the discourse patterns and world view in much of Anglo-Canadian and Anglo-American society.

Literacy as it is practiced in European-based education — essay-text literacy in the phrase used above — is connected to a reality set or world view that Scollon and Scollon term 'modern consciousness'. This reality set is consonant with particular discourse patterns, ones quite different from the discourse patterns used by the Athabaskans. As a result, the acquisition of this sort of literacy is not simply a matter of learning a new technology, it also involves association with values, social practices, and ways of knowing that conflict with those of the Athabaskans. Thus, Scollon and Scollon argue, literacy of the essay-text sort may be experienced by Athabaskans as a form of interethnic communication. And much of their book is devoted to an analysis of the problems and misunderstandings involved in interethnic communication.

As the following three examples reveal, Athabaskans differ at various points from mainstream Canadian and American English speakers in how they engage in discourse. First, Athabaskans have a high degree of respect for the individuality of others and carefully guard their own individuality. Thus, they prefer to avoid conversation except when the point of view of all participants is well known. On the other hand, English speakers feel that the main way to get to know other people's point of view is through conversation with them.

Second, for Athabaskans, persons in subordinate positions do not display, or show off; rather, they observe the person in the superordinate position. For instance, adults, as either parents or teachers, are supposed to display abilities and qualities for the child to learn. However, in mainstream American society, children are supposed to show off their abilities for teachers and other adults.

Third, the English idea of 'putting your best foot forward' conflicts directly with an Athabaskan taboo. In situations of unequal status relations, English speakers normally try to display themselves in the best light possible. They also tend to speak highly of the future and try to present a career or life trajectory of success and planning. This English system is very different from the Athabaskan system, in which it is considered inappropriate and bad luck to anticipate good luck, to display oneself in a good light, to predict the future, or to speak unfavorably of another's luck.

Scollon and Scollon list many other differences, including differences in systems of pausing that ensure that English speakers in an interethnic encounter select most of the topics and do most of the talking. The net result of these communication problems is that each group ethnically stereotypes the other. English speakers come to believe that Athabaskans are unsure, aimless, incompetent, and withdrawn. Athabaskans come to believe that English speakers are boastful of their abilities, sure they can predict the future, careless with luck, and far too talkative.

Scollon and Scollon characterize the different discourse practices of Athabaskans and English speakers in terms of two different world views, or 'forms of consciousness': bush consciousness (connected with survival values in the bush) and modern consciousness (this latter taken partly from Berger, Berger, & Kellner, 1973). These forms of consciousness are 'reality sets' in the sense that they are cognitive orientations toward the everyday world, including the learning of that world. Anglo-Canadian and American mainstream culture has adopted a model of literacy, based on the values of essayist prose style, that is highly compatible with modern consciousness.

In essayist prose, the important relationships to be signaled are those between sentence and sentence, not those between speakers nor those between sentence and speaker. For a reader this requires a constant monitoring of grammatical and lexical information. With the heightened emphasis on truth value, rather than social or rhetorical conditions, comes the necessity to be explicit about logical implications. A significant aspect of essayist prose style is the fictionalization of both the audience and the author. The reader of an essayist text is not an ordinary human being, but an idealization, a rational mind formed by the rational body of knowledge of which the essay is a part. By the same token the author is a fiction, since the process of writing and editing essayist texts leads to an effacement of individual and idiosyncratic identity. Scollon and Scollon show the relation of these essayist values of modern consciousness by demonstrating that they are variants of the defining properties of the modern consciousness as given by Berger, Berger & Kellner (1973).

For the Athabaskan, writing in this essayist mode can constitute a crisis in ethnic identity. To produce an essay would require the Athabaskan to produce a major display, which would be appropriate only if the Athabaskan was in a position of dominance in relation to the audience. Both the audience and the author are fictionalized in essayist prose, and the text becomes decontextualized. This means that a contextualized, social relationship of dominance is obscured. When the relationship of the communicants is unknown, the Athabaskan prefers silence. The paradox of prose for the Athabaskan, then, is that contextualized communication between known author and audience is compatible with Athabaskan values, but not good essayist prose. To the extent that prose becomes decontextualized and thus good essayist prose, it becomes uncharacteristic of Athabaskans to seek to communicate. The Athabaskan set of discourse patterns is to a large extent mutually exclusive of the discourse patterns of essayist prose.

Scollon and Scollon go on to detail a number of narrative and non-narrative uses of language in Athabaskan culture, showing how each of these is in turn shaped by the Athabaskan reality set, especially respect for the individual and care about intervention in others' affairs (including their knowledge and beliefs). For example, riddles, which are an important genre in Athabaskan culture, are seen as schooling in guessing meanings, in reading between the lines, in anticipating outcomes, and in indirectness. In short, riddles provide a schooling in nonintervention. And in the best telling of a narrative 'little more than the themes are suggested and the audience is able to interpret those themes as highly contextulized in his own experiences' (p. 127). This is, of course, just the reverse of the decontextualization valued by essayist prose.

Heath and *Ways With Words*

Heath's already classic *Ways With Words* (1983) is an ethnography study of how literacy is embedded in the cultural context of three communities in the Piedmont Carolinas in the United States: Roadville, a white working-class community that has been part of mill life for four generations; Trackton, a working-class black community whose older generation was brought up on the land but which now is also connected to mill life and other light industry; and mainstream, middle-class, urban-oriented blacks and whites.

Heath analyzes the ways these different social groups 'take' knowledge from the environment, with particular concern for how 'types of literacy events' are involved in this taking. *Literacy events* are any event involving print, such as group negotiation of meaning in written texts (e.g. an ad), individuals 'looking things up' in reference books or writing family records in the Bible, and the dozens of other types of occasions when books or other written materials are integral to interpretation in an interaction. Heath interprets these literacy events in relation to the *larger sociocultural patterns* which they may exemplify or reflect, such as patterns of care-giving roles, uses of space and time, age and sex segregation, and so forth.

The oral/literate contrast makes little sense because in fact many social groups, even in high-technology societies, fall into such mixed categories as residual orality (Ong, 1982) or restricted literacy (Goody, 1977). The members of many US communities, though they may write and read at basic levels, have little occasion to use these skills as taught in school. Much of their daily lives is filled with literacy events in which they must know how to respond orally to written materials. Different social groups do this in different ways. How the members of a community use print to take meaning from the environment and how they use knowledge gained from print are interdependent with the ways children learn language and are socialized in interaction with peers and care givers. Language learning and socialization are two sides of the same coin (Ochs & Schieffelin, 1984). Thus, Heath concentrates on how children in each community acquire language and literacy in the process of becoming socialized into the norms and values of their communities.

As school-oriented, middle-class parents and their children interact in the preschool years, adults give their children, through modeling and specific instruction, ways of using language and of taking knowledge from books which seem natural in school and in numerous other institutional settings such as banks, post offices, businesses, or government offices.

To illustrate this point, Heath (1982) analyzes the bedtime story as an example of a major literacy event in mainstream homes. (All citations below are to this article, which contains much of the same material as *Ways With Words*.) The bedtime story sets patterns of behavior that recur repeatedly through the life of mainstream children and adults at school and in other institutions. In the bedtime story routine, the parent sets up a 'scaffolding' dialogue (see Cazden, 1979) with the child by asking questions like *What is X?* and then supplying verbal feedback and a label after the child has vocalized or given a nonverbal response. Before the age of 2, the child is thus socialized into the 'initiation-reply-evaluation' sequences so typical of class-room lessons (e.g. Mehan, 1979; Sinclair & Coulthard, 1975).

In addition, reading with comprehension involves an internal replaying of the same types of questions adults ask children about bedtime stories, and *what*-explanations are replayed in the school setting in learning to pick out topic sentences, write outlines, and answer standardized tests. Through the bedtime story routine and many similar practices in which children learn not only how to take meaning from books but also how to talk about it, they repeatedly practice routines which parallel those of classroom interaction: 'Thus, there is a deep continuity between patterns of socialization and language learning in the home culture and what goes on at school' (p. 56).

Children in both Roadville and Trackton were unsuccessful in school, despite the fact that both communities placed a high value on success in school. Roadville adults did read books to their children, but they did not extend the habits of literacy events beyond book reading. For instance, they did not, upon seeing an event in the real world, remind children of similar events in a book or comment on such similarities and differences between a book and real events.

The strong Fundamentalist bent of Roadville tended to make the members of this community view any fictionalized account of a real event as a *lie*. Since they regarded reality as being better than fiction, they did not encourage the shifting of the context of items and events characteristic of fictionalization and abstraction. They tended to choose books which emphasized nursery rhymes, alphabet learning, and simplified Bible stories. Even the oral stories that Roadville adults told, and that children modeled, were grounded in the actual. These stories, which were drawn from personal experience, were tales of transgression which made the point of reiterating the expected norms of behavior.

Thus, Roadville children were not practiced in decontextualizing their knowledge or in fictionalizing events known to them and shifting them about into other frames. In school, they were rarely able to take knowledge learned in one context and shift it to another; they did not compare two items or events and point out similarities and differences.

Trackton presents a quite different language and social environment. Babies in Trackton, who were almost always held during their waking hours, were constantly in the midst of a rich stream of verbal and nonverbal communication. Aside from Sunday school materials, there were no reading materials in the home just for children; adults did not sit and read to children. Children did, however, constantly interact verbally with peers and adults.

Adults did not ask children *What is X?* questions, but rather analogical questions calling for nonspecific comparisons of one item, event, or person with another (e.g. *What's that like?*). Though children could answer such questions, they could rarely name the specific feature or features which made two items or events alike. Parents did not believe they had a tutoring role and did not simplify their language for children, as mainstream parents do, nor did they label items or features of objects in either books or the environment at large. They believed children learned when they were provided with experiences from which they could draw global, rather than analytically specific, knowledge.

Children seemed to develop connections between situations or items by gestalt patterns, analogues, or general configuration links, not by specification of labels and discrete features in the situation. They did not decontextualize; rather, they heavily contextualized nonverbal and verbal language. Trackton children learned to tell stories by rendering a context and calling on the audience's participation to join in the imaginative creation of the story. In an environment rich with imaginative talk and verbal play, they had to be aggressive in inserting their stories into an ongoing stream of discourse. Fictionalizaiton, imagination, and verbal dexterity were encouraged.

Indeed, group negotiation and participation were prevalent features of the social group as a whole. Adults read not alone but in a group. For example, someone might read from a brochure on a new car while listeners related the text's meaning to their experiences, asking questions and expressing opinions. The group as a whole would synthesize the written text and the associated oral discourse to construct a meaning for the brochure.

At school, most Trackton children failed not only to learn the content of lessons but also to adopt the social interactional rules for school literacy events. Print in isolation carried little authority in their world, and the kinds of questions asked about reading books were unfamiliar (for example, *what*-explanations). The children's abilities to link two events or situations metaphorically and to recreate scenes were not tapped in school. In fact, these abilities often caused difficulties because they enabled children to see parallels teachers did not intend and, indeed, might not have recognized until the children pointed them out. By the time in their edcuation when their imaginative skills and verbal dexterity could really pay off (usually after the elementary years), they had failed to gain the necessary written composition skills they would need to translate their analogical skills into a channel teachers could accept.

Heath's characterization of Trackton, Roadville, and mainstreamers leads us to see not a binary (oral/literate) contrast, but a set of features that cross-classifies the three groups in various ways. Each group shares various features with the other groups but differs from them in other ways: The mainstream group and Trackton both valued imagination and fictionalization, while Roadville did not; Roadville and Trackton both shared a disregard for decontextualization not shared by mainstreamers. Both mainstreamers and Roadville, but not Trackton, believed parents have a tutoring role in language and literacy acquisition (they read to their children and asked questions that required labels). However, Roadville shared with Trackton, not the mainstream, an experiential, nonanalytic view of learning (children learn by doing and watching, not by having the process broken down into its smallest parts). As we add more groups to the comparison, for example, the Athabaskans (who share with Trackton parents a regard for gestalt learning and storage of knowledge but differ from them in the degree of self-display they allow), we will get more complex cross-classifications.

In *Ways With Words,* Heath has suggested that in order for a non-mainstream social group to acquire mainstream, school-based literacy practices, with all the oral and written language skills this implies, individuals, whether children or adults, must 'recapitulate', at an appropriate level for their age of course, the sorts of literacy experiences the mainstream child has had at home. Unfortunately, schools as currently constituted tend to be good places to practice mainstream literacy once you have its foundations, but they are not good places to acquire those foundations.

Heath suggests that this foundation, when it has not been set at home, can be acquired by apprenticing the individual to a school-based literate person (the teacher in a new and expanded role), who must break down essay-text literacy into its myriad component skills and allow the student to practise them repeatedly. Such skills involve the ability to give *what*-explanations; to break down verbal information into small bits of information; to notice the analytic features of items and events and to be able to recombine them in new contexts, eventually to offer *reason*-explanations; and finally to take meaning from books and be able to talk about it.

Heath has actually had students, at a variety of ages, engage in ethnographic research with the teacher (e.g. studying the use of language or languages or of writing and reading in their communities) as a way of learning and practising the various subskills of essay-text literacy (e.g. asking questions; taking notes; discussing various points of view, often with people with whom the student does not share a lot of mutual knowledge; writing discursive prose and revising it with feedback, often from nonpresent readers).

As pointed out earlier, essay-text values are in fact best exemplified in the ideology and practice, ideally, of academic work. Heath's approach obviously fits perfectly with Scribner & Cole's (1981) practice account of literacy. And, in line with Street's (1984) ideological approach to literacy, it claims that individuals who have not been socialized into the discourse practices that constitute mainstream, school-based literacy must eventually be socialized into them if they are ever to acquire them. The component skills of this form of literacy must be practiced, and one cannot practice a skill one has not been exposed to or engage in a social practice one has not been socialized into (which is what most nonmainstream children are expected to do in school).

At the same time, however, we must remember Scollon and Scollon's (1981) warning that for many social groups this practice will mean a change of identity and the adoption of a reality set at odds with their own at various points. There is a deep paradox here — and there is no facile way of removing it, short of changing our hierarchical social structure and the school systems that by and large perpetuate it.

Conclusion: Literacy and the English Teacher

The literature on orality and literacy is rife with implications for teachers of English, most of which I hope are readily apparent from the preceding discussion. Let me conclude, however, by touching on some major themes. Teachers of English are not, in fact, teaching English, and certainly not English grammar, or even 'language'. Rather, they are teaching a set of discourse practices, oral and written, connected with the standard dialect of English.

Language and literacy acquisition are forms of socialization, in this case socialization into mainstream ways of using language in speech and print, mainstream ways of taking meaning, of making sense of experience. Discourse practices are always embedded in the particular world view of a particular social group, they are tied to a set of values and norms. In learning new discourse practices, a student partakes of this set of values and norms, this world view. Furthermore, in acquiring a new set of discourse practices, a student may be acquiring a new identity, one that at various points may conflict with the student's initial acculturation and socialization.

Different literacy practices allow the student to practice different, quite specific skills, and the student indeed gets better at these. Literacy in and of itself leads to no higher order, global cognitive skills; all humans who are acculturated and socialized are already in possession of higher order cognitive skills, though their expression and the practices they are embedded in will differ across cultures.

Essay-text literacy, with its attendant emphasis on the syntactic mode and explicitness, while only one cultural expression of literacy among many, is connected with the form of consciousness and the interests of the powerful in our society. As Western technology and literacy spread across the globe, this form of consciousness is influencing, interacting with, and often replacing indigenous forms all over the world; hence such remarks as 'Western yardsticks are relevant everywhere because all men must become Western or perish' (Musgrove, 1982: 42).

We should not fool ourselves into thinking that access to essay-text literacy automatically ensures equality and social success or erases racism or minority disenfranchisement. But, nonetheless, English teachers are gatekeepers: Short of radical social change, there is no access to power in the society without control over the discourse practices in thought, speech, and writing of essay-text literacy and its attendant world view.

English teachers can cooperate in their own marginalization by seeing themselves as 'language teachers' with no connection to such social and political issues. Or they can accept the paradox of literacy as a form of interethnic communication which often involves conflicts of values and identities, and accept their role as persons who socialize students into a world view that, given its power here and abroad, must be looked at critically, comparatively, and with a constant sense of the possibilities for change. Like it or not, English teachers stand at the very heart of the most crucial educational, cultural, and political issues of our time.

Acknowledgments

My thinking about orality, literacy, and related issues has been greatly influenced, over the last few years, by conversations with Courtney Cazden (Harvard University), David Dickinson (Tufts University), Ruth Nickse (Boston University), and Sarah Michaels (Harvard and the University of Massachusetts, Boston), to all of whom I am deeping indebted. I am also indebted to Shirley Brice Heath, Michael Cole, Dell Hymes, and Karen Watson-Gegeo for the lucidity and importance of their written work, which, apparent or not, has influenced me a great deal.

References

Abrahams, R. D. (1964) *Deep Down in the Jungle: Negro Narrative Folklore from the Streets of Philadelphia.* Harboro, PA: Folklore Associates.
— (1970) *Positively Black.* Englewood Cliffs, NJ: Prentice-Hall.
— (1976) *Talking Black.* Rowley, MA: Newbury House.
Berger, P., Berger, B. and Kellner, H. (1973) *The Homeless Mind: Modernization and Consciousness.* New York: Random House.
Cazden, C. (1979) Peekaboo as an instruction model: Discourse development at home and at school. *Papers and Reports in Child Language Development* 17, 1–29.

Chafe, W. (1982). Integration and involvement in speaking, writing, and oral literature. In D. Tannen (ed.) *Spoken and Written Language: Exploring Orality and Literacy* (pp. 35–53). Norwood, NJ: Ablex.

Cook-Gumperz, J. (1986) Literacy and schooling: An unchanging equation? In J. Cook-Gumperz (ed.) *The Social Construction of Literacy* (pp. 16–44). Cambridge: Cambridge University Press.

Donald, J. (1983) How illiteracy became a problem (and literacy stopped being one). *Journal of Education* 165, 35–52.

Douglas, M. (1973) *Natural Symbols*. Harmondsworth, England: Penguin.

Erickson, F. (1984) Rhetoric, anecdote, and rhapsody: Coherence strategies in a conversation among black American adolescents. In D. Tannen (ed.) *Coherence in Spoken and Written Discourse* (pp. 81–154). Norwood, NJ: Ablex.

Evans-Pritchard, E. E. (1937) *Witchcraft, Oracles and Magic Amongst the Azande*. Oxford: Clarendon Press.

— (1951) *Social Anthropology*. London: Routledge & Kegan Paul.

Gee, J. P. (1985) The narrativization of experience in the oral style. *Journal of Education* 167, 9–35.

— (1986) Literate America on illiterate America: A review of Jonathan Kozol's *Illiterate America*. *Journal of Education* 168, 126–40.

— (in press) Units in the production of narrative discourse. *Discourse Processes*.

Gilmore, P. (1985) 'Gimme room': School resistance, attitude, and access to literacy. *Journal of Education* 167, 111–28.

Givon, T. (1979) *On Understanding Grammar*. New York: Academic Press.

Goody, J. (1977) *The Domestication of the Savage Mind*. Cambridge: Cambridge University Press.

Goody, J. and Watt, I. P. (1963) The consequences of literacy. *Comparative Studies in History and Society* 5, 304–45.

Gould, S. J. (1977) *Ontogeny and Phylogeny*. Cambridge, MA: Harvard University Press.

Graff, H. J. (1979) *The Literacy Myth: Literacy and Social Structure in the 19th Century City*. New York: Academic Press.

Greenfield, P. (1972) Oral or written language: The consequences for cognitive development in Africa, U.S. and England. *Language and Speech* 15, 169–78.

Gumperz, J. J. (1986) Interactional social linguistics in the study of schooling. In J. Cook-Gumperz (ed.) *The Social Construction of Literacy* (pp. 45–68). Cambridge: Cambridge University Press.

Havelock, E. A. (1963) *Preface to Plato*. Cambridge, MA: Harvard University Press.

— (1982) *The Literate Revolution in Greece and its Cultural Consequences*. Princeton, NJ: Princeton University Press.

Heath, S. B. (1982) What no bedtime story means: Narrative skills at home and at school. *Language in Society* 11, 49–76.

— (1983) *Ways With Words*. Cambridge: Cambridge University Press.

Hildyard, A. and Olson, D. (1978) *Literacy and the Specialization of Language*. Unpublished manuscript, Ontario Institite for Studies in Education.

Horton, R. (1967) African traditional thought and Western science. *Africa* 37, 1–2.

Hymes, D. (1981) *'In Vain I Tried to Tell You': Essays in Native American Ethnopoetics*. Philadelphia: The University of Pennsylvania Press.

Kochman, T. (1981) *Black and White Styles in Conflict*. Chicago: University of Chicago Press.

Kozol, J. (1985) *Illiterate America*. Garden City, NY: Anchor Press/Doubleday.

Labov, W. (1972) *Language in the Inner City*. Philadelphia: University of Pennsylvania Press.

Levi-Bruhl, L. (1910) *Les Fonctions Mentales dans les Sociétés Inférieures.* Paris: F. Alcan.

Levi-Strauss, C. (1963) *Structural Anthropology.* New York: Basic Books.

— (1966) *The Savage Mind.* Chicago: The University of Chicago Press.

Lord, A. B. (1960) *The Singer of Tales.* Cambridge, MA: Harvard University Press.

Luria, A. R. (1976) *Cognitive Development: Its Cultural and Social Foundations* (M. Cole, ed., and M. Lopez-Morillas & L. Solotaroff, trans.). Cambridge, MA: Harvard University Press.

Mehan, H. (1979) *Learning Lessons.* Cambridge, MA: Harvard University Press.

Michaels, S. (1981) 'Sharing time': Children's narrative styles and differential access to literacy. *Language in Society* 10, 423–42.

Musgrove, F. (1982) *Education and Anthropology: Other Cultures and the Teacher.* New York: John Wiley.

Ochs, E. and Schieffelin, B. B. (1984) Language acquisition and socialization: Three developmental stories and their implications. In R. Shweder and R. LeVine (eds) *Culture Theory: Essays on Mind, Self and Emotion* (pp. 276–320). Cambridge: Cambridge University Press.

Olson, D. R. (1977) From utterance to text: The bias of language in speech and writing. *Harvard Education Review* 47, 257–81.

Ong, W. J. and Ong, S. J. (1982) *Orality and Literacy: The Technologizing of the Word.* London: Methuen.

Parry, M. (1971) *The Making of Homeric Verse: The Collected Papers of Milman Parry* (A. Parry, ed.). Oxford: Clarendon Press.

Richardson, R. C., Jr, Risk, E. C. and Okun, M. A. (1983) *Literacy in the Open Access College.* San Francisco: Jossey Bass.

Sapir, E. (1921) *Language.* New York: Harcourt Brace & World.

Scollon, R. and Scollon, S. B. K. (1981) *Narrative, Literacy and Face in Interethnic Communication.* Norwood, NJ: Ablex.

Scribner, S. and Cole, M. (1973) Cognitive consequences of formal and informal education. *Science* 182, 553–9.

— (1981) *The Psychology of Literacy.* Cambridge, MA: Harvard University Press.

Sinclair, J. M. and Coulthard, R. M. (1975) *Toward an Analysis of Discourse.* New York: Oxford University Press.

Smitherman, G. (1977) *Talkin' and Testifyin': The Language of Black America.* Boston: Houghton Mifflin.

Street, B. V. (1984) *Literacy in Theory and Practice.* Cambridge: Cambridge University Press.

Wertsch, J. V. (1985) *Vygotsky and the Social Formation of Mind.* Cambridge, MA: Harvard University Press.

12 Educational Language Planning in England and Wales: Multicultural Rhetoric and Assimilationist Assumptions

MICHAEL STUBBS

Britain is often recognised as a country with profoundly monolingual assumptions and a widespread apathy towards learning other languages. This paper is a case study of some major changes which are currently taking place in the British education system. These changes involve a great deal of discussion of language issues, both in official documents and in the press, and they do have some bright spots, notably:

— for the first time, learning a modern foreign language will be compulsory for all secondary school pupils
— an element of language studies (language awareness) will be a compulsory component within the English curriculum.

However, despite much government rhetoric about increased opportunities for linguistic diversity, I will conclude pessimistically, that basic attitudes are unchanged, and that there are major attempts to further strengthen the dominant position of Standard English in Britain, rather than to attempt a more balanced relationship between English and other languages.

The essential theme of the article is expressed by Williams (1965: 145) in his discussion of the selective tradition in British education:

> . . . the way in which education is organized can be seen to express, consciously and unconsciously, the wider organization of a society, so that what has been thought of as *simple distribution* is in fact an active shaping to particular social ends.

His comment about distribution is intended to apply to selections of content in the curriculum, and therefore applies equally to the way in which languages are chosen for the education system.

The essential structure of the argument is provided by a very pointed and aggressive attack in current government language policy, formulated by Rosen (quoted in the *Times Education Supplement,* 24 June 1988): 'liberal words (which are used) to disguise sinister messages of state coercion.'

In this paper, I discuss to what extent such judgements are true, and conclude that they are, to a large extent, justified. There is much talk in government statements about ethnic diversity and about opportunities for children to study a wider range of languages. But much of this looks like empty rhetoric when seen against the background of:

— other statements
— the lack of resources to implement such policies
— the complete absence of any overall language planning.

(For other articles with the same basic argument that there is a gap between the rhetoric and the reality, between appealing formulations which give only an illusion of change and social facts, see Skutnabb-Kangas 1989, and several papers in Skutnabb-Kangas & Commins (eds) 1988, especially Tosi, 1988, who discusses the 'depressingly vague and ambiguous notion' of multicultural education in the UK.)

The Education Reform Act (ERA) and the 'National' Curriculum

This paper discusses only England and Wales: Scotland and Northern Ireland have different education systems, and the Secretary of State for Education and Science (i.e. the Minister of Education) has responsibility only for England and Wales. He cedes this responsibility to the Secretary of State for Wales in Welsh matters, including the Welsh language in schools. I will comment further below on this geographical definition of language matters in Britain.

The organization of education in England and Wales has changed very sharply since 1988, when the ERA came into force: this is the largest piece of educational legislation (hundreds of pages in length) since the Education Act of 1944, and makes very large scale changes to the organization of primary, secondary and tertiary education. One of the main planks of current British conservative government policy is the National Curriculum. This is a misnomer, since it applies only to state schools in England and Wales. (Private schools may follow it if they wish.) However, it is within the so-called National Curriculum that a great deal of language planning is taking place, not explicitly and overtly, but in a fragmented and uncoordinated way, so that its effects are more difficult to monitor and predict.

What mainly concerns us here is that previously there was no National Curriculum in schools. Pre-1988, in the years BNC (before the National Curriculum):

— many educational responsibilities were delegated to around 110 Local Education Authorities (LEAs)
— the curriculum in schools was the responsibility of individual schools, departments and teachers (with examination boards effectively controlling the content of the curriculum for upper secondary age pupils).

Whereas now:

— there is enormous centralization of control over the content and assessment of the curriculum: the Act gives the Secretary of State about 400 new powers with which to manage the whole system.

These changes have taken place very fast indeed, with only minimum consultation with teachers and others. Amongst very many other provisions, the ERA established a National Curriculum comprising English, mathematics, science, technology, history, geography, one modern foreign language, music, art and physical education, and, in Wales, Welsh.

I will discuss here the work of various government committees (only some of which were overtly concerned with language), whose work amounts to *de facto* language planning. My main references will be to the following Reports and Orders:

    1975 Bullock (DES, 1975)
    1985 Swann (DES, 1985)
    1988 Kingman (HMSO, 1988)
    1989 Cox (DES, 1989a)
    1989 Orders for Modern Foreign Languages (DES, 1989b)
    1990 Harris (DES, 1990)

There is no national language planning commission (as there has been, for example, in Australia: Clyne, 1988). CDE (1982) is a very clear Australian statement on the inadequacy of uncoordinated, *ad hoc* responses to language diversity, and on the need for an explicit national language policy, with clear discussion of the different roles of languages in the country, local, national and international.

It has not been customary for the British government to do any language planning at all. For example, it has collected no statistics of languages spoken in the UK in the 10-yearly censuses (except for Welsh, Scottish Gaelic and Irish). Figures, where they have been collected at all, have been collected at Local Education Authority level (e.g. LMP, 1985; Bourne, 1989a, b; and see Printon (ed.), 1986, who gives some basic statistics from various sources.)

However, language planning has suddenly simply started to be done, on a very large scale. But it is not generally presented as such: it is seen merely as a natural concomitant of the National Curriculum, an inevitable effect of the work of various government committees concerned with English and foreign language teaching. Language planning is introduced by the back door. The approach is uncoordinated, perhaps deliberately so: it could be denied that this is language planning at all.[1] It is either a muddle or a conspiracy, depending on your wider view of British history. But certainly, when there is no explicit policy, it is more difficult to monitor the language rights of different groups.

Skutnabb-Kangas and Phillipson (1989: 8) point out that countries differ significantly in the degrees of explicitness with which language rights are formulated. Britain is far at the implicit end. (See Figure 1.) The British government has always avoided any basic policy commitments on languages (except for Welsh). It is, I think, a widespread and justifiable view of the Thatcher government, but also more widely of British politics, that there is a lack of underlying theory: things are done in an *ad hoc,* pragmatic, piecemeal fashion. But an absence of a policy is a policy, whether intended or not. And an indifference to languages is likely to lead to an endorsement of the status quo.

It is doubtful, in fact, if the term *language planning* would mean anything at all to most people (including most politicians and educationalists) in Britain. It might mean 'teaching English to immigrants' or 'choosing which foreign languages to teach in schools'. The majority could probably not conceive what else it might mean, because of the profoundly monolingual assumptions which are regarded as natural in Britain.

Language planning of a far-reaching kind has, then, suddenly started to be done, via different committees which are isolated from each other. One effect of the lack of explicit planning is that advice and decision making are all split. The Swann Report (1985) was about the education of minority group children. The Kingman Report (1988) was about English language in the mother tongue curriculum.[2] The Cox Report (1989) was about teaching English as a mother tongue in the National Curriculum.[3] The Harris Report is about modern foreign languages in the National Curriculum. But no committee has had a national language policy *per se* as part of its terms of reference. And there are large areas, obviously relevant to general policy, which are not covered at all in the present reforms: e.g. adult literacy; the education of the deaf; language disabilities; translation and interpretation services, in the courts or social services.

Consultation is also muddled and split. Therefore groups of subject teachers or bilingual speakers have to make the same points over and over again to different committees. They have no participation rights, and the process of divide and rule leads to exhaustion and demoralization.

The Swann Report (DES, 1985)

The Swann Committee was set up to advise not on language planning, but on the role of education in race relations and equal opportunities. The concern was with social cohesion, in a situation where the government was deeply worried about possible race riots in an ethnically divided country. The Committee recommended a policy of mainstreaming: i.e. of giving bilingual children better access to the curriculum, by having them taught, with support, alongside their peers, rather than being withdrawn to separate remedial language classes or special language centres (as had been the strategy to deal with large waves of immigrant children into Britain from the 1960s). The policy of mainstreaming is now widely accepted.

But this change is, by definition, limited to schools with multilingual populations. Swann's general recommendations about the need for all children, in whatever area, to learn about the multilingual nature of Britain, have hardly been put into effect, and have had little effect on the dominant culture (Verma (ed.), 1989). The Cox Report (DES, 1989a: 2.8) recommends that the curriculum for all pupils should include informed discussion of the multi-cultural nature of British society, whether or not the individual school is culturally mixed. This may be a pious hope. It may also be phrased too vaguely in terms of 'multilingualism', with no specific demands about languages.

The Kingman Report (DES, 1988)

In the immediate run up to the National Curriculum, the Kingman Committee was set up to recommend on English language teaching. This was widely perceived as having to do with grammar teaching, though the Kingman Report itself inteprets the issue more widely, as indeed its terms of reference required it to do.

The Report proposes a model of language comprising: the forms of the English language (essentially phonology, graphology, syntax and discourse), communication and comprehension, acquisition and development, and variation. This is a standard type of model, very familiar to linguists. Much of it is, however, almost incomprehensible to many English teachers, who have received little or no training in English language or linguistics.

In addition, the model has come under heavy attack. It provides an extraordinary description of language variation, which is seen as historical and geographical, but not social. No social class or ethnic divisions are mentioned, although social class is obviously a major concomitant of language diversity in Britain. (The Cox Report also avoids the term 'social class', and talks coyly of 'social groups'.) The implicit denial of social class differences in the Kingman Report is clearly politically loaded; it is also simply false. The language of a particular class is passed off as the language of the nation.

But there is considerable confusion in the Kingman Report over whether the Committee are talking of the English language or of languages in general. For example, consider these paragraphs (p. 33, paras 1 and 2):

> It is the purpose of this chapter to illustrate the relevance of the language model to English teaching . . . Children arrive at their first school able to use at least their own spoken language.

For many children in Britain, this will be a language other than or in addition to English, but there is no unambiguous statement that English can be better understood in relation to other languages. (Contrast Cox, 2. 7–12.) Since the educational recommendations are not clearly focussed on language learning needs in general, the effect is to give more weight, yet again, to English.

On the surface, the Kingman Report appears moderate and liberal, though many analyses (e.g. Cameron & Bourne, 1989: 12–13) see it as authoritarian. It recommends social cohesion around one variety of English. It uses a rhetoric of language entitlement and language rights, and of freedom and democracy (e.g. pp. 2, 3, 4, 7, 10, 11), which gives the Report its superficially liberal pluralist tone. (In other areas of education, the government stresses parents' rights.) Talk of individual language rights makes the correct moral noises, but it has no legislative basis, and is therefore empty. There is talk of entitlement, but not of the discrimination which many children face; and talk of equality of opportunity, but not equality of outcome. (Cf. Rampton, 1989 on the 'entitlement' rhetoric; and Skutnabb-Kangas & Phillipson, 1989 on the myth that language rights are a reality in many countries.)

Language and Nationality

In the debate over language and nation, the Kingman Report is a key ideological text (Cameron & Bourne, 1989). The focus was on a claimed crisis of falling standards. 'Grammar' carried an enormous symbolic weight of authority, hierarchy, order, tradition, and elitism. The Report has been widely interpreted as taking an authoritarian, national unity position, ethnocentric and nostalgic, with the covert function of strengthening and protecting English.

A characteristic of the current debate in Britain about language, especially English in the National Curriculum, is the enormous press coverage which the Kingman and Cox Reports have had, and essential to an understanding of the debate is the nature of the rhetoric which is used. For example, *The Times* leading article (30 April 1988), when Kingman was published, wrote:

> English ought to be the queen of the curriculum for any British child. It is one of the things that define his or her nationality.

This claimed relationship between language and nationality, which has very little basis in British law, occurs very frequently. Marenbon (1987) is published by the Centre for Policy Studies, a right-wing think tank set up by Margaret Thatcher and Keith Joseph in 1974. Marenbon ends his attack on current trends in English teaching in this way:

> . . . in the future of its language there lies the future of a nation.

The Kingman Report itself uses a general formulation (p. 43, para 32):

> . . . language above all else is the defining characteristic of an individual, a community, a nation.

There are certainly many cases in the world where language has been the focus of separatist, nationalist demands. But the Kingman Report is presenting as the only, obvious, 'natural' view, what is, in fact, a particular 19th century European Romantic view (Leith, 1989), that a language expresses individual, creative, poetic genius (there is a lot of literary criticism in the Report on biblical translations, Shakespeare and Dickens), and the Volksgeist, the genius of a people.

The Cox Report (DES, 1989a)

The main job of the Cox Committee was to recommend programmes of study and attainment targets for English mother tongue teaching from 5 to 16. Its recommendations have been amended, after limited consultation, by the National Curriculum Council, and turned into law. The Report also contains other chapters on Standard English, linguistic terminology, knowledge about language, equal opportunities, bilingual children, and Wales: these chapters have no statutory force.

There is no space here for a detailed account of the very substantial debates around teaching English as a mother tongue. (For more detailed analysis of the Cox Report see Stubbs, 1989.) The Report is discussed elsewhere in this article for its relevance to the other languages of England.

The essential general point is that the ERA defines separate subjects on the school curriculum: 'English' is different from 'Modern Foreign Languages'. Different Committees are responsible for the curriculum, with only poorly defined requirements of 'cross curricular themes' between subjects. It has been pointed out that the list of subjects in the National Curriculum is almost identical to the list of subjects for grammar schools proposed in the early 1900s.

Modern Foreign Languages in the National Curriculum: Statutory Orders

In connection with the ERA, the government has published Statutory Orders (DES, 1989b), which came into effect in August 1989, specifying which languages may be taught in the National Curriculum. Nineteen languages are listed as possible foundation subjects, to be taught between 11 and 16 years (probably for 4 periods per week).

The positive aspect is that, for the first time, a modern foreign language will be compulsory for all secondary age pupils, whereas previously a foreign language has been seen as a subject for the academic elite. This new 'languages for all' policy is a major step forward, in the context of facilitating communication between citizens of EC countries. However, there are several aspects of the policy which are disappointing.

The permitted languages are in two schedules. Schedule 1 contains the working languages of the EC (minus English). These are unconditionally specified as foundation subjects, and schools must offer at least one:

> Danish, Dutch, French, German, Modern Greek, Italian, Portuguese, Spanish.

Schedule 2 contains 11 languages, which are a mixture of international languages and languages of major linguistic minorities in Britain. As long as they offer an EC language, schools may in addition offer one or more of:

> Arabic, Bengali, Chinese (Cantonese or Mandarin), Gujerati, Modern Hebrew, Hindi, Japanese, Panjabi, Russian, Turkish, Urdu.

The schedules do explicitly give legal status to a relatively wide range of languages, and one must welcome the formal recognition of non-European languages. This enhancement of their status may look very progressive in a European context, where non-European languages are often totally unrecognised except in low status 'migrant worker programmes'. But it has been quickly pointed out that the schedules also establish a caste system of grade 1 and grade 2 languages. (See also below on some of the implications of territorial descriptions such as 'non-European'.)

Again, we have a proposal which appears superficially to encourage language diversity. However, there are problems:

— Children are obliged to study only one language in the National Curriculum: they may study second and subsequent languages, but outside the National Curriculum, and very little time is available outside the compulsory subjects. In practice, the opportunity to study a second language will seldom be available.
— The publication of such lists creates the expectation of adequate resourcing, but, in fact, no resourcing is available for the wider range of languages proposed. There are no teachers of Danish or Dutch, for example. Nor are there any incentives to offer schedule 2 languages. French will therefore continue to be taught because there are teachers of French. The government has published schedules of languages, to which it can rhetorically refer in talking of opportunities for pupils, but it has shown no commitment to turning the schedules into reality.
— In practice, there are few resources to teach much apart from French. But there is actually a current shortage even of French teachers, and this is when over 60 per cent of pupils now drop French at age 14. Under the National Curriculum, they will be obliged to continue with a language until 16, and the teacher shortage will therefore be more acute.
— Although 19 languages are listed, others are thereby excluded: schools need special permission to teach them. The central specification of particular languages is inevitably a partial and arbitrary estimation of future needs, but no mechanisms are proposed whereby the schedules might be changed. In general, the Orders fossilize provision. The schedules embody a superficial and mechanical definition of Europe: simply 1992 as visualized in 1989. If Turkey or Sweden join the EC, for example, does the government have to change the law? After the events of summer and autumn 1989, this view of Europe looks very dated indeed.

The Orders are accompanied by a non-statutory Circular (DES 9/89) which contains a brief discussion of which languages are of relevance to Britain. There is a weak classification into: working languages of the EC, major trading languages, and languages used by ethnic communities in Britain. But there is no real theory of such language types or functions. (Again, contrast CDE, 1982).

Watertight categories are clearly useless, and any theory would have to allow multiple categorization (Clyne, 1988). Starting categories might be:

— traditional foreign languages, i.e. languages for which teachers are available
— community/heritage languages
— languages of neighboring countries and/or trading partners
— EC languages

— world/international languages, e.g. languages used for scientific communication
— classical languages (which are completely omitted from the National Curriculum)
— 'easy' versus 'difficult' languages, e.g. languages with a non-Roman
writing system (though such a description may be very ethno- or Euro-
centric).

It would not be possible to define such categories in more than a common
sense way. In fact, it is evident that the categories above are not neutral,
since they signal the status of languages: *international language* sounds
important, *community language* less so. But planners and decision makers
need such categories because they imply policies and actions.

The Circular attempts no basic justifications for language education
(Clyne, 1988: 278), in terms, for example, of social justice, enrichment for
all British citizens, or the maintenance of languages already spoken in Britain. Even on cost-benefit grounds, the economic arguments look very
shortsighted: there is likely to be an enormous waste, allowing languages
already spoken in the home and community to be eroded, whilst starting
from scratch to teach other languages in schools and colleges. Only a narrow
version of economic strategies in relation to Britain's external relations is
clearly spelled out.

This will need careful analysis of the implications of some very simple
facts. For example, in Europe, German is the first language in terms of numbers of speakers, and of the number of different countries in which it is the
main language (Germany, Austria and Switzerland, with sizeable numbers
of speakers in other countries). In the world, in terms of numbers of speakers, German ranks below English, Spanish and Portuguese (and many other
languages) (Ammon, in Coulnas, 1991).

The Circular gives only a very sketchy rationale, based on personal motivations (practical skills, understanding of other cultures), and national motivations (economic and cultural, trade, tourism and international relations).
This needs to be substantially developed by an analysis of increased personal
mobility, of increased opportunities to meet migrants and tourists, of the
increasing importance of languages in international life, including increased
access to radio, television and films in other languages, etc. Nor is there anything but the vaguest discussion of the internationalization of business and
commercial life in which an adult is very likely to have to use a foreign language, but probably not the one s/he learned at school (Trim, 1989). The
implications of the global village are hardly recognised.

In a word, there is still great confusion over what modern foreign languages are *for* in British schools. The range of political, social and historical

factors which lead to lists of languages such as those in the schedules must be publicly debated and justified. Language planning depends on a problem being defined, alternative solutions being formulated, so that they can be evaluated, and so that one can then be chosen and implemented, and its implementation in turn evaluated (Ó Riagáin, in Coulnas, 1991).

In addition, the rationale for teaching heritage/community languages is very different from teaching traditional modern foreign languages (in practice, French and German), and very different programmes of study are needed. Expectations of linguistic competence could be much higher than with ab initio teaching of a foreign language. The main motivations may be cultural and or religious, and the maintenance of a language spoken in the local community.

In summary, the overt ideology has changed in favour of widening the available languages. But when this rhetoric is translated into concrete actions in institutions, little will change. If anything, the present status quo could be even more rigid than at present, because some aspects of it are now enshrined in law. English exists in a web of institutions, woven even tighter in England and Wales by the National Curriculum.

In a review of language planning in the USA from the 1960s to the 1980s, Fishman (1981: 516, 522) reaches pessimistic conclusions, very similar to this article:

> *plus ça change, plus c'est la même chose.* On the surface a great deal has changed . . . but basically ours is not a society whose peculiar genius is along the line of linguistic sophistication, sensitivity or concern . . . the exasperated know-nothingism of 'this is, after all, an English-speaking country' . . . Language maintenance . . . is not part of public policy because it is rarely recognised as being in the public interest.

Modern Foreign Languages in the National Curriculum: The Harris Committee

The National Curriculum Modern Foreign Languages Working Group was set up in September 1989, to design the programmes of study and attainment targets which will come into force from Autumn 1992.

The press statement, from the Education Minister at the DES who introduced the Committee, emphasised, in a narrow way, the 'challenge of 1992' and the need for languages in 'today's increasingly competitive world'. The Committee's terms of reference were, however, wider than many people had predicted: the group was asked both to reconsider the two schedules of languages and also whether only one language in secondary education is appropriate. At the time of writing (March 1990), the Committee has produced an interim report, which does not significantly change the terms of the debate.

Welsh

The Welsh Act of 1967 asserted the 'equal validity' of English and Welsh, and gave both languages equal status in legal proceedings. However, when the effects of the Act were reviewed 10 years later, it was concluded that such legislation had not strengthened Welsh. This required active promotion in all domains. The National Curriculum Welsh Working Group envisages a variety of different kinds of provision: Welsh medium education, Welsh mother tongue teaching, and Welsh as a second language within English medium education. In 1988, only 13 per cent of young primary age Welsh children were fluent in Welsh. The proportion of bilinguals does not therefore look very different in Wales and in England.

But the legal situation of Welsh in Wales is very different from the situation of other languages in England or Wales. A particular form of territoriality principle, with unfortunate consequences, is used for Welsh in Wales (Cameron & Bourne, 1989; Bourne, 1989a, b). Geography is used to define provision and rights. Welsh has legal status only in Wales, so that as soon as a Welsh speaker crosses the border into England those rights vanish for that individual. This territorial conception of language rights is not only enshrined in law: it is the conception which has been acceptable to Welsh language activists themselves. (The territorial view is, of course, found widely elsewhere under very different political circumstances: many separatist political demands are based on a language-territory claim; even in Switzerland, despite the notion of a multilingual federation, languages are linked to territory. Nelde & Watts, in Coulnas, 1991.)

The Welsh Act is the only explicit legislation in the UK concerning language rights, and is therefore significant for its covert implications for other languages. And this discourse of national boundaries has dangerous implications. The territorial conception may well have benefited Welsh itself, but has created unfortunate precedents for other languages. If Welsh is the natural language of Wales, then it seems to follow that English is the natural language of England, and that languages in general belong to territories not to speakers. Since the languages of England (e.g. Asian languages, Chinese, etc.) have geographical homes elsewhere, then they have no natural home in Britain. Their speakers belong elsewhere, and should presumably forget their languages or return to where they came from. They certainly cannot expect any language rights in Britain. This seems to be the unacceptable logic of this way of thinking.

It is such assumptions which have to be extracted from covert statements. The Kingman Report (e.g. p. 30) also sees languages as things which spread over territories:

> As populations are dispersed and separated, they typically develop regular regional changes in their language forms. These changes may mark different dialects (or eventually different languages).

This expresses a strange model of populations 'dispersing', independently of other populations who might be making them disperse: agency is strangely missing. Further, there is no notion that, having dispersed, the populations might come into contact with other populations who speak different languages. Language *contact* often leads to language *convergence*.

The Other Languages of England and Wales

Bhatt & Martin-Jones (1989) summarize the changing policies concerning minority languages in Britain. The major waves of immigration into Britain in the 1960s were accompanied by firmly assimilationist assumptions: Britain should respect, but could not be expected to perpetuate, different cultural values. Groups were seen as a problem needing compensatory English teaching: bilingualism was seen as bewildering for the individuals involved (DES, 1971: 9). The Bullock Report (1975) took a liberal pluralist view that minority languages are a resource and a right: in a famous statement (quoted by Cox, DES, 1989a: 2.7), they asserted that children should not be expected to cast off the language and culture of the home as they cross the school threshold. The EC Directive (EC, 1977) on the education of the children of migrant workers was interpreted by the DES (1981) as requiring an exploration of how minority languages might be taught inside or outside school, but not as the right of children to have such tuition. In the 1980s, there was discussion of the possibility of minority languages in three places in the curriculum: as examination subjects in secondary schooling; as bilingual support in the classroom, especially for young children in reception classes; and as a resource in language awareness courses. (Tosi, 1988 provides a comparable analysis, of a rhetoric which shifts from 'assimilation' to 'integration', with little changing but the words.)

Surveys of minority languages spoken in Britain tend to stress their diversity. For example, the Cox Report (10.3) emphasises that:

> The 1987 Languages Survey conducted by ILEA (Inner London Education Authority) found 23 per cent of the Authority's school population using a language other than or in addition to English at home, with 170 different languages spoken by its pupils.

This argument is probably a strategic blunder, because is makes planned provision seem impossible (Bourne, 1989a, b). In fact, of the 170 languages spoken by London school children, 37 languages were spoken only by one child, and the overall distribution of the languages was very uneven. For example, Bengali accounted for over 20 per cent of bilingual children (some 12,600 pupils), who were concentrated in certain areas. There were large numbers of speakers of Bengali, Gujerati, Panjabi and Urdu, and substantial numbers of Turkish, Greek and Chinese speaking children. In England some 5 per cent of children are bilingual, but in many schools over 60 per cent of the children speak the same language other than English, and in some schools it is over 90 per cent. Such a presentation of the figures makes planned provision seem much more realistic.

It is important, in a wider European context, to stress that such children are not from migrant worker or immigrant families. They are not *Gastarbeiter* or *Wanderarbeiter*. They are second or third generation British citizens.

Pupils who have recently arrived in the UK may be exempted for only 6 months from the National Curriculum, but the DES (Circular 15/89) expects such exemptions to be very rare. Even if exempted, they are still entitled to a 'broad and balanced' curriculum: i.e. there are no explicit language recommendations even here (that they should receive special English language teaching help, for example). Otherwise, bilingual children are subject to the same programmes of study and attainment targets as any other pupils. This might seem on the face of it, like equality of treatment. But again, the point is that there are no general principles for language education, only specific programmes of study which pupils have to follow. The *ad hoc* language planning is hidden. Furthermore, bilingual children do not anywhere get credit for their knowledge of two (or more) languages.

The Kingman Report (p. 58, para. 17) dismisses bilingual children in a single paragraph, saying simply that the Report is concerned with English as L1, and that English as L2 is outside their terms of reference. This is an extremely weak argument, and arguably quite false. The Committee's terms of reference asked them to advise on a model of the English language which could inform 'all aspects of English teaching', but the committee narrowed its own terms of reference quite sharply.

The Cox Committee, in contrast, was given much more sharply defined guidance by the Secretary of State, and contested it by trying to find a better formulation. However, the formulations which it did find stand only as an assertion of principle, with no financial backing or legislative force. They amount only to recommendations that other languages should be valued and respected.

In a statement (in the Notes of further guidance to the Chair of the Committee) the Secretary of State said this, in an extraordinary paragraph on equal opportunities:

> The group should take account of the ethnic diversity of the school populations and society at large, bearing in mind the cardinal point that English should be the first language and medium of instruction for all pupils in England.

In this unprecedentedly explicit statement, English is given priority, and the assumption appears to be that bilingual education is ruled out in Britain: only English-medium education is assumed (except for bilingual schools in Wales). Furthermore, the assumption appears to be that English should become (?) the 'first language' of children themselves: the monolingual assumptions underlying this statement are quite extraordinary. Language loss appears to be recommended. Given that the paragraph is about 'equal opportunities', it is just double speak.

The statement is contested in the Cox Report itself, but only weakly. The Report points out that English is not the first language of all children. But it admits that English is the 'first language' of the education system. Overall, the rhetoric is one of rights and entitlements. It appears tolerance- and promotion-oriented: and some of the minority languages are explicitly listed in the schedules. But there is no actual promotion or financial support. Such languages may be a subject on the curriculum, but not a language of instruction. There is no explicit right even to use such languages in education (or any other institution). There is only weakly supported co-existence in very narrow domains.

Assimilationist Assumptions

Researchers (e.g. LMP, 1985) have struggled to have linguistic diversity accepted as the norm on a continuum from dialects of English to languages other than English. And some of these ways of talking have been picked up in government reports. The overt rhetoric is often of ethnic diversity and multiculturalism, but always held in check by ethnocentric and assimilationist assumptions.

Schools have always been the most powerful mechanism in assimilating minority children into mainstream cultures Skutnabb-Kangas & Phillipson (1989) discuss the symbolic violence involved in a shift from physical to psychological control over groups of people. This is a new and more sophisticated control, which recognises ethnic diversity, but confines it to the home, which pays lip service to multilingualism, but is empty liberal rhetoric. They argue that declarations of language rights must be explicit. Even overt permission does not protect languages: compare the lack of effect of the Welsh Language Act cited above. Languages are oppressed, not by active opposition, but by lack of resources (also Phillipson, 1989).

There are no social justice arguments used in favour of minority languages. There is no thought of whose interests are served, or of what policy for language provision would be formulated by a speaker of one of the minority languages, from the point of view of the bilingual him or herself. (See Rawls, 1972.)

There is an unstated premise: that the situation of the monolingual majority should be altered as little as possible. Language planning (such as it is) avoids any challenge to the practice of the currently privileged. The policies operate systematically and consistently to the advantage of speakers of Standard English. But this is nowhere stated: this is the advantage of *not* having a language policy. Implicit ideologies are used to legitimate unequal resources. The discourse of multiculturalism excludes questions of social, economic and political power.

In a swingeing attack on such situations in different countries, Skutnabb-Kangas & Phillipson (1989) talk of the implicit paranoia ideology of a country which is monolingual in an international language. Multilingualism is thought to be inevitably negative, and one widely held, but seldom explicitly expressed, myth or assumption, is that 'many languages divide a nation' (Skutnabb-Kangas & Phillipson, 1989: 55). There is an implicit assumption that societal monolingualism is the norm and that language diversity means conflict. Behind the rhetoric, *bilingual* is often a euphemism for 'Black' and 'poor'.

Educational statements often refer to societal multilingualism as a fact. For example, the Secretary of State's notes of guidance to the Cox Committee refer to:

> the ethnic diversity of the school population and society at large.

But they tend not to refer to individual bilingualism as a goal. In the present context, this goal is formulated only with reference to Welsh in Wales.

Knowledge About Language

One bright spot on the horizon is the explicit requirement that language study itself, or language awareness, become an explicit part of English teaching. A prerequisite of successful foreign language learning is a positive attitude towards multilingualism. The monolingual ideology must be contested if the aim is to be a more linguistically aware nation.

Widdowson (1989) discusses Britain as a profoundly monolingual nation which has no concept of multilingualism as an asset. The pervasive attitude is of cultural and linguistic self-sufficiency, and of a contempt of anything foreign which does not contribute to material well-being. As an example of ethnocentric complacency and prejudice, he quotes an article in *The Sun* with the headline *Di foxed by Frog Lingo*. The article reported Princess Diana sympathising with children at the British school in Paris because of their difficulties in learning French: i.e. the language of the country they were living in . . . This was reported with indulgent tolerance and approval. Widdowson makes the point that simply putting an obligatory language in the National Curriculum will not magically improve the image of modern languages: it might just provoke mass disaffection. (Esarte-Sarries, 1989 reports research on primary age children's stereotypes of France and the French: onion sellers in stripey shirts. At the end of a depressing article, she makes the point that 'the continuation of negative attitudes amongst secondary boys was disquieting'.)

Along with supporting chapters on Standard English and Linguistic Terminology, the Cox Report has a complete chapter on knowledge about language. This will become an obligatory part of programmes of study in Speaking and Listening, Writing and Reading from ages 11 to 16, covering forms of language, language variation and language in social institutions.

A major problem, however, will be teachers' own lack of knowledge and confidence in this area. The Bullock, Kingman and Cox Reports all point out that almost 30 per cent of teachers of English as a mother tongue have no qualifications in English past their own schooling, and that such teachers are responsible for about 15 per cent of all English teaching. Bourne (1989b) points out that many teachers of English as a second language have come from other subjects, and are not much better qualified. And Kingman and Cox both point to the huge teacher training programme which is necessary if teachers themselves are to know enough about language to teach about it coherently. A £15 million training programme is now underway: possibly a drop in the ocean of prejudice and stereotypes, but at least a start. Even this programme is being developed by and for English teachers themselves. Modern language and community language teachers are certainly not systematically involved. Again, there is monolingual vision.

Conclusions

Language planning is, by definition, interventionist, goal-oriented, and institutional. It ought to be explicit and, ideally, systematic (Christian, 1988:

197). The British government now has a highly interventionist policy in the state education system: but the nature of their intervention in language planning is not explicit, even if it is conscious and deliberate. It is goal-oriented, but its goals are often unclear. It is pervasive, but it is neither systematic nor rational. It is not based on an careful analysis of the range of relevant factors and of the desired outcomes. The alternatives are not clearly laid out: there are, for example, no genuine consultations between central government, local authorities and smaller groups with different language interests. And I see little possibility of the present British government, in the current political climate, setting up the national language commission which would be necessary to move beyond the *ad hoc,* uncoordinated and disguised language planning which is taking place.

Nevertheless, ideologies are never static. Hegemonies are constantly adjusted and renegotiated. Although little is likely to change in the profoundly monolingual assumptions in Britain, the ways in which the linguistic domination is maintained have changed rapidly and significantly. These mechanisms therefore require analysis, to discover where they might be challenged.

Rational argument is clearly not enough on its own. Linguists have been exposing linguistic myths for years, with some genuine effects, but only in restricted domains, such as initial teacher training. What is required may include a range of small-scale strategies and publicity campaigns aimed at changing people's attitudes. Over time, modest changes in the image of other languages might affect people's assumptions about languages and their speakers. For example, British television is gradually using more subtitles in place of voice-overs when speakers of languages other than English are broadcast. In this small way, other languages gain a higher profile in a natural way, people get used to hearing them, and sometimes understanding them, if only a little. Such initiatives should be encouraged. In addition, languages need institutional support: for example, university chairs in minority languages are a concrete sign that they are valued in British society. British academics, as a whole, have done little to encourage such developments, or even to prevent cuts in the few such chairs which have existed.

Concessions have been made, in British law, to Welsh in Wales, and this could support movements for change elsewhere, if alliances could be forged. The ideology of multilingualism is strong at local levels, where approaches to language diversity are unavoidable, but it is hampered by lack of central resourcing. Relations with the European Community have had some effect: witness the schedules of languages in the National Curriculum. The British government has previously used the decentralized education system as an excuse for not acting (e.g. on the EC Directive on the education of the children of migrant workers), but with a highly centralized system, it no longer has this excuse.

When the possibilities for rational and systematic planning are so restricted, then perhaps small, *ad hoc* strategies are the best hope. In general, more linguists should be encouraged to get involved with the policy making and to influence decisions where they are made.

Summary

This article has discussed the failure of current British government policies to address the dilemma of pluralism: how can a country both sustain cultural differences and also promote national unity? (Widdowson, 1989). The symbolic functions of language as both a separatist and a unifying force are evident from the media hype and hysteria which accompanied the publication of the Kingman and Cox Reports (Stubbs, 1989). But there is no planning for the possible co-existence of the lower order bonds of community and of the higher order bonds of national unity: no discussion of pluralist Gemeinschaft and national Gesellschaft (Fishman, 1981).

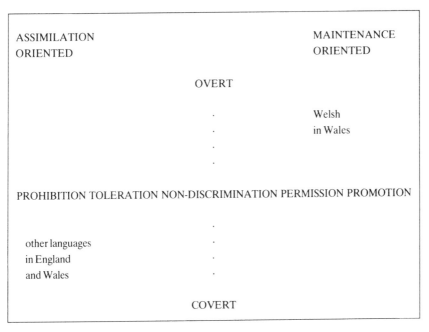

Figure 1 After Skutnabb-Kangas & Phillipson, 1989

A great deal of language policy is currently being formulated in England and Wales, but, due to a lack of an explicit general statement, and the (deliberate?) fragmentation of the consultation process, it is difficult to see its implications. The present article is a very partial study of some of the mechanisms which legitimate the dominance of one language over others. The partial nature of the analysis is partly due to the very speed at which the legislative changes are taking place in the British education system.

Skutnabb-Kangas & Phillipson (1989) have provided a way of charting the positions on language rights adopted in different countries. For example, Phillipson (1988) points out that discrimination against languages may be *overt* (e.g. a language may be prohibited in schools), or *covert* (e.g. certain languages are simply not used in schools or teacher training), or *conscious* (e.g. teachers tell their pupils not to use their home languages in case this interferes with their learning of another language), or *unconscious* (e.g. English is just assumed to be the 'natural' language for education or whatever). They also provide a way of mapping the positions adopted by different countries in their language planning provisions: Figure 1 provides a brief summary of my argument.

Acknowledgements

I have learned a great deal about the topics discussed here from Jill Bourne, both from her published work and from her detailed critical comments on an earlier draft of this paper. I have also drawn on papers by Ben Rampton and Ros Mitchell submitted as evidence to the DES on language issues. I am grateful to Gabi Keck, Robert Phillipson and Tove Skutnabb-Kangas for critical comments on an earlier draft. Many points made in discussions at the conference in Bad Homburg have also been integrated into the argument.

Notes

1. The term *language planning* is used explicitly by Peter Gannon, HMI, Secretary of the Kingman Committee (Gannon, 1988).
2. I will use the term *English mother tongue* in places in this article. But the term is misleading, since many English teachers teach children who have mother tongues other than English.
3. I was a member of the Cox Committee.

References

Bhatt, A. and Martin-Jones, M. (1989) Bilingualism, inequality and the language curriculum. Paper read at British Association for Applied Linguistics Annual Meeting, University of Lancaster, September 1989.

Bourne, J. (1989a) The teaching of languages in the English school system. Paper read to European Colloquium on Language Planning Policies in a Context of Cultural Pluralism, Brussels, May 1989.

— (1989b) *Moving into the Mainstream: LEA Provision for Bilingual Pupils.* London: NFER-Nelson.

Bourne, J. and Bloor, T. (eds) (1989) *Kingman and the Linguists.* Committee for Linguistics in Education (Mimeo).

Cameron D. and Bourne, J. (1989) Grammar, nation and citizenship: Kingman in linguistic and historical perspective. *Language and Education* 2, 3, 147–60.

CDE (Commonwealth Dept of Education) (1982) *Towards a National Language Policy.* Canberra.

Christian, D. (1988) Language planning: The view from linguistics. In F. J. Newmeyer (ed.) *Language: The Socio-Cultural Context.* Cambridge: Cambridge University Press.

Clyne, M. (1988) Australia's national policy on languages and its implications. *Journal of Educational Policy* 3, 3, 273–80.

Coulnas, F. (ed.) (1991) *A Language Policy for the European Community: Prospects and Quandaries.* Berlin/New York: Mouton de Gruyter.

DES (Dept of Education and Science) (1971) *The Education of Immigrants.* Education Survey 13. London: HMSO.

— (1975) *A Language for Life* (Bullock Report). London: HMSO.

— (1981) *Directive of the Council of the European Community on the Education of the Children of Migrant Workers.* Circular 5/18. London: DES.

— (1985) *Education For All* (Swann Report). London: HMSO.

— (1988) *Report of the Committee of Inquiry into the Teaching of English Language* (Kingman Report). London: HMSO.

— (1989) *English for Ages 5 to 16* (Cox Report). London: DES and Welsh Office.

— (1989b) *The Education (National Curriculum) (Modern Foreign Languages) Order 1989.* Statutory Instruments, 825. London: HMSO.

— (1990) *National Curriculum Modern Foreign Languages Working Group. Initial Advice.* London: DES and Welsh Office.

European Community (1977) *Council Directive on the Education of the Children of Migrant Workers.* 77/486/EEC. Brussels: EC.

Esarte-Sarries, V. (1989) 'Onions and stripey tee-shirts' or how do primary pupils learn about France? *British Journal of Language Teaching* 27, 2, 65–71.

Fishman, J. (1981) Language policy: Past, present and future. In C. A. Ferguson and S. Brice Heath (eds) *Language in the USA.* Cambridge: Cambridge University Press.

Gannon, P. (1988) Kingman: Setting the scene. In E. Ashworth and L. Masterman (eds) *Responding to Kingman.* University of Nottingham (Mimeo).

Lawlor, S. (1988) *Correct Core.* London: Centre for Policy Studies.

Leith, D. (1989) *Three Criticisms.* In Bourne and Bloor (eds).

Letwin, O. (1988) *Aims of Schooling.* London: Centre for Policy Studies.

LMP (Linguistic Minorities Project) (1985) *The Other Languages of England.* London: Routledge & Kegan Paul.

Marenbon, J. (1987) *English Our English.* London: Centre for Policy Studies.

Phillipson, R. (1988) Linguicism: Structures and ideologies in linguistic imperialism. In Skutnabb-Kangas and Cummins (eds).

— (1989) Human rights and the delegitimation of dominant languages. Paper presented at Fourth International Conference on Minority Languages, Ljouwert/Leeuwarden, June 1989.

Printon, V. (ed.) (1986) *Facts and Figures: Languages in Education.* London: Centre for Information on Language Teaching and Research.

Rampton, B. (1989) Almost passionate in its advocacy: Kingman on entitlement. In Bourne and Bloor (eds.)

Rawls, J. (1972) *A Theory of Justice.* Oxford: Oxford University Press.

Skutnabb-Kangas, T. (1989) Legitimating or delegitimating new forms of racism: The role of researchers. Paper presented at Fourth International Conference on Minority Languages, Ljouwert/Leeuwarden, June 1989.

Skutnabb-Kangas, T. and Cummins, J. (eds) (1988) *Minority Education: From Shame to Struggle*. Avon: Multilingual Matters.

Skutnabb-Kangas, T. and Phillipson, R. (1989) *Wanted! Linguistic Human Rights*. *Rolig-Papir* 44. University of Roskilde (Mimeo).

Stubbs, M. (1989) The state of English in the English state: Reflections on the Cox Report. *Language and Education* 3, 4, 235–50.

Tosi, A. (1988) The jewel in the crown of the modern prince. In Skutnabb-Kangas and Cummins (eds).

Trim, J. L. M. (1989) Language teaching in the perspective of the predictable requirements of the Twenty-First century. Prepared for AILA for submission to UNESCO.

Verma, G. (ed.) (1989) *Education for All: A Landmark in Pluralism*. London: Falmer.

Widdowson, H. G. (1989) Language in the National Curriculum (Unpublished lecture). Institute of Education: University of London.

Williams, R. (1965) *The Long Revolution*. Harmondsworth: Penguin.

13 The Beginnings of English Literary Study in British India[1]

GAURI VISWANATHAN

This paper is part of a larger inquiry into the construction of English literacy education as a cultural ideal in British India. British parliamentary documents have provided competing evidence for the central thesis of the investigation: that humanistic functions traditionally associated with the study of literature — for example, the shaping of character or the development of the esthetic sense or the disciplines of ethical thinking — are also essential to the process of sociopolitical control. My argument is that literary study gained enormous cultural strength through its development in a period of territorial expansion and conquest, and that the subsequent institutionalization of the discipline in England itself took on a shape and an ideological content developed in the colonial context.

In what follows, I propose to outline the preliminary stages of the historical process by which literature was made serviceable to British political interests — a process, I may add, that is replete with numerous ironies, contradictions, and anomalies. I have titled my essay 'The Beginnings of English' rather than, say 'The Rise of English' or 'The Growth of English' to emphasize two things: first, my interest is in seeking out the historical moment at which English literature as a subject for study made its appearance in India, a moment that can be identified as a 'beginning' which, in Edward Said's formulation, 'includes everything that develops out of it, no matter how eccentric the development or inconsistent the result';[2] and second, my method of doing so is by describing the historical conditions which enabled that appearance in the first place, indeed even necessitated it.

English literature came into India, howsoever inperceptibly, with the passing of the Charter Act of 1813. This act, which renewed the East India Company's charter for commercial operations in India, produced two major changes in Britain's role with respect to its Indian subjects: one was the assumption of a new responsibility towards native education, and the other was a relaxation of controls over missionary work in India.

The pressure to assume a more direct responsibility for the welfare of the natives came from several sources. The earlier and perhaps more significant one, decisively affecting the future course of British administrative rule in India, was the English Parliament. Significantly, the goal of civilizing the natives was far from being the central motivation in these first official efforts at educational activity. Parliamentary involvement with Indian education had a rather uncommon origin in that it began with the excesses of their own countrymen in India. The extravagant and demoralized life-styles of the East India Company servants, combined with their ruthless exploitation of native material resources, had begun to raise serious and alarming questions in England about the morality of British presence in India. It was an issue that was too embarrassing for Parliament to ignore without appearing to endorse Company excesses. But unable to check the activities of these highly placed 'Nabobs', or wealthy Europeans whose huge fortunes were amassed in India, it sought instead to remedy the wrongs committed against the natives by attending to their welfare and improvement.

Yet however much parliamentary discussions of the British presence in India may have been couched in moral terms, there was no obscuring the real issue, which remained political not moral. The English Parliament's conflict with the East India Company was a long-standing one, going back to the early years of trading activity in the East Indies when rival companies clashed repeatedly in a bid to gain exclusive rights to trade in the region. Besides, the English Parliament was becoming alarmed by the danger of having a commercial company constituting an independent political power in India. By 1757 the East India Company had already become virtual master of Bengal, and its territorial influence was growing steadily despite numerous financial problems besetting it. But in the absence of any cause for interference in the activities of the Company, the British Crown could conceivably do little to reorganize the Company's system of administration and win control of its affairs. Not until the last quarter of the eighteenth century, when reports of immorality and depravity among Company servants started pouring in, did Parliament find an excuse to intervene, at which point, in the name of undertaking responsibility for the improvement of the natives, it began to take a serious and active interest in Indian political affairs. It was a move that was to result in a gradual erosion of the unchallenged supremacy of the Company in India.

One cannot fail to be struck by the peculiar irony of a history in which England's initial involvement with the education of the natives derived not from a conviction of native immorality as the later discourse might lead one to believe, but from the depravity of their own administrators and merchants. In Edmund Burke's words, steps had to be taken to 'form a strong and solid security for the natives against the wrongs and oppressions of British subjects resident in Bengal'.[3] While the protectiveness contained in this remark may seem dangerously close to an attitude of paternalism, its immediate effect was beneficial, as it led to a strengthening of existing native institutions and traditions to act as a bulwark against the forces of violent change unleashed by the British presence.

This mission to revitalize Indian culture and learning and protect it from the oblivion to which foreign rule might doom it merged with the then current literary vogue of 'Orientalism' and formed the mainstay of that phase of British rule in India known as the 'Orientalist' phase. Orientalism was adopted as an official policy partly out of expediency and caution and partly out of an emergent political sense that an efficient Indian administration rested on an understanding of Indian culture. It grew out of the concern of Warren Hastings, governor-general from 1774 to 1785, that British administrators and merchants in India were not sufficiently responsive to Indian languages and Indian traditions. The distance between ruler and ruled was perceived to be so vast as to evoke the sentiment that 'we rule over them and traffic with them, but they do not understand our character, and we do not penetrate theirs. The consequence is that we have no hold on their sympathies, no seat in their affections'.[4] Hastings' own administration was distinguished by a tolerance for the native customs and by a cultural empathy unusual for its time. Underlying Orientalism was a tacit policy of reverse acculturation, whose goal was to train British administrators and civil servants to fit into the culture of the ruled and to assimilate them thoroughly into the native way of life.

Opposing Orientalism was the countermovement of Anglicism, which gained ascendancy in the 1830s. Briefly, Anglicism grew as an expression of discontent with the policy of promoting the Oriental languages and literatures in native education. In its vigorous advocacy of Western instead of Eastern learning, it came into sharp conflict with the proponents of Orientalism, who vehemently insisted that such a move would have disastrous consequences, the most serious being the alienation of Indians from British rule. To understand the forces enabling the shift from Orientalism to Anglicism, it is necessary to distinguish the various political and commercial groups entering the Indian scene. Warren Hastings was succeeded in the governor-generalship by Lord Cornwallis (1786–1793), who found himself at the helm of a government seriously compromised by financial scandals and deteriorating standards. For this state of affairs the new governor-general squarely laid the blame on the earlier policy of accommodation to the native culture. In his view the official indulgence towards Oriental forms of social organization, especially government, was directly responsible for the lax morals of the Company servants. If the Company had sorely abused its power, what better explanation was there than the fact that the model of Oriental despotism was constantly before their eyes? To Cornwallis, the abuse of power was the most serious of evils afflicting the East India Company, not only jeopardizing the British hold over India, but worse still, dividing the English nation on the legitimacy of the colonial enterprise.

The most pressing task therefore was to ensure that no further abuse would occur. In the process of working towards this end, Cornwallis evolved a political philosophy that he believed would be consistent with British commercial aims. His theoretical position was that a good government was held together not by men but by political principles and laws, and in these alone rested absolute power. Dismissing the Oriental system as deficient in a strong political tradition (and in this belief Cornwallis was doing no more than echoing a view that was common currency), he turned to English principles of government and jurisprudence for setting the norms of public behavior and responsibility by which administrators were to function. Determined to run a government that would remain free of corrupting influences from the native society, Cornwallis concentrated his entire energies on the improvement of European morals on English lines. The natives engaged his attention only minimally; for the most part, he appeared wholly content to leave them in their 'base' state in the belief that their reform was well beyond his purview.

Clearly, the first steps towards anglicization wereaimed at tackling the problem of corruption within the ranks. To this extent, Anglicism began as an entirely defensive movement. But even in this form it was not without elements of aggression towards the native culture, as is apparent in certain measures that Cornwallis adopted to streamline the government. Convinced that contact with natives was the root cause of declining European morals, he resolved to exclude all natives from appointment to responsible posts, hoping by this means to restore the Englishman to his pristine self and rid him once and for all of decadent influences. Predictably, the exclusion of Indians from public office had serious repercussions on Anglo-Indian relations. The personal contact that Englishmen and Indians had enjoyed during Hastings' administration vanished with Cornwallis, and the result was that a more rigidified master-subject relationship set in. One historian, Percival Spear, has gone so far as to suggest that this event marks the point at which there developed 'that contempt for things and persons Indian . . . and which produced the views of a Mill or a Macaulay'.[5]

With Cornwallis charting an apparently serious course for administrative rule on English principles, one would expect Anglicism as a cultural movement to have triumphed much earlier than it actually did (i.e. the 1830s). Its momentum was badly shattered, however, by the cultural policy of his immediate successors, a group of skilled and politically astute administrators who had all at one time served under Lord Wellesley, a governor-general (1798–1805) noted for his caution and reserve, and later under the Marquess of Hastings under whose governor-generalship (1812–23) British rule was more firmly consolidated. Conservative in their outlook and fiercely Romantic in their disposition, these accomplished officers — John Malcolm, Thomas Munro, Charles Metcalf, and Mountstuart Elphinstone — had no use for the impersonal bureacratic system of government carved out for India by Cornwallis. While Cornwallis had no particular interest in either promoting or discouraging Oriental learning, as long as Englishmen were not compelled to go through its studies, his successors by no means shared his indifference. Indeed, they were shrewd enough to see that it was entirely in their interest to support Orientalism if it meant the preservation of the feudal character of British rule. At the same time they were too conscious of England's by then strengthened position in India to resort to the promotion of native culture as a purely defensive measure. Rather, Orientalism represented for them the logical corollary of a precise and meticulously defined scheme of administration. In that scheme, the British government was to function as a paternal protectorate governing India not by direct rule (that is, through the force of British law) but through various local functionaries. In other words, the Cornwallis system of centralized administration was spurned in favor of one which was more diffuse, and operated through a network of hierarchical relationships between British officers at one level and between the British and the Indians on another. Now in order to draw the Indians into this hegemonic structure, it was imperative for the British administration to maintain an alliance with those who formed the traditional ruling class. This was essential partly to conciliate the indigenous elite for their displaced status but partly also to secure a buffer zone for absorbing the effects of foreign rule, which, if experienced directly by the masses, might have an entirely disastrous impact.

This scheme of administration was at once more personal and more rigidly stratified in its conception. It was further bolstered by the philosophy that no political tradition could be created anew or superimposed on another without a violent rejection of it by the preexisting society. For a new political society to emerge, it was argued that the native tradition and culture had to provide the soil for its growth. The imagery of grafting that permeated the discourse around this time pointed to an emerging theory of organicism that conceived of political formation as part of a process of cultural synthesis.[6]

This phase of British rule, roughly spanning the first two decades of the nineteenth century, acquires a special significance in this narrative for marking the historical moment when political philosophy and cultural policy converged to work towards clearly discernible common ends. The promotion of Orientalism no less than Anglicism became irrevocably tied from this point onwards to questions of administrative structure and governance: for example, how were Indian subjects to be imbued with a sense of public responsibility and honor, and by what means could the concept of a Western-style government best be impressed on their minds to facilitate the business of state?

Such questions also implied that, with the reversal of the Cornwallis policy of isolationism from Indian society and the hierarchical reordering of the Indian subjects for administrative purposes, the problem of reform was no longer confined to the British side but extended more actively to the Indian side as well. The more specialized functions devolving upon a government now settling down to prospective long-term rule brought the Indians as a body of subjects more directly into the conceptual management of the country than was the case in either Hastings' or Cornwallis' time. As a result, the 'Indian character' suddenly became a subject of immense importance, as was the question of how it could best be moulded to suit British administrative needs.

But curiously it was on this last point that Orientalism began to lose ground to Anglicism. For even though it appeared to be the most favorable cultural policy for a feudal-type administration, its theoretical premises were seriously undermined by the gathering tide of reform that accompanied the restructuring of government. It is well worth remembering that this was a government that had grown acutely aware of both its capacity for generating change (thus far internally) and its own vested authority over the natives. The Orientalist position was that a Western political tradition could be successfully grafted upon the native without having to direct itself towards the transformation of that society along Western lines. But as a theory it found itself at odds with the direction of internal consolidation along which British rule was moving. The strengthening of England's position in India, as exemplified by a recently coordinated and efficient administrative structure, put the rulers under less compulsion to direct change inward than to carry over the reformist impulse to those over whom they had dominion.

That tendency was reinforced by two outside developments. One was the opening of India to free trade in 1813, which resulted in the Private Trade and City interests steadily exerting stronger influence on the Crown at the expense of Indian interest. The 'Private Traders' had no tradition of familiarity with India behind them and were more prone to taking decisions that reflected their own biases and assumptions about what was good for their subjects than what the existing situation itself demanded.

A second and more important influence in the thrust towards reform was exerted by a group of missionaries called the Clapham Evangelicals, who played a key role in the drama of consolidation of British interests in India. Among them were Zachary Macaulay, William Wilberforce, Samuel Thornton, and Charles Grant, and to these men must be given much of the credit for supplying British expansionism with an ethics of concern for reform and conversion. Insisting that British domination was robbed of all justification if no efforts were made to reform native morals, the missionaries repeatedly petitioned Parliament to permit them to engage in the urgent business of enlightening the Indians. Unsuccessful with the earlier Act of 1793 that renewed the Company's charter for a twenty-year period, the missionaries were more triumphant by the time of the 1813 resolution, which brought about the other major event associated with the Charter Act: the opening of India to missionary activity.

Although chaplains had hitherto been appointed by the East India Company to serve the needs of the European population residing in India, the English Parliament had consistently refused to modify the Company charter to allow missionary work in India. The main reason for government resistance was an apprehension that the Indians would feel threatened and eventually cause trouble for England's commercial ventures. Insurrections around the country were invariably blamed on proselytizing activity in the area. The fear of further acts of hostility on religious grounds grew so great that it prompted a temporary suspension of the Christianizing mission. In keeping with the government policy of religious neutrality, the Bible was proscribed and scriptural teaching forbidden.

The opening of India to missionaries, along with the commitment of the British to native improvement, might appear to suggest a victory for the missionaries, encouraging them perhaps to anticipate official support for their Evangelizing mission. But if they had such hopes, they were to be dismayed by the continuing checks on their activities, which grew impossibly stringent. Publicly, the English Parliament demanded a guarantee that large-scale proselytizing would not be carried out in India. Privately, though, it needed little persuasion about the distinct advantages that would flow from missionary contact with the Indians and their 'many immoral and disgusting habits'.

Though representing a convergence of interests, these two events — of British involvement in Indian education and the entry of missionaries — were far from being complementary or mutually supportive. On the contrary, they were entirely opposed to each other both in principle and in fact. The inherent constraints operating on British educational policy are apparent in the central contradiction of a government committed to the improvement of the people while being restrained from imparting any direct instruction in the religious principles of the English nation. The encouragement of Oriental learning, seen initially as a way of fulfilling the ruler's obligations to the subjects, seemed to accentuate rather than diminish the contradiction. For as the British swiftly learned to their dismay, it was impossible to promote Orientalism without exposing the Hindus and Muslims to the religious and moral tenets of their respective faiths — a situation that was clearly not tenable with the stated goal of 'moral and intellectual improvement'.

This tension between increasing involvement in Indian education and enforced noninterference in religion was productively resolved through the introduction of English literature. Significantly, the direction to this solution was present in the Charter Act itself, which ambiguously stated that 'a sum of not less than one lac of rupees shall be annually applied to the revival and improvement of literature, and the encouragement of the learned natives of India'.[7] While the use of the word 'revival' may weight the interpretation on the side of Oriental literature, the almost deliberate imprecision suggests a more fluid government position in conflict with the official espousal of Orientalism. Over twenty years later Macaulay was to seize on this very ambiguity to argue that the phrase clearly meant Western literature, and denounced in no uncertain terms attempts to interpret the clause as a reference to Oriental literature:

> It is argued, or rather taken for granted, that by literature, the Parliament can have meant only Arabic and Sanskrit literature, that they never would have given the honourable appellation of a learned native to a native who was familiar with the poetry of Milton, the Metaphysics of Locke, the Physics of Newton; but that they meant to designate by that name only such persons as might have studied in the sacred books of the Hindoos all the uses of cusa-grass, and all the mysteries of absorption into the Deity.[8]

Macaulay's plea on behalf of English literature had a major influence on the passing of the English Education Act in 1835, which officially required the natives of India to submit to its study. But English was not an unknown entity in India at that time, for rudimentary instruction in the language had been introduced more than two decades earlier. Initially, English did not supersede Oriental studies but was taught alongside it. Yet it was clear that it enjoyed a different status, for there was a scrupulous attempt to establish separate colleges for its study. Even when it was taught within the same college, the English course of studies was kept separate from the course of Oriental study, and was attended by a different set of students. The rationale was that if the English department drew students who were attached only to its department and to no other (that is, the Persian or the Arabic or the Sanskrit), the language might then be taught 'classically' in much the same way that Latin and Greek were taught in England.

Though based on literary material, the early British Indian curriculum in English was primarily devoted to language studies. However, by the 1820s the atmosphere of secularism in which these studies were conducted became a major case for concern to the missionaries who were premitted to enter India after 1813. One missionary in India, Rev. William Keane, argued that while European education had done much to destroy 'heathen' superstition, it had not substituted any moral principle in its place. The exclusion of the Bible had a demoralizing effect, he claimed, for it tended to produce evils in the country and to give the native mind:

unity of opinion, which before it never had . . . and political thoughts, which they get out of our European books, but which it is impossible to reconcile with our position in that country, political thoughts of liberty and power, which would be good if they were only the result of a noble ambition of the natural mind for something superior, but which when they arise without religious principles, produce an effect which, to my mind, is one of unmixed evil.[9]

The missionaries got further support from an unexpected quarter. The military officers who testified in the parliamentary sessions on Indian education joined hands with them in arguing that a secular education in English would increase the natives' capacity for evil because it would elevate their intellects without providing the moral principles to keep them in check. Major-General Rowlandson of the British Army warned, 'I have seen native students who had obtained an insight into European literature and history, in whose minds there seemed to be engendered a spirit of disaffection towards the British Government'.[10] While obviously the missionaries and the military had different interests at stake, with the latter perhaps not quite as interested in the souls of the heathen as the former, they were both clearly aiming at the same goal: the prevention of situations leading to political disunity or lawlessness. The alliance between the two undoubtedly proved fruitful insofar as it loosened the British resistance to the idea of religious instruction for the natives and made them more conscious of the need to find alternate modes of social control.

In English social history the functions of providing authority for individual action and belief and of dispensing moral laws for the formation of character had traditionally been carried out through the medium of church-controlled educational institutions. The aristocracy maintained a monopoly over access to church-dominated education and instituted a classical course of studies that it shared with the clergy, but from which the middle and working classes were systematically excluded. The classical curriculum under church patronage in England became indentified as a prerequisite for social leadership and, more subtly, as the means by which social privilege was protected. This alliance between church and culture consecrated the concept of station in life and directly supported the existing system of social stratification: while the classical curriculum served to confirm the upper orders in their superior social status, religious instruction was given to the lower orders to fit them for the various duties of life and to secure them in their appropriate station. The alliance between church and culture was thus equally an alliance between ideas of formative education and of social control.

As late as the 1860s, the 'literary curriculum' in British educational establishments remained polarized around classical studies for the upper classes and religious studies for the lower. As for what is now known as the subject of English literature, the British educational system had no firm place for it until the last quarter of the nineteenth century, when the challenge posed by the middle classes resulted in the creation of alternative institutions devoted to 'modern' studies.

It is quite conceivable that educational development in British India may have run the same course as it did in England, were it not for one crucial difference: the strict controls on Christianizing activities. Clearly, the texts that were standard fare for the lower classes in England could not legitimately be incorporated into the Indian curriculum without inviting violent reactions from the native population, particularly the learned classes. And yet the fear lingered in the British mind that without submission of the individual to moral law or the authority of God, the control they were able to secure over the lower classes in their own country would elude them in India. Comparisons were on occasion made between the situation at home and in India, between the 'rescue' of the lower classes in England, 'those living in the dark recesses of our great cities at home, from the state of degradation consequent on their vicious and depraved habits, the offspring of ignorance and sensual indulgence', and the elevation of the Hindus and Muslims whose 'ignorance and degradation' required a remedy not adequately supplied by their respective faiths.[11] Such comparisons served to intensify the search for other social institutions to take over from religious instruction the function of communicating the laws of the social order.

Provoked by missionaries on the one hand and fears of native insubordination on the other, British administrators discovered an ally in English literature to support them in maintaining control of the natives under the guise of a liberal education. With both secularism and religion appearing as political liabilities, literature appeared to represent a perfect synthesis of these two opposing positions. The idea evolved in alternating stages of affirmation and disavowal of literature's derivation from and affiliation with Christianity as a social institution. What follows is a description of that process as reconstructed from the minutes of evidence given before the British Parliament's Select Committee, and recorded in the 1852–53 volume of the *Parliamentary Papers*. These proceedings reveal not only an open assertion of British material interests but also a mapping out of strategies for promoting those interests through representations of Western literary knowledge as objective, universal, and rational.

The first stage in the process was an assertion of structural congruence between Christianity and English literature. Missionaries had long argued on behalf of the shared history of religion and literature, of a tradition of belief and doctrine creating a common culture of values, attitudes, and norms. They had ably cleared the way for the realization that as the 'grand repository of the book of God' England had produced a literature that was immediately marked off from all non-European literatures, being 'animated, vivified, hallowed, and baptized' by a religion to which Western man owed his material and moral progress. The difference was rendered as a contrast between:

> the literature of a world embalmed with the Spirit of Him who died to redeem it, and that which is the growth of ages that have gloomily rolled on in the rejection of that Spirit, as between the sweet bloom of creation in the open light of heaven, and the rough, dark recesses of submarine forests of sponges.[12]

This other literature was likened to Plato's cave, whose darkened inhabitants were 'chained men . . . counting the shadows of subterranean fires'.

If not in quite the same eloquent terms, some missionaries tried to point out to the government that though they pretended to say they taught no Christianity, they actually taught a great deal, for it was virtually impossible to take Christianity out of an English education, and much more of scriptual teaching was imparted than was generally admitted. The Rev. W. Keane tried to persuade officials that:

> Shakespeare, though by no means a good standard, is full of religion; it is full of the common sense principles which none but Christian men can recognize. Sound Protestant Bible principles, though not actually told in words, are there set out to advantage, and the opposite often condemned. So with Goldsmith, Abercrombie on the Mental Powers, and many other books which are taught in the schools; though the natives hear they are not to be proselytized, yet such books have undoubtedly sometimes a favourable effect in actually bringing them to us missionaries.[13]

The missionary description was appropriated in its entirety by government officers. But while the missionaries made such claims in order to force the government to sponsor teaching of the Bible, the administrators used the same argument to prove English literature made such direct instruction redundant. Several steps were initiated to incorporate selected English literary texts into the Indian curriculum on the claim that these works were supported in their morality by a body of evidence that also upheld the Christian faith. In their official capacity as members of the Council on Education, Macaulay and his brother-in-law Charles Trevelyan were among those engaged in a minute analysis of English texts to prove what they called the 'diffusive benevolence of Christianity' in them. The process of curricular selection was marked by weighty pronouncements on the 'sound Protestant Bible principles' in Shakespeare, the 'strain of serious piety' in Addison's *Spectator* papers, the 'scriptural morality' of Bacon and Locke, the 'devout sentiment' of Abercrombie, the 'noble Christian sentiments' in Adam Smith's *Moral Sentiments* (which was hailed as the 'best authority for the true science of morals which English literature could supply').[14] The cataloguing of shared features had the effect of convincing detractors that the government could effectively cause voluntary reading of the Bible and at the same time disclaim any intentions of proselytizing.

But while these identifications were occurring at one level, at another level the asserted unity of religion and literature were simultaneously disavowed, as evidenced in a series of contradictory statements. The most directly conflicting of these maintained, on the one hand, that English literature is 'imbued with the spirit of Christianity' and 'interwoven with the words of the Bible to a great degree' so that 'without ever looking into the Bible one of those natives must come to a considerable knowledge of it merely from reading English literature'.[15] But in the same breath a counterclaim was made that English literature 'is not interwoven to the same extent with the Christian religion as the Hindoo religion is with the Sanskrit language and literature'.[16] Charles Cameron, who succeeded Macaulay as President of the Council on Education, attempted to provide an illustration for the latter position by arguing that though Milton assumed the truth of Christianity, his works did not bear the same relation to the doctrines of Christianity as did Oriental literature to the tenets of the native religious systems. But when pressed by his examiners to explain the point further, he refused to elaborate, admitting only 'a difference in degree'.[17]

It is certainly possible to interpret the contradiction as an unimportant and inconsequential instance of British ambivalence or inconsistency of policy. But to do so is to ignore a subtle but palpable shift in emphasis from the centrality of universal Christian truths to the legitimacy and value of British authority. Mediating this shift was a relativization of the notion of truth, producing a heightened emphasis upon the intellectual motive in literary instruction. The difference that Cameron hesitated to specify had long before been named by several missionaries when they termed Western literature a form of intellectual production, in contrast to Oriental literature which, they claimed, set itself up as a source of divine authority. The Serampore Baptist missionary William Carey best expressed the missionary viewpoint when he lamented, in comparing the Hindu epic the *Mahabharata* to Homer, that '[were] it, like his Iliad, only considered as a great effort of human genius, I should think it is one of the first productions in the world, but alas! it is the ground of Faith to Millions of men; and as such must be held in the utmost abhorrence'.[18]

The distinction served to emphasize the arbitrariness of the Oriental conception of truth, which derived its claims from the power of the explicator (that is, the maulvis and the pundits, the class learned in Arabic and

Sanskrit) to mediate between the popular mind and sacred knowledge. From the viewpoint of a government seeking entry into the native system, the distinction had a powerful political appeal, for it proposed an idea that turned into an effective political strategy: If the native learned classes had arrogated all power to decipher texts unto themselves by blurring the lines between literature and religion, an erosion of that power base was bound to ensue, so the reasoning went, if the authority vested in the explicator were relocated elsewhere — that is, if authority were reinvested in a body of texts presented as objective, scientific, rational, empirically verifiable truth, the product not of an exclusive social or political class but of a consciousness that spoke in a universal voice and for the universal good.

The Protestant Reformation provided an historical model for the reloca- tion of authority in the body of knowledge represented by English literary texts. In its deliberations on the curriculum the Council on Indian Education seized on the analogy between the British presence in India and the Reforma- tion in Europe to make two related arguments, which are here summarized from the reports issued from 1840 to 1853: One, the characterization of English literature as intellectual production suggested a different process of reading, requiring the exercise of reason rather than unquestioning faith. The history of the 'despotic Orient' was adequate proof from the British viewpoint that a literature claiming to provide divine revelation diluted the capacity of the individual mind to resist the manipulations of a priestly caste. By the terms of this argument, not only did Oriental literature lull the indi- vidual into a passive acceptance of the fabulous incidents as actual occurr- ences; more alarmingly, the acceptance of mythological events as factual description stymied the mind's capacity to extrapolate a range of meanings for analysis and verification in the real world. The logic of associating reason with an approach to literary texts as types of human activity was a simple one: The products of human consciousness must submit to interpretation because their creating subject is man not God, man in all his imperfection and fallibility. Because interpretation by definition entails a plurality of response, the receiving mind is pressured all the more to weight the truth- value of each possibility, thereby activating rational processes of discrimina- tion and judgment — intellectual skills unanimously held to be utterly alien to a literature conceived as divine agency.

Two, as an example of human invention drawing its material from a rationally perceived world, English literature disciplined the mind to think and reason from the force of evidence. The Cartesian influence is especially strong in this description, particularly in the argument that the element of doubt attending upon the senses sets the mind in a state of intellectual fer- ment, forcing it to do battle with error until a full knowledge of the truth is reached. Since an individually realized truth would have proceeded through the stages of rational investigation — of detached observation, analysis, verification, and application — its claims to universal, objective knowledge were unquestionably greater, it was concluded, than the claims to truth of received tradition.

Given the elaborate manner in which English literature was set up as the highest example of empirical reasoning, its transformation into scientific, rational, and objective truth was all but a *fait accompli*. The Scottish missionary Alexander Duff, for example, had no difficultly in defining the literature of England as a group of texts that supplied a complete course of knowledge free of error in every branch of inquiry, literary, scientific, and theological. By contrast, the literature of India, he claimed, could not produce 'a single volume on any one subject that is not studded with error, far less a series of volumes that would furnish anything bearing the most distant resemblance to a complete range of information in any conceivable department of useful knowledge'.[19] The force of his argument lay in offering a definition of literature that linked it with the production of scientific knowledge and the material improvement of the material conditions of mankind. By the same token, the definition dismissed the notion of literature as the transmission and perpetuation of cultural tradition, the argument by which the learned classes had retained their hold over the native population.

But having said this, Duff raised by implication a perplexing, more complicated set of questions: to what extent would the earlier identification of English literature with Christianity cause problems for the promotion of identification with science? Was it possible to have a sustained unity of the moral and the intellectual imperatives given the constraints placed upon evolving a coherent educational policy for British India? Or were the claims of religion and science — the former urging devotion to the articles of faith laid down by the established church and the latter to a secular, nonpartisan conception of knowledge — so irreconcilable that only the temporary suspension of the one would permit the practical realization of the other?

Charles Cameron's reticence may take on more meaning in the context of this imperative, for his unspoken assumption was that the distinctiveness of English literature lay in its double stance towards reason and faith, utility and tradition, empiricism and revelation — a stance obscuring its affiliations with institutional religion (and the entire system of social and political formation of which it was a part) through its appeal to an objective, empirical reality. In other words, the political significance of English literature rested on its inclining one's thoughts towards religion while maintaining its secular nature. But to make explicit through instruction what was better off understood as an *implicit* relation was not only to undercut the operational value of this double stance: it was to lay open to native questioning the validity of the knowledge to be imparted. Native resistance to the truth of Christianity had always been a cause of immense frustration for missionaries, who often complained that they had to adopt a different, more demanding style of instruction in India. The Serampore missionary William Carey, for instance dejectedly wrote that the rhetorical fervour of his lessons was often wasted on an audience that demanded proofs and demonstrations in its place. The government was more shrewd in assessing the source of the difficulty, and sensed that the natives resisted missionary claims not merely because they conflicted with perceptions derived from their own religions, but because the intention of conversion so overlay the content of instruction as to render its truth-value immaterial.

To disperse intention, and by extension authority in related fields of knowledge and inquiry proposed itself as the best means of dissipating native resistance. As one government publication put it, 'If we lay it down as our rule to teach only what the natives are willing to make national, viz., what they will freely learn, we shall be able by degrees to teach them all we know ourselves, without any risk of offending their prejudices'.[20] One of the great lessons taught by Gramsci, which this quotation amply corroborates, is that cultural domination operates by consent, indeed often preceding conquest by force. 'The supremacy of a social group manifests itself in two ways', he writes in the *Prison Notebooks,* 'as "domination" and as "intellectual and moral leadership" . . . It seems clear . . . that there can, and indeed must be hegemonic activity even before the rise of power, and that one should not count only on the material force which power gives in order to exercise an effective leadership'.[21] He argues that consent of the governed is secured primarily through the moral and intellectual suasion, a strategy clearly spelled out by the British themselves: 'The Natives must either be kept down by a sense of our power, or they must willingly submit from a conviction that we are more wise, more just, more humane, and more anxious to improve their condition than any other rulers they could have'.[22]

Implicit in this strategy is a recognition of the importance of self-representation, an activity crucial to what the natives 'would freely learn'. The answer to this last question was obvious to at least one member of the Council on Education: the natives' greatest desire, averred C. E. Trevelyan, was to raise themselves to the level of moral and intellectual refinement of their masters; their most driving ambition, to acquire the intellectual skills that confirmed their rulers as lords of the earth. Already, he declared, the natives had an idea that 'we have gained everything by our superior knowledge; that it is this superiority which has enabled us to conquer India, and to keep it; and they want to put themselves as much as they can upon an equality with us'.[23] If the assumption was correct that individuals willingly learned whatever they believed provided them with the means of advancement in the world, a logical method of overwhelming opposition was to demonstrate that the achieved material position of the Englishman was derived from the knowledge contained in English literary, philosophical, and scientific texts, a knowledge accessible to any who chose to seek it.

In effect, the strategy of locating authority in these texts all but effaced the sordid history of colonialist expropriation, material exploitation, and class and race oppression behind European world dominance. Making the Englishman known to the natives through the products of his mental labour served a valuable purpose in that it removed him from the plane of ongoing colonist activity — of commercial operations, military expansion, administration of territories — and de-actualised and diffused his material presence in the process. In a crude reworking of the Cartesian axiom, production of thought defined the Englishman's true essence, overriding all other aspects of his identity — his personality, actions, behaviour. His material reality as a subjugator and alien ruler was dissolved in his mental output; the blurring of the man and his works effectively removed him from history. As the following statement suggests, the English literary text functioned as a surrogate Englishman in his highest and most perfect state: '[The Indians] daily converse with the best and wisest Englishmen through the medium of their works, and form ideas, perhaps higher ideas of our nation than if their intercourse with it were of a more personal kind.'[24] The split between the material and the discursive practices of colonialism is nowhere sharper than in the progressive rarefaction of the rapacious, exploitative, and ruthless actor of history into the reflective subject of literature.

How successful was the British strategy? That is clearly a topic for another paper, though it is worth noting that the problematics of colonial representations of authority have been brilliantly analyzed by Homi Bhabha in a recent article in *Critical Inquiry* (Fall, 1985). His essay 'Signs Taken for Wonders' provides a compelling philosophical framework for analyzing native interrogation of British authority in relation to the 'hybridization' of power and discourse, the term Bhabha uses to describe the nontransparency of the colonial presence and the problems created thereby in the recognition of its authority. Though my purpose in this paper has primarily been to describe a historical process rather than to do a microanalysis of the techniques of power, the question of effectiveness of strategy is never far removed. Indeed, the fact that English literary study had its beginnings as a strategy of containment raises a host of questions about the interrelations of culture, state, and civil society and the modes of assertion of authority within that network of relations. Why, if the British were the unchallenged military power in India, was the exercise of direct force discarded as a means of maintaining social control? What accounts for the British readiness to turn a disciplinary branch of knowledge to perform the task of administering the natives? What was the assurance that a disguised form of authority would be more successful in quelling a potential rebellion among the natives than a direct show of force? Why introduce English in the first place only to work at strategies to balance its secular tendencies with moral and religious ones?

These questions suggest a vulnerability in the British position that is most sharply felt when the history of British Rule is read in the light of the construction of an ideology. There is little doubt that a great deal of strategic manoeuvring went into the creation of a blueprint for social control in the guise of a humanistic programme of enlightenment. But merely to acknowledge this fact is not enough, for there is yet a further need to distinguish between strategy as unmediated assertion of authority and strategy as mediated response to situational imperatives. That is to say, it is important to decide whether British educational measures were elaborated from an uncontested position of superiority and strength, and as such are to be read as unalloyed expressions of ethnocentric sentiment, or whether that position itself was a fragile one which it was the role of educational decisions to fortify; given the challenge posed by historical contingency and confrontation.

I believe the difference is a crucial one, affecting not only the method we employ to study ideology but also the kinds of conclusions we reach. I have argued in this paper that the introduction of English literature represented an embattled response to historical and political pressures: to tensions between the English Parliament and the East India Company, between Parliament and the missionaries, between the East India Company and the native elite classes. It is possible to study strategic effectiveness using only the techniques of literary, textual analysis, but it is equally possible that in the process the two kinds of strategies are reduced to a single category from which are excluded extratextual considerations, such as the exigencies of the political and historical situation, the variable power relationships between different groups, the specific composition, affiliation, and vested interests of the 'ruling class' over different periods of time. No doubt responsiveness both to historical change and to the subtleties of discursive practice at one and the same time requires unusual methodological skill and sophistication, and I am aware that this essay comes nowhere near achieving this goal. But I do hope that what will have emerged is a sense of the interpenetration of different kinds of histories — social, cultural, political, literary. For this interpenetration to be studied in all its richness and diffuseness, it is obvious that no single model of analysis will suffice. Rather, the goal of future research must be to strive for a combination of models.

Notes

1. This chapter is a composite of two articles: 'The beginnings of English literary study in British India', *Oxford Literary Review,* 9, 1987 and 'Currying favor: The politics of British educational and cultural policy in India, 1813–1854', *Social Text,* Fall, 1988.

2. Said, Edward W. (1975) *Beginnings: Intention and Method* (p. 12). 1985 rpt. New York: Columbia University Press.
3. Ninth Report of Select Committee on the Affairs of India, 1783; quoted in Eric Stokes (1959) *The English Utilitarians and India* (p. 2). Oxford: Clarendon Press.
4. Adam, William, *Reports on Vernacular Education in Bengal and Bihar* (p. 340) Third Report. Calcutta: Calcutta University Press.
5. Spear, Percival (1965) *Oxford History of Modern India, 1740–1975* (p. 89). Oxford: Oxford University Press.
6. Cf. 'To allure the learned natives of India to the study of European science and literature, we must, I think, engraft this study upon their own established methods of scientific and literary institutions, and particularly in all the public colleges or schools maintained or encouraged by government, good translations of the most useful European compositions on the subjects taught in them, may, I conceive, be introduced with the greatest advantage'. Paper by J. H. Harrington, June 19, 1814, quoted in *Adam's Reports on Vernacular Education in Bengal and Bihar* (p. 310).
7. Great Britain, *Parliamentary Debates* 1813, Vol. 26, p. 1027.
8. Macaulay, Thomas B. (1935) *Speeches* (p. 345). G. M. Young (ed.). London: Oxford University Press.
9. Great Britain, *Parliamentary Papers,* 1852–53, Vol. 32, p. 301. Evidence of the Rev. W. Keane.
10. *Ibid.*
11. Great Britain, *Parliamentary Papers,* 1852–53, Vol. 29, p. 190. Minute of Marquess of Tweeddale on Education, 4 July 1846.
12. *Madras Christian Instructor and Missionary Record,* Vol. 11, No. 4 (September 1844), p. 195.
13. Great Britain, *Parliamentary Papers,* 1852–53, Vol. 32, p. 302. Evidence of the Rev. W. Keane.
14. All references are from *Parliamentary Papers,* 1852–53, Vol. 32.
15. Great Britain, *Parliamentary Papers,* 1852–53, Vol. 32, p. 185. Evidence of Charles Trevelyan.
16. Great Britain, *Parliamentary Papers,* 1852–53, Vol. 32, p. 287. Evidence of Charles Cameron.
17. *Ibid.*
18. Northampton MS. — William Carey to Andrew Fuller, 23 April 1796; quoted in M. A. Laird, *Missionaries and Education in Bengal, 1793–1837* (p. 56). Oxford: Clarendon Press.
19. Great Britain, *Parliamentary Papers,* 1852–53, Vol. 32, p. 412. Evidence of Alexander Duff.
20. Sharp, Henry (ed.) (1920) *Selections from Educational Records, Part I, 1781–1839.* Calcutta: Superintendent Government Printing, India.
21. Gramsci, Antonio, *Selections from the Prison Notebooks of Antonio Gramsci* (p. 57). Quintin Hoare and Geoffrey Nowell Smith (eds) 1971. London: Lawrence and Wishart.
22. Minute of J. Farish dated 28 August 1838; Poll. Dept, Vol. 20/795, 1837–39 (Bombay Records); quoted in B. K. Boman-Behram (1942) *Educational Controversies of India: The Cultural Conquest of India Under British Imperialism* (p. 239). Bombay: Taraporevala Sons & Co.
23. Great Britain, *Parliamentary Papers,* 1852–53, Vol. 32, p. 187. Evidence of Charles Trevelyan.
24. Trevelyan, C. E. (1838) *On the Education of the People of India* (p. 176). London: Lo, Orme, Brown, Green, and Longmans.

14 Gender, Language and the Politics of Literacy

KATHLEEN ROCKHILL

> I don't want to be a housekeeper all my life. I would like to be somebody,
> you know . . . I would like to go out to talk to people, to work, to do
> something interesting, to help somebody. It's terrible, because they say,
> 'You are the woman. You have to stay in the home, you have to do dinner.
> You have to do *everything*'.

Maria feels confined to her home all day by a husband who refuses her permission to leave the house. Isolated, alone, she despairs that she is 'no one'. Her husband stopped her from attending English classes because, she says, he was jealous that she was going to meet someone else. She tries to talk to her mother and sisters but they tell her she must do as her husband says. She dreams of running away with her young child, escaping to Mexico where she would be able to work as a beautician. Maria passionately echoes the voices of many other Hispanic immigrant women whom we interviewed in Los Angeles. True, there are variations, but the theme of longing, cross-cut by confinement, runs throughout.

Maria's yearning stands in stark contrast to the professional discourse of adult education which points to a 'lack of motivation' as a major explanation for adult non-participation in literacy programs. As Gillette & Ryan observe:

> Certainly, we know far more today than we did two decades ago about the organisation of literacy activities. But *the most fundamental requirement is still the desire of the participant to learn* and, second only to that, the will of the instructor to teach. (Quoted in Fordham (1985), p. 17, emphasis added.)

If the distance between Maria's urgent desire and their dispassioned analysis is enormous, even greater is the chasm between her experience and the mounting panic in the United States about the threat posed by the swelling numbers of illiterates. Typical in tone is the position expressed by the director of the Mayor's Committee on Literacy in Philadelphia warning that the millions of illiterate Americans are 'hostages to a problem of frightening dimensions':

> Frightening because adult illiteracy costs billions of dollars each year
> . . . Frightening because it is embedded in the social landscape of
> crime, drug abuse and hopelessness in a land of plenty. Frightening
> because of the tremendous human cost . . . for the parent who cannot
> read to her [sic] child and the senior citizen who cannot read the Bible.
>
> But frightening, too, because of the debilitating effect of illiteracy on
> our ideals of citizenship and liberty. Is it any wonder that with one of
> five adults unable to fully read a newspaper that voter turnout has
> steadily fallen to record lows? (*New York Times,* 13 September 1986,
> p. 17).

From positions of male power, voices resonate around the world, warning us that illiteracy is dangerous, a threat to liberty, to economic and technological development and to the moral well-being of society. Who hears the cries of longing, sealed within the confines of four walls, exhausted by overwork and worry, spoken in a language ruled 'illegal', by women with no right to speak in public, let alone in their own homes?

The purpose of this paper is to bring these voices into the same space and to explore why, apart from the obviously concealed fact that their languages are different, they don't speak the same language. More precisely, this article considers how literacy has been constructed as power in discourses of power (i.e. professional, social science, government) and contrasts those frames with the ways in which women who cannot read and write English well, live literacy and power in their everyday lives. An underlying theme is that politics, education and literacy must be reconceptualised if women's experience, as well as the experiences of adult second language learners, are to be taken into account.

While the focus is upon gender the work shows that the way women live sexual oppression is integrally connected to the ways they live race, class and ethnicity. The point is that these are not experienced as a series of 'commatised' background variables but they are lived together in the mosaic of people's lives.

It is difficult to find studies that consider the simultaneity of gender, race, ethnicity and class as lived. In their review of four leading journals of educational research in the US, Grant & Sluter (1986) conclude that most studies treat these as separate factors. I agree that 'integrationist' research is needed. However, if we are to accomplish this, we must cease thinking about race, gender, etc. as discrete categories of individual attributes which in some (mysterious) way signal social context, and instead think about them in terms of power relations which are lived through the construction of our subjectivities. As the work of Foucault suggests, this means thinking differently about power as 'coextensive and continous with life . . . [as] linked with a production of truth — the truth of the individual himself [sic]' (1982: 783). In the words of Biddy Martin:

> Power comes from below; it is induced in the body and produced in every social interaction. It is not exercised negatively from the outside, though negation and repression may be one of its effects. *Power in the modern world is the relation between pleasures, knowledge and power as they are produced and disciplined.* (Martin, 1982: 6, emphasis added.)

To study how power operates to maintain domination, we must take into consideration the concrete, everyday material practices and social relations which regulate our subjectivities, as well as the symbolic and ideological meaning structure through which we interpret our experience. A full range of feminist inquiry is pointing us in these directions. Noteworthy are studies of how class and gender are lived (for example, MacKinnon, 1981; McRobbie, 1982; Radway, 1984; Smith, 1977; Steedman, 1986; Walkerdine, 1984). While studies that include race and ethnicity are rarer, the work of Davis (1983), Ng (1986), Silvera (1983) and Westwood (1984) is highly suggestive. Some of this work is beginning to signal the ways in which sexuality, especially the dream of salvation through romance, is fundamental to how women live 'class' materially, as well as psychologically and culturally.

The focus upon literacy in the lives of Hispanic women in Los Angeles provides a dynamic arena for seeing how power is lived through the everyday practices, social regulations and images of desire which govern their sexuality and use of language. It is noteworthy that Hispanic women in general, and Mexicans in particular, have completed fewer years of formal schooling than any other group signalled out in official US statistics (Hunter & Harman, 1979). Through contrasting the experiences of these women with a range of public and social science discourses about literacy, the importance of language and literacy in power relations, whether at the national, state, local, familial or intimate male/female level of interaction, is revealed.

This article is based upon research into literacy which I initially began in 1972 when I received funding from the US Office of Education to study the phenomenon of school drop-out. In 1979, what was to become a very significant shift in my work occurred when the National Institute of Education funded my continuing study of illiteracy, with the proviso that I concentrate upon non-English-speaking adults. At the time, I welcomed the shift, for the years of prior work had shown me how many of those targeted by current literacy policies were limited-English-speaking adults. This was even more dramatically the case in Los Angeles, the city to which I had recently moved.

In this paper, I draw upon life history interviews conducted by me and my co-workers with approximately 50 'working class', Spanish-speaking adults who had settled on the west side of Los Angeles. The interviews included a detailed inventory of situations in which the person was confronted with the English language and a description of how these situations were handled. Augmentation by a community ethnography, including systematic interviews of social and health service personnel, has allowed me to situate the person's experience and better understand how knowing/not knowing English structures the daily interactions, practices and choices. The simultaneous attention paid to professional, social science, policy and media discourses about language and literacy has provided yet another view on how adults who are not fluent in English have been constructed as illiterate.

The Santa Monica-Venice-West Los Angeles area was selected because of extensive community contacts and because of the increasing numbers of Spanish-speaking people settling in a vicinity where English is the dominant language. Numbers are difficult to pin down, for so much of the recent Hispanic in-coming population is undocumented — 'illegal aliens' in the view of most of the English-speaking public. In 1980, the official census figures for Los Angeles put the number of Hispanics at 27% of the population, as non-Hispanic whites declined to 48% of the total (*New York Times,* 24 August 1986, p. E5). With estimates of illegal immigration ranging from 2 to 12 million, and dramatically increasing since the economic crisis of Mexico in 1982, one can be assured that the numbers are much higher than actually recorded. In one of the rare studies of Hispanics who have moved to the west side of Los Angeles, we found that almost without exception, anyone who had entered the country since 1975 is undocumented (Rockhill, 1982).

With this background, I now want to turn to the various ways in which literacy has been practised and interpreted as power.

Literacy as Power

Literacy is power. While most would agree that this equation is too simplistic, it is still the assumption that dominates most discourses about literacy. The power of literacy has been framed primarily in terms of economic development, equality of opportunity and the possibilities of liberty and democracy.

Whereas once literacy was pluralistic in conception, and there were a multiplicity of literacies associated with specific skills, during the processes of state formation, industrialisation and the movement toward mass schooling in 19th century North America, literacy began to take on symbolic and ideological dimensions that went far beyond being able to read and write

(Graff, 1981; Soltow & Stevens, 1981). As literacy became associated with liberty, 'illiterates' carried the burden of society's evils. In the process, literacy, schooling, education, and intelligence also became inextricably linked to a morality of individual responsibilities for economic well-being (Cook-Gumperz, 1986). As such, literacy is an excellent example of the individualising and totalising power of the modern state described by Foucault (1982). This shift from 'literacies' to 'literacy' as ideology is integral to its use as means of governance. Whereas once the state feared the development of literacy among the working class, by the mid-nineteenth century, literacy was being mandated as a means of social and moral regulation in industrialised countries (for example, see Corrigan & Gillespie, 1978; Corrigan & Sayer, 1986).

In a major extension of the use of literacy to regulate people, since the 1960s the State's differentiation between literates and illiterates has been the means by which adult educational services have been organised for poor people. In the United States, literacy is provided through adult basic education (ABE), a federal program that developed as part of the 'War on Poverty'. Since the early 1970s, a central aspect of adult education's campaign for federal funds has involved demonstrating the high rate of illiteracy in the country. This has been accomplished by radically redefining literacy in terms of the 'functional' tasks that must be performed in order to effectively function in life. Pragmatically, this has meant measuring performance on a range of documentary-related tasks that involve complex reading skills. In the first study of its kind, the Adult Performance Level Study found 23 million functional illiterates, 56% of whom were Spanish surnamed (Adult Performance Level, 1975). Today's estimates are higher, ranging from 23 to 27 million adults, with another 20 million categorised as borderline.

As 'functional' literacy definitions become more enmeshed in highly questionable ideological uses of social science to justify particular forms of governance, they feed into the moralistic and jingoistic politics which underlie proclamations about the high rate of illiteracy in the US. This is epitomised in the current national crusade against illiteracy which has involved the unprecedented use of the media. So ABC-TV launches its 'battle cry' against illiteracy with host Peter Jennings standing in the Library of Congress, telling viewers that illiteracy threatens both our national security and our ideals: 'Literacy and Liberty . . . the two are inextricably linked'. He recites the 'appalling' statistics: 20 million adult Americans are illiterate; 20 million more read at or below the eighth-grade level' (*New York Times,* 30 September 1986, p. 25). The connections to morality are nowhere clearer than in Education Secretary William J. Bennett's drive to establish 'moral literacy' as a fundamental teaching of schools and colleges (*New York Times,* 10 October 1986, p. 1; 31 October 1986, p. 18).

Although the panic about immigration is not mentioned in the moral panic about literacy, the two come together in the latest laws that affect the foreign born. The most dramatic of these is the California law which declares English to be the official language. The law is aimed at making all bilingual services illegal (*New York Times,* 26 November 1986, p. 12). Since these services are crucial to limited English-speakers, overnight, by executive fiat, another several million will, operationally, become 'functionally illiterate'. This racist mandate reflects the general national hysteria about the erosion of America's standards, and the swelling numbers of 'illegal aliens' who are seen as a drain on an already troubled economy. (The reported poverty rate among Hispanics — those counted! — has risen to 29%, *New York Times,* 4 September 1986, p. 11). The angry charge of white Americans is that recent immigrants have been unwilling to learn English. This is not true. Everyone we interviewed talked of repeated efforts to learn English, with virtually everyone having attended classes soon after arrival. But, sustained attendance is extremely difficult and complex, especially for women, as shall be seen below.

Only a few days before the California referendum on language was passed by a two-thirds majority, President Reagan signed a new national policy on immigration. The 'Alien Law', grants legal status to those who can prove continuous *illegal* residence in the country for five years prior to 1982. So people who have had to continuously prove that they were *not* present, now have to prove their illegality to the government. In addition to the risk of deportation if they are found to be ineligible for legal status, they are subject to taxation for all non-reported income (pay stubs are the primary way of proving continuous residency), *and* required to demonstrate proficiency in English (*New York Times,* 26 October 1986, p. 1; 7 November 1986, p. 8). The meaning of the latter has not yet been made clear, but the provision of more English classes is seen to be essential (*New York Times,* 26 November 1986, p. Y12).

The provision of opportunities to overcome 'illiteracy' is seen as central to the liberty of the individual, as well as the nation. Focusing attention upon illiterates is a strategy used by educators of conservative as well as progressive political persuasions in order to fight for the economic support necessary to expand programs. Expansion is legitimised as essential to 'equality of opportunity'. The equality argument complements the social control/moral regulation position in that both speak to the necessity of enhancing individual freedom through regulation (for 'his' own good!) The complementarity of the positions depends upon theoretical and ideological dichotomies between self and society, agency and structure. Thus, as the argument goes, freedom is increased through the social provision of more educational opportunities from among which the individual, as agent, is morally obligated to choose. The adult educator's responsibility is clear — to fight for the provision of more education — and once this is accomplished, to mobilise and motivate adults to participate in the 'opportunities' so provided (Bhola, 1985; Dave, 1976; Jarvis, 1986). Lodged firmly in liberal conceptions of the rational individual and benevolent state, it is argued that the way through structural inequities is to bring 'marginal' adults into the mainstream. (For a critique of how this ideology was used to obliterate working class education in the USA, see Rockhill, 1985.) With the provision of 'opportunities', success is dependent only upon individual capacity and motivation. This is the litany that pervades the literature of adult education. Literacy becomes a basic prerequisite to equality, to individual success. As such, it becomes a commodity, an object, an 'it' to be acquired.

Theories of inequality decontextualise and split apart the learner from what is to be learned, as well as from the forms and structures through which 'it' is provided. In the process of establishing literacy as a universalistic formula through which equality can be realised, literacy is treated as though it occurs in a vacuum. Thus, all learners are treated as the same, but symbolically are dichotomised as literate or illiterate — that is, learners or non-learners — and literacy is established as an isolatable, measurable, uniform, 'thing', a skill or commodity that can be acquired if one only has the necessary motivation to participate in learning opportunities or literacy programs. That is, literacy is treated as though it is outside the social and political relations, ideological practices, and symbolic meaning structures in which it is embedded.

Inequality theories do not take difference into account in a way that can get at how inequality is constructed and domination is reproduced and lived in the power relations of everyday life. Instead, quite the opposite occurs as lived differences and the practices that give rise to them are concealed and sealed behind conceptions that mask, categorise and mark. This is vividly exemplified in the labeling of one in five adults as functionally illiterate. In establishing literacy as a uniform, clearly discernible 'fact', the related 'facts', that a large proportion of the adults classified as illiterate are not fluent in English — and that more than half of these are women — are ignored. So we fail to see how literacy is integral to gender, cultural and language politics, for literacy means, at the very least, reading and writing in the *dominant* language. Concealed by the banner of liberty and equality is the ethnocentrism, racism, and sexism inherent in literacy policies.

More radical conceptions of literacy as power argue that literacy can empower, through collective action and the enhancement of individual capacity. There have been numerous international declarations on the right to learn, the right to read, the right to literacy (e.g. UNESCO, 1985). Yet, as Limage argues, 'literacy has never been formally enshrined as a basic human right' (1985). In his stirring call, Kozol (1986) urges 'illiterate' adults to get angry, to lobby, to organise, to demand to receive the education to which they are entitled.

Those who argue for literacy in terms of empowerment do not challenge the dominant ideology which constructs vast numbers of people as illiterate, thereby rendering them powerless. Like liberals who argue in terms of equality of opportunity, more radical voices are also lodged within the unifying ideology that sees illiteracy as the characteristic that keeps people powerless. So Kozol reasons: 'When illiterate people are powerless, when they see their children rendered powerless, when they recognize that one essential aspect of that impotence is inability to read and write, to understand, *to know* . . .' (p. 92). Although Kozal goes on to attribute this condition to social injustice rather than ignorance, he does not disagree with the ideology of mass adult illiteracy and its equation with powerlessness and ignorance.

Theories of resistance have romanticised 'the culture of the poor' without considering how it, too, is pervaded by dominant ideology, as well as differences and contradictions (Walker, 1986). Power is undifferentiatedly connected to structure and conceptualised as out there, not lived in our subjectivities and the concrete relations of everyday life. In contrast, empowerment is connected to agency and resistance. If we accept that power is multiple and pervades our subjectivities, which are also multiple, then we must ask: resistance to what? in what form? The people we interviewed asserted that learning to read and write English was crucial to getting ahead, *and* they said that, it was unnecessary, for one could get by OK without it, *and* one could never learn enough for it to make a real difference in their lives. Yet, the women especially yearn to learn the language. 'God willing, I will learn one day', runs like a refrain throughout their interviews. Is their goal to become empowered? to act in accord with their rights? to resist? — if so, who, what and how do they resist? Conceptions of empowerment, resistance and rights do not capture the way the women we interviewed talk about their longing for literacy; how they think about their lives, what is meaningful to them, or the conflicts they live. These conceptions do not reveal how power is lived in the concrete material practices, relationships, or dreams of women. Empowerment arguments are directed at participation in the 'public' spheres of national, economic, political and, to some extent, cultural activities (Fordham, 1975; Kozol, 1986). Totally absent from consideration is empowerment in the so called private sphere of the home, including religious, family, sexual and male/female relations.

Literacy as Communicative Form and Practice

An important bridge in the agency/structure, empowerment/power dichotomies is the idea that literacy is socially constructed in the practices of everyday interaction. In this view, literacy is seen in terms of cultural and communicative practices and patterns, which take place in face-to-face interactions and are situated in different types of communicative settings (Cook-Gumperz, 1986; Darville, 1987; Heath, 1983; Sola & Bennett, 1985). Key to this developing body of research is the idea that literacy is multiple and that it involves different forms of communication. While the effects of moral regulation, social control and universally prescribed, functional standards for performance are recognised as central to the social construction of literacy requirements, the shift in focus to what actually happens as people do the work of literacy production and performance gives rise to questions that signal how literacy is actually lived in concrete practices and daily interactions. Rather than measure people's deficiency with respect to an abstract performance standard, this work relies upon ethnographies of community and classroom interaction to see how it is that people *do* communicate and accomplish 'communicative competence'. While this approach addresses questions of language difference, the concentration has been upon differences in dialects within the same language. The distinction is not always clear-cut, however, as the approach emphasizes that dialects are embedded in a range of communicative patterns that signal different cultural meanings, as well as different language structures.

The significance of this research is that it recognises a multiplicity of literacies, which makes it possible to ask questions about the nature of power relationships among them. Thus far, inquiry into relations of power has been limited to showing that the literacy requirements of schooling and 'mainstream' culture differ from and are invested with more power than those of life in the community and home. The work of Bennett (1983), and Sola & Bennett (1985), is exceptional in that they begin to probe into 'the relationships of power, communicative practice and consciousness'. In their studies of Hispanic students learning English, they conclude that, 'the struggle for voice . . . is an important piece of a larger struggle between a majority community and the classes that rest on the labour of the community. This is the struggle for hegemony over the productive processes of consciousness formation' (Sola & Bennett, 1985: 109). Hence, they argue that literary practices are riddled by power relations which reflect broader struggles for domination, struggles (re)enacted in face-to-face interactions.

While Sola & Bennett do not address the question of functional literacy, the implications are major. Most obvious is the question of how, from among a range of skills, certain ones become privileged as functional requirements and how these conform to particular cultural, gender and ideological prescriptions. A related point is that the latest emphasis upon functional literacy privileges documentary reading over any other practice, in the process creating a passive stance (Levine, 1982), as well as a tacit acceptance of the governance procedures through which lives are socially regulated. Furthermore, a successful decoding of the forms requires a comprehensive understanding of how the American system works, as well as an astute knowledge of how to 'safely' replicate experience in acceptable documentary form. The series of interactions that immigrant women in particular have with bureaucracies is much more complex than 'filling in the blanks' on an information sheet. In an account of immigrants working their way through the health care system, I trace the multiplicity of interlocking, ambiguous, bureaucratic regulations with which they must be familiar in order to know and collect the benefits for which they are eligible. These were bizarre to immigrants who had come from cultures where help is exchanged through relationships of reciprocity rather than doled out through bureaucracies, and where the condition of establishing eligibility is mutual trust and caring, not proving that one is not ineligible (Rockhill, 1984).

The significance of the dimension of meaning, cultural form and the power relations in which they are embedded is crucial to understanding the experience of language difference, where one's world is necessarily structured by possibilities of communication. The primary way of getting by is to restrict one's range of activities to the Spanish-speaking community. That this is not solely a function of language furthers the argument that language means more than words. These words must be situated in terms of the regulatory processes of society, especially those that affect legal status, health, housing and work possibilities. Then, too, there is the desire to live among those with whom one can communicate, who share similar values and provide an informal network of support.

Literacy as Gendered

The vividness with which language and gender structure the possibility of literacy is nowhere clearer than in the situation of women who speak little English, especially since access to schooling is highly problematic. Because there are two primary ways of learning a second language — through informal interactions in mixed language settings *or* through formal study in school situations, adults who cannot readily participate in formal schooling situations have to depend upon informal contact with spoken and written English to acquire the language. Where access to schooling is restricted, access to various public domains where the second language is spoken becomes crucial to the eventual acquisition of literacy, and vice versa — that is, where access to 'the public' is restricted, schooling is more crucial. Because women are restricted in both cases, literacy becomes highly problematic for them.

In my research, I've come to see that the situation of women with respect to literacy is defined by a pervasive male/female power dynamic, cross-cut by differing constructions of masculinity and femininity, that are not considered in the literature. In fact, with rare exception, discourses about literacy, whether about power, skills or social relations, are strangely silent on the questions of gender or of women — especially strange since women are the primary participants in literacy programs. This may be shifting with UNESCO's (1985) signalling women as a primary 'target population'.

A developing feminist critique is beginning to raise questions about the traditional occupations and roles for which women are being prepared through functionally-defined literacy programs (Bhasin, 1984; Ellis, 1984; Horsman, 1986; Ramdas, 1985; Riria, 1983). To make the obvious point, literacy is much more than a set of reading and writing skills — literacy is always about something and it is a language — it cannot be separated from the content or the linguistic form of the texts read, or the social and pedagogic politics of their production and reading. Perhaps the most vulnerable to feminist critique are the 'life skills' components of basic literacy and job preparedness programs through which women are taught how to dress and perform properly (Morton, 1985). The extent to which women's literacy practices, including participation in schooling, are ruled by the men in their lives, is yet to be systematically documented, although examples are a taken-for-granted part of our popular culture (for example, the film, *Educating Rita*). As Ramdas (1985) argues, 'there must be a clear recognition of the role played by men in preventing women from going out of their homes . . .' (p. 103).

The study we conducted in Los Angeles points to gender differences in everyday literacy practices, as well as the integral relationship between the sexual oppression of women and literacy. The most striking pattern is that the women we interviewed tend to use and to depend more upon the written word, whereas men acquire and use more spoken English. This has a great deal to do with the silencing of women, their confinement to the domestic sphere, and the structure of work available to people who speak little English. Women talk of being afraid to speak, ashamed of not knowing English. Men stress the importance of talking, of making themselves understood by whatever means necessary.

The men we interviewed feel at ease in 'the public' in a way that women do not. The public takes on a special meaning — it is either a male ethnic grouping, or the public world where English is spoken, a world that women venture into only if they must in order to go to church, to work or to attend to the family's needs. Men own the public; women do not go out of the house without their approval, and if they do go out, there is no public place for them to congregate, unless it is at work — or at school — and this is part of the threat that school poses to the gendered traditions of the people — for it is a public place where women can potentially meet other people.

Women rarely go out alone; whenever possible they go with a child, relative or friend. Even if they are going to school, they will not go unless they have someone to go with. Confinement to the home is reinforced by the vulnerability they feel due to not knowing English well enough to defend themselves, especially true in the high-crime districts in which they live. Having few options to pick up spoken English, the cycle of vulnerability spirals.

Women do most of the literacy work of the household. In addition to the uses of literacy involved in housework, they attend to the purchase of goods, as well as transactions around social services, public utilities, health care and the schooling of children. In our detailed inventory of English-language situations in everyday life, women report handling almost all of those which involve the use of the written word. Through detailed repetition, some acquire specific sets of literacy skills. Where community workers provide help to those who seek it, the woman acts as the mediator. It was very difficult to get accounts of the literacy work that women do in maintaining their homes and families. They don't notice it; literacy is another piece of the invisibility of women's work.

When women enter the public domain where the English language is spoken, they do so in ways that involve specific transactions in a variety of situations which do not occur on a regular basis. They do not experience frequent, repeated contact in linguistically similar situations, so they cannot learn to speak English through this work. Whenever possible, they go with someone who can help them with English, as well as with the bureaucratic regulations they will encounter.

The work available to women is an extension of their work at home and does not provide them with the opportunity to learn English in the same way that men can. The men who learn more English, work in situations where they have contact with the English-speaking public. Examples are work in construction, gardening, small restaurants and stores. After working with friends or relatives for awhile, who help them learn the ropes and the language, men can sometimes manage to get together enough capital to strike out on their own. The range of work options open to women is much more limited, including their access to any form of capital. The choices narrow down to domestic or factory work. The latter usually means working in a Spanish-speaking job ghetto at tasks that require minimal interaction. Unless a domestic worker happens upon a very unusual employer who helps her to learn English, she is confined to the home where she works and often lives in isolation, learning only the few English words that are specific to housework, or to serving the family.

As the confinement of women to the home suggests, the gendered politics of literacy is about more than male/female differences in everyday communicative practices. These differences are constructed culturally and socially, through the delegation of women to the 'private' sphere. Literacy is integral to the power dynamic between men and women, to material differences in the options available to them, and to man's domination of woman through her sexuality.

Violence was common in the lives of the women we interviewed. Expressions of male violence typically included the charges that the women were 'stupid', 'illiterate', 'whores'. I believe that the linkage of these words is symbolically significant, signifying that to be a woman and illiterate is to be a stupid whore; whereas to be literate is to be a 'lady' — men feel legitimated in dominating whores in a way that they do not with ladies — to control their woman they keep her illiterate, and accuse her of being a whore if she goes out of the home, leaving her no exit. The converse is the fear that if she does go to school, she will become a 'lady' and leave him.

Several women related stories of being physically beaten; some flee their homes, some call the police and a few turn to the priest — but most remain silent, too ashamed and afraid to give any more than a fleeting glimpse of the violence they live — a violence enshrined as normal by the family, church and other social institutions. Over the course of months, Modesta talked of plans she and her husband had to attend English classes — plans which never materialised. Then one night, she broke down and sobbed, offering a hushed explanation: 'He drinks a lot. He is very much like a man. Right now, things aren't going very well for us. He loves his children very much but he treats me badly. Very badly.'

In my original work, I did not connect these and other stories of violence with the question of literacy or of learning English. Now I see it as central. Over the years, I have been struck by a multiplicity of anecdotes about women whose husbands would not allow them to go to school. We need to know more about what it means to live in the face of male rage and violence. In my case, when I lived daily in the face of threat, never knowing what act would be interpreted as a transgression, an attack upon MALE RIGHT or power (Corrigan, 1986), I did all I could not to set off that rage and withdrew into the safety of a kind of death. While not all of the women talked of violence, several of those to whom I became closer over the course of my research talked, painfully, angrily, of similar experiences of violence, sometimes explicitly directed against their going to school. Their situations differed from mine in that they had fewer options. In addition, the fear of their husbands seemed lodged in the worry that their wives would be influenced by contact with 'gringos' — both men and women — and thus challenge their family traditions. Men who have higher educations and/or are in more daily contact with the English-speaking world tended to be more supportive of their wives learning English.

Women express a strong desire to take classes in order to learn English. They do but, except for the young and highly educated, they stop attending. The typical pattern is one of several attempts. They explain stopping in terms of the enormous pressures of their daily lives, including resistance at home. They talk about worry, anxiety, too much on their minds and feeling too old to concentrate upon the difficult and time-consuming endeavour of learning the language. The hope that one day conditions will be right lingers on:

> I am thinking of going to school within the next year. I went a few years ago, but I didn't continue . . . you always regret it for not going to school, and for not learning . . .

Gladys frames learning English in terms of going to school and learning. There is a point at which taking classes is no longer a question of learning English but of going to school. Initial efforts to learn the language are framed in terms of self-defence, of survival. This shifts to a frame of 'advancement', of getting ahead. It is important to understand this distinction in order to understand how it is that literacy can be both the taken-for-granted work of women and a threat. As long as the reading and writing or spoken English which are learned are seen as the rudiments of survival, there is no threat. Learning and education are a different matter; they carry a symbolic dimension of movement into a better, more powerful class and culture — another world, another life, which is both desired and feared. As has been noted, the symbolic significance of literacy is connected with its attachment to schooling. For the women we interviewed, schooling brings with it the possibility of becoming a 'lady' — somebody.

Once literacy carries with it the symbolic power of education, it poses a threat to the power relations in the family. Men need to feel in control; not only does this mean having more power than their wives, but controlling what they think and do. This is especially so when the man feels little or no power at work, or is not the family's primary breadwinner. Furthermore, immigrant men are denied alternative forms of social status and are confronted by the chauvinism of an alien culture. The shock of immigration, in and of itself, can be demasculinising. Finally, in a culture where machismo reigns, the man is easily threatened by any sign of the woman's independence. The words of Maria echo the feelings of many: 'I don't want a macho. I want a man'.

Women are more likely to develop their English literacy skills once they are separated or divorced. Several of the women we interviewed had left their husbands because of violence. They talk hopefully of changing their lives through education, especially those who are younger and know enough English so that they can see the possibility of finding a different kind of work.

Women do not think of their experience in terms of rights. When they tell their stories, they tell about their children and their husbands. In the trauma of immigration, they recede into the background; fighting for survival, they turn toward their children for hope, and measure progress in terms of the family's acquisition of material goods. As the husband struggles to hold on to signs of power and social status in a demasculinising situation, the woman painfully learns to put her dreams aside and do what she must to supplement the family's income. So Elena tells us:

> I consider myself to be a successful woman because I went to the school and they told me that my son was the best and that he likes to study. That is a triumph for me. And then, my husband says to me, 'My work is going better and better'. This is also a success for me.

When women do talk about going to school, they frame it in terms of desire, not rights. Women in their late teens and early twenties and/or women who are living alone, have the desire to learn enough English to go to school and find 'office work'. The dream is to be a secretary or a receptionist — but it is more than this — it is to enter the world of middle class America, to wear dresses and high heels, to look and be the female image they see smiling back at them in magazines, on their TV screens and billboards. That these jobs are highly literacy dependent is part of the dream — and the 'reality' that they live. For women, there is no middle level work, where speaking, reading and writing skills are used but do not have to be highly developed. The women we interviewed cannot learn enough English to move into the next strata of jobs open to them. There are few ways out of domestic or factory work — except through sustained schooling, and they cannot do this unless they are supported, in some way, to participate. As we have seen, quite the opposite is true.

Conclusion

The politics of literacy are integral to the cultural genocide of a people, as well as the gendering of society. The construction of literacy is embedded in the discursive practices and power relationships of everyday life — it is socially constructed, materially produced, morally regulated, and carries a symbolic significance which cannot be captured by its reduction to any one of these. Literacy is caught up in the material, racial and sexual oppression of women, *and* it embodies their hope for escape. For women, it is experienced as *both,* a threat and a desire — to learn English means to go to school

— to enter a world that holds the promise of change and, because of this, threatens all that they know.

Literacy is women's work, but not women's right. They do the work of literacy in the privacy of their homes, but they do not have the right to change — to be 'somebody' — their husbands object, sometimes forcefully. They live in a very ambiguous situation: they cannot do what they are socialy mandated to do — and want to do — to learn English — to go to school.

The dependence of women upon schooling to learn English is related to their exclusion from forms of work or other forms of activity where they might learn the language informally. The question that literacy poses for Hispanic women cannot be separated from the ways in which language structures their world, the symbolic significance of schooling, and the ways that both of these are defined by culturally prescribed practices of sexism. Because the professional and social science discourses about literacy have decontextualised it from lived experience, none of the foregoing has been evident. To frame literacy in terms of equality of opportunity, rights, or empowerment is absurd in the face of a fist — or, less dramatically, in a gendered society where the conception of rights is alien to women who have been told all their lives that they must obey and care for others.

This account began by posing the question of what might happen if the voices of Hispanic immigrant women, educational professionals and public policy makers, each of whom is speaking to the question of literacy from very different perspectives, were brought into the same space. In doing so, we've seen how alien the view of those in positions of power is to the experiences of the Hispanic women interviewed. To portray 'illiterates' as a threat to the American tradition of liberty, as unmotivated to learn, unwilling to participate in educational opportunities which would provide the conditions necessary to promote equality and/or as not seeing how literacy can empower them is to never have heard the urgent plea of Maria and others. Their cries of yearning have been systematically excluded. Despite the 'fact' that Hispanic women probably have the highest rate of 'illiteracy' of any group in the USA, they are not the 'illiterates' imaged by those who have turned their attention to this issue. The rhetoric suggests that the unarticulated image is that of a male — be he black, white or an 'illegal alien'.

In order to see women, and to understand their experiences with literacy, we need to look at how language in general, as well as the particularities of reading and writing English, enter into their everyday lives. It is also important to look at schooling, both in terms of its symbolic meaning and the material realities in women's lives. To seriously act upon the principle of literacy or learning as a right — or even a possibility — for women, it is necessary to reconceptualise how 'the political' and 'the educational' are constituted so that the primary sites of oppression in their lives are not systematically excluded from our politics or our classrooms. Our work suffers from a splitting between the public and the private which reinforces precisely the same gendered practices through which women are oppressed in their everyday lives. The gendered politics of literacy reflect these practices. If we open the doors of our minds to the power of the fist, the power of the sexual, the power of the family, church and other cultural forms, perhaps we can begin to find ways to address the contradictory constructions of women's subjectivities with respect to literacy/learning/education. They are in a double bind: to act upon their desire for change requires a choice that few feel they can make — a choice between love, family, home and violent upheaval. However violent the love they live may be, for most, the unknown of the latter is the more threatening.

References

Adult Performance Level Project (1975) *Adult Functional Competency: A Summary.* Austin: University of Texas.

Bennett, Adrian T. (1983) Discourses of power, the dialectics of understanding, the power of literacy. *Journal of Education* 165, 53–74.

Bhasin, K. (1984) The why and how of literacy for women: Some thoughts in the Indian context. *Convergence* 17 (4), 37–43.

Bhola, H. S. (1985) A policy analysis of adult literacy promotion in the Third World: An accounting of promises made and promises fulfilled. Unpublished manuscript.

Cook-Gumperz, J. (1986) Literacy and schooling: An unchanging equation? In J. Gook-Gumperz (ed.) *The Social Construction of Literacy.* London: Cambridge University Press.

Corrigan, P. (1986) Masculinity as right: Some thoughts on the geneology of 'rational violence'. Unpublished manuscript.

Corrigan, P. and Gillespie, V. (1978) *Class Struggle, Social Literacy and Idle Time: The Provision of Public Libraries in England as a Case Study in 'the Organisation of Leisure with Indirect Results'.* Brighton: Moyes Labour History Monographs.

Corrigan, P. and Sayer, D. (1986) *The Body Politic to the National Interest: English State Formation in Comparative and Historical Perspective.* Forthcoming.

Darville, R. (1987) The language of experience and the literacy of power. Forthcoming.

Dave, R. H. (1976) Foundations of lifelong education: Some methodological aspects. In R. H. Dave (ed.) *Foundations of Lifelong Education.* Oxford: Pergamon Press.

Davis, Angela Y. (1983) *Women, Race and Class.* New York: Vintage Books.

Ellis, P. (1984) Women, adult education and literacy: A Caribbean perspective. *Convergence* 17 (4), 44–53.

Fordham, Paul (ed.) (1985) *One Billion Illiterates, One Billion Reasons for Action: Report on the International Seminar 'Co-operating for Literacy'.* West Berlin, October 1983. Bonn: International Council for Adult Education and Deutsche Stiftung fur internationale Entwicklung.

Foucault, Michel (1982) The subject and power. *Critical Inquiry* 8, 777–95.

Graff, Harvey J. (1981) Literacy, jobs, and industrialization: The nineteenth century. In H. J. Graff (ed.) *Literacy and Social Development in the West: A Reader* (pp. 232–60). London: Cambridge University Press.

Grant, C. A. and Sleeter, C. E. (1986) Race, class and gender in education research: An argument for integrative analysis. *Review of Education Research* 56, 195–211.

Heath, Shirley B. (1983) *Ways with Words: Language, Life and Work in Communities and Classrooms*. London: Cambridge University Press.

Horsman, J. (1986) Illiteracy in the context of women's lives in Nova Scotia. Thesis proposal. Ontario Institute for Studies in Education.

Hunter, Carman St. J. and Harman, D. (1979) *Adult Illiteracy in the United States*. New York: McGraw-Hill.

Jarvis, Peter (1986) *Sociological Perspectives on Lifelong Education and Lifelong Learning*. Athens: University of Georgia.

Kozol, Jonathan (1985) *Illiterate America*. New York: New American Library.

Levine, Kenneth (1982) Functional literacy: Fond illusions and false economies. *Harvard Educational Review* 52, 249–66.

Limage, Leslie J. (1980) Illiteracy in industrialized countries: A sociological commentary. *Prospects* 10, 141–55.

MacKinnon, C. A. (1981) Feminism, marxism, method and the state: An agenda for theory. In N. O. Keohane, M. Z. Rosalda and B. C. Gelpi (eds) *Feminist Theory: A Critique of Ideology* (pp. 1–30). Chicago: The University of Chicago Press.

Martin, Biddy (1982) Feminism, criticism, and Foucault. *New German Critique* 27, 3–30.

McRobbie, Angela (1982) The politics of feminist research: Between talk, text and action. *Feminist Review* 12, 46–57.

Morton, Janet (1985) Assessing vocational readiness in low-income women: An exploration into the construction and use of ideology. MA thesis. Ontario Institute for Studies in Education.

Ng, Roxana (1986) The documentary construction of 'immigrant women' in Canada (forthcoming).

Radway, Janice (1984) *Reading the Romance: Women, Patriarchy and Popular Culture*. Chapel Hill: The University of North Carolina Press.

Ramdas, L. (1985) Illiteracy, women and development. *Adult Education and Development*. German Adult Education Association, No. 24, 95–105.

Riria, J. (1983) Co-operating for literacy — the perspective of women, presented at the Berlin Conference, Co-operating for Literacy.

Rockhill, Kathleen (1982) Language learning by Latino immigrant workers: The socio-cultural context. Washington, DC, unpublished report to National Institute of Education.

— (1984) Health crises in the lives of non-English-speaking Latino immigrants: language, legalities and trusted advocates. Unpublished manuscript.

— (1985) The liberal perspective and the symbolic legitimation of university adult education in the USA. In R. Taylor, R. Rockhill and R. Fieldhouse (eds) *University Adult Education in England and the USA* (pp. 123–74). London: Croom Helm.

Silvera, Makeda (1983) *Silenced*. Toronto: Williams-Wallace.

Smith, Dorothy E. (1977) *Feminism and Marxism: A Place to Begin, a Way to Go*. Vancouver: New Star Books.

Sola, M. and Bennett, A. T. The struggle for voice: Narrative literacy and consciousness in an east Harlem school. *Journal of Education* 167, 88–110.

Soltow, Lee and Stevens, Edward (1981) *The Rise of Literacy and the Common School in the United States*. Chicago: University of Chicago Press.

Steedman, Carolyn (1986) *Landscape for a Good Woman: A Story of Two Lives*. London: Virago.

Walker, J. C. (1986) Romanticising resistance, romanticising culture: Problems in Willis's theory of cultural production. *British Journal of Sociology of Education* 7, 59–80.

Walkerdine, Valerie (1984) Some day my prince will come . . . young girls and the preparation for adolescent sexuality. In A. McRobbie and M. Neva (eds) *Gender and Generation*. New York: Macmillan.

Westwood, Sallie (1984) *All Day, Every Day: Factory and Family in the Making of Women's Lives*. London: Pluto Press.

UNESCO (1985) *Final Report*. Fourth International Conference on Adult Education. Paris, 19–29 March 1985. Paris: UNESCO.

15 The Adult Literacy Process as Cultural Action for Freedom[1]

PAULO FREIRE

Every Educational Practice Implies a Concept of Man and the World

All educational practice implies a theoretical stance on the educator's part. This stance in turn implies — sometimes more, sometimes less explicitly — an interpretation of man and the world.

Teaching adults to read and write must be seen, analysed and understood in this way. The critical analyst will discover in the methods and texts used by educators and students practical value options which betray a philosophy of man, well or poorly outlined, coherent or incoherent.

Let us consider the case of primers used as the basic texts for teaching adults to read and write. We begin with the fact, inherent in the idea and use of the primer, that it is the teacher who chooses the words and proposes them to the learner. Insofar as the primer is the mediating object between the teacher and students, and the students are to be 'filled' with words the teachers have chosen, one can easily detect a first important dimension of the image of man which here begins to emerge. It is the profile of a man whose consciousness is 'spatialized', and must be 'filled' or 'fed' in order to know.

This 'digestive' concept of knowledge, so common in current educational practice, is found very clearly in the primer.[2] Illiterates are considered 'under-nourished', not in the literal sense in which many of them really are, but because they lack the 'bread of the spirit'. Consistent with the concept of knowledge as food, illiteracy is conceived of as a 'poison herb', intoxicating and debilitating persons who cannot read or write. Thus, much is said about the 'eradication' of illiteracy to cure the disease. In this way, deprived of their character as linguistic signs constitutive of man's thought-language, words are transformed into mere 'deposits of vocabulary' — the bread of the spirit which the illiterates are to 'eat' and 'digest'.

The 'nutritionist' view of knowledge perhaps also explains the humanitarian character of certain Latin American adult literacy campaigns. If millions of men are illiterate, 'starving for letters', 'thirsty for words', the word must be *brought* to them to save them from 'hunger' and 'thirst'. The word, according to the naturalistic concept of consciousness implicit in the primer, must be 'deposited', not born of the creative effort of the learners. As understood in this concept, man is a passive being, the object of the process of learning to read and write, and not its subject. As object his task is to 'study' the so-called reading lessons, which in fact are almost completely alienating and alienated, having so little, if anything, to do with the student's sociocultural reality.

It would be a truly interesting study to analyse the reading texts being used in private or official adult literacy campaigns in rural and urban Latin America. It would not be unusual to find among such texts sentences and readings like the following random samples.

A asa é da ave The wing is of the bird.
Eva viu a uva Eva saw the grape.
O galo canta The cock crows.
O cachorro ladra The dog barks.
Maria gosta dos animais Mary likes animals.
João cuida das arvores John takes care of the trees.

O pai de Carlinhos se chama Antonio. Carlinhos é um bom menino, bem comportado e estudioso Charles's father's name is Antonio. Charles is a good, well-behaved and studious boy.

Ada deu o dedo ao urubu? Duvido, Ada deu o dedo a arara . . . [3]
Se você trabalha com martelo e prego, tenha cuidado para nao furar o dedo. If you hammer a nail, be careful not to smash your finger.

Peter did not know how to read. Peter was ashamed. One day, Peter went to school and registered for a night course. Peter's teacher was very good. Peter knows how to read now. Look at Peter's face. [These lessons are generally illustrated.] Peter is smiling. He is a happy man. He already has a good job. Everyone ought to follow his example.

In saying that Peter is smiling because he knows how to read, that he is happy because he now has a good job, and that he is an example for all to follow the authors establish a relationship between knowing how to read and getting good jobs which, in fact, cannot be borne out. This naïveté reveals, at least, a failure to perceive the structure not only of illiteracy, but of social phenomena in general. Such an approach may admit that these phenomena exist, but it cannot perceive their relationship to the structure of the society in which they are found. It is as if these phenomena were mythical, above and beyond concrete situations, or the results of the intrinsic inferiority of a certain class of men. Unable to grasp contemporary illiteracy as a typical manifestation of the 'culture of silence', directly related to underdeveloped structures, this approach cannot offer an objective, critical response to the challenge of illiteracy. Merely teaching men to read and write does not work miracles; if there are not enough jobs for men able to work, teaching more men to read and write will not create them.

Analysis of these texts reveals, then, a simplistic vision of men, of their world, of the relationship between the two, and of the literacy process which unfolds in that world.

Their authors do not recognize in the poor classes the ability to know and even create the texts which would express their own thought-languages at the level of their perception of the world. The authors repeat with the texts what they do with the words, i.e. they introduce them into the learners' consciousness as if it were empty space — once more, the 'digestive' concept of knowledge.

Still more, the a-structural perception of illiteracy revealed in these texts exposes the other false view of illiterates as marginal men.[4] Those who consider them marginal must, nevertheless, recognize the existence of a reality to which they are marginal — not only physical space, but historical, social, cultural, and economic realities — i.e. the structural dimensions of reality. In this way, illiterates have to be recognized as beings 'outside of', 'marginal to' something, since it is impossible to be marginal to nothing. But being 'outside of' or 'marginal to' necessarily implies a movement of the one said to be marginal from the centre, where he was, to the periphery. This movement, which is an action, presupposes in turn not only an agent but also his reasons. Admitting the existence of men 'outside of' or 'marginal to' structural reality, it seems legitimate to ask: Who is the author of this movement from the centre of the structure to its margin? Do so-called marginal men, among them the illiterates, make the decision to move out to the periphery of society? If so, marginality is an option with all that it involves: hunger, sickness, rickets, pain, mental deficiencies, living death, crime, promiscuity, despair, the impossibility of being. In fact, however, it is difficult to accept that 40 per cent of Brazil's population, almost 90 per cent of Haiti's, 60 per cent of Bolivia's, about 40 per cent of Peru's, more than 30 per cent of Mexico's and Venezuela's, and about 70 per cent of Guatemala's would have made the tragic *choice* of their own marginality as illiterates. If, then, marginality is not by choice, marginal man has been expelled from and kept outside of the social system and is therefore the object of violence.

In fact, however, the social structure as a whole does not 'expel', nor is marginal man a 'being outside of'. He is, on the contrary, a 'being inside of', within the social structure, and in a dependent relationship to those whom we falsely call autonomous beings, inauthentic beings-for-themselves.

A less rigorous approach, one more simplistic, less critical, more technicist, would say that it was unnecessary to reflect about what it would consider unimportant questions such as illiteracy and teaching adults to read and write. Such an approach might even add that the discussion of the concept of marginality is an unnecessary academic exercise. In fact, however, it is not so. In accepting the illiterate as a person who exists on the fringe of society, we are led to view him as a sort of 'sick man', for whom literacy would be the 'medicine', to cure him, enabling him to 'return' to the 'healthy' structure from which he has become separated. Educators would be benevolent counsellors, scouring the outskirts of the city for the stubborn illiterates, runaways from the good life, to restore them to the forsaken bosom of happiness by giving them the gift of the word.

In the light of such a concept — unfortunately, all too widespread — literacy programmes can never be efforts toward freedom; they will never question the very reality which deprives men of the right to speak up — not only illiterates, but all those who are treated as objects in a dependent relationship. These men, illiterate or not, are, in fact, not marginal. What we said before bears repeating: they are not 'beings outside of'; they are 'beings for another'. Therefore the solution to their problem is not to become 'beings inside of', but men freeing themselves; for, in reality, they are not marginal to the structure, but oppressed men within it. Alienated men, they cannot overcome their dependency by 'incorporation' into the very structure responsible for their dependency. There is not another road to humanization — theirs as well as everyone else's — but authentic transformation of the dehumanizing structure.

From this last point of view, the illiterate is no longer a person living on the fringe of society, a marginal man, but rather a representative of the dominated strata of society, in conscious or unconscious opposition to those who, in the same structure, treat him as a thing. Thus, also teaching men to read and write is no longer an inconsequential matter of *ba, be, bi, bo, bu,* of memorizing an alienated word, but a difficult apprenticeship in naming the world.

In the first hypothesis, interpreting illiterates as men marginal to society, the literacy process reinforces the mythification of reality by keeping it opaque and by dulling the 'empty consciousness' of the learner with innumerable alienating words and phrases. By contrast, in the second hypothesis — interpreting illiterates as men oppressed within the system — the literacy process, as cultural action for freedom, is an act of knowing in which the learner assumes the role of knowing subject in dialogue with the educator. For this very reason, it is a courageous endeavour to demythologize reality, a process through which men who had previously been submerged in reality begin to emerge in order to re-insert themselves into it with critical awareness.

Therefore the educator must strive for an ever greater clarity as to what, at times without his conscious knowledge, illumines the path of his action. Only in this way will he truly be able to assume the role of one of the subjects of this action and remain consistent in the process.

The Adult Literacy Process as an Act of Knowing

To be an act of knowing the adult literacy process demands among teachers and students a relationship of authentic dialogue. True dialogue unites subjects together in the cognition of a knowable object which mediates between them.

If learning to read and write is to constitute an act of knowing, the learners must assume from the beginning the role of creative subjects. It is not a matter of memorizing and repeating given syllables, words and phrases, but rather of reflecting critically on the process of reading and writing itself, and on the profound significance of language.

Insofar as language is impossible without thought, and language and thought are impossible without the world to which they refer, the human word is more than mere vocabulary — it is word-and-action. The cognitive dimensions of the literacy process must include the relationships of men with their world. These relationships are the source of the dialectic between the products men achieve in transforming the world and the conditioning which these products in turn exercise on men.

Learning to read and write ought to be an opportunity for men to know what *speaking the word* really means: a human act implying reflection and action. As such it is a primordial human right and not the privilege of a few, as I point out in my 'La alfabetazación de adultos'. Speaking the word is not a true act if it is not at the same time associated with the right of self-expression and world-expression, for creating and re-creating, of deciding and choosing and ultimately participating in society's historical process.

In the culture of silence the masses are 'mute', that is, they are prohibited from creatively taking part in the transformations of their society and therefore prohibited from being. Even if they can occasionally read and write because they were 'taught' in humanitarian — but not humanist — literacy campaigns, they are nevertheless alienated from the power responsible for their silence.

As an event calling forth the critical reflection of both the learners and educators, the literacy process must relate *speaking the word* to *transforming reality,* and to man's role in this transformation. Perceiving the significance of that relationship is indispensable for those learning to read and write if we are really committed to liberation. Such a perception will lead the learners to recognize a much greater right than that of being literate. They will ultimately recognize that, as men, they have the right to have a voice.

The adult literacy process as an act of knowing implies the existence of two interrelated contexts. One is the context of authentic dialogue between learners and educators as equally knowing subjects. This is what schools should be — the theoretical context of dialogue. The second is the real, concrete context of facts, the social reality in which men exist.

In the theoretical context of dialogue, the facts presented by the real or concrete context are critically analysed. This analysis involves the exercise of abstraction, through which, by means of representations of concrete reality, we seek knowledge of that reality. The instrument for this abstraction in our methodology is codification,[5] or representation of the existential situations of the learners.

Codification, on the one hand, mediates between the concrete and theoretical contexts (of reality). On the other hand, as knowable object, it mediates between the knowing subjects, educators and learners, who seek in dialogue to unveil the 'action-object wholes'.

The first stage of decodification[6] — or reading — is descriptive. At this stage, the 'readers' — or decodifiers — focus on the relationship between the categories constituting the codification. This preliminary focus on the surface structure is followed by problematizing the codified situation. This leads the learner to the second and fundamental stage of decodification, the comprehension of the codification's 'deep structure'. By understanding the codification's 'deep structure' the learner can then understand the dialectic which exists between the categories presented in the 'surface structure', as well as the unity between the 'surface' and 'deep' structures.

In our method, the codification initially takes the form of a photograph or sketch which represents a real existent, or an existent constructed by the learners. [Editor's note: an example of a codification might be a picture of a slum, or of labourers working.] When this representation is projected as a slide, the learners effect an operation basic to the act of knowing: they gain distance from the knowable object. This experience of distance is undergone as well by the educators, so that educators and learners together can reflect critically on the knowable object which mediates between them. The aim of decodification is to arrive at the critical level of knowing, beginning with the learner's experience of the situation in the 'real context'.

The learners, rather than receive information about this or that fact, analyse aspects of their own existential experience represented in the codification.

In the process of decodifying representations of their existential situations and perceiving former perceptions, the learners gradually hesitatingly and timorously place in doubt the opinion they held of reality and replace it with a more and more critical knowledge.

Let us suppose that we were to present to groups from among the dominated classes codifications which portray their imitation of the dominators' cultural models — a natural tendency of the oppressed consciousness at a given moment.[7] The dominated persons would perhaps, in self-defence, deny the truth of the codification. As they deepened their analysis, however, they would begin to perceive that their apparent initiation of the dominators' models is a result of their interiorization of these models and, above, all, of the myths about the 'superiority' of the dominant classes which cause the dominated to feel inferior. What in fact is pure interiorization appears in a naïve analysis to be imitation. Basically, as I point out in *Pedogagy of the Oppressed,* when the dominated classes reproduce the dominators' style of life, it is because the dominators live 'within' the dominated. The dominated can eject the dominators only by getting distance from them and objectifying them. Only then can they recognize them as their antithesis, as Fanon says.

To the extent, however, that interiorization of the dominator's values is not only an individual phenomenon, but a social and cultural one, ejection must be achieved by a type of cultural action in which culture negates culture. That is, culture, as an interiorized product which in turn conditions men's subsequent acts, must become the object of men's knowledge so that they can perceive its conditioning power.

When the creation of a new culture is appropriate but impeded by interiorized cultural 'residue', this residue, the myths, must be expelled by means of culture. Cultural action and cultural revolution, at different stages, constitutes the modes of this expulsion.

The learners must discover the reasons behind many of their attitudes toward cultural reality and thus confront cultural reality in a new way. The learners' capacity for critical knowing — well beyond mere opinion — is established in the process of unveiling their relationships with the historical-cultural world *in* and *with* which they exist.

Such education must have the character of commitment. It implies a movement from the concrete context which provides objective facts, to the theoretical context where these facts are analysed in depth, and back to the concrete context where men experiment with new forms of praxis.

When we consider adult literacy learning or education in general as an act of knowing, we are advocating a synthesis between the educator's maximally systematized knowing and the learners' minimally systematized knowing — a synthesis achieved in dialogue. The educator's role is to propose problems about the codified existential situations in order to help the learners arrive at an increasingly critical view of their reality. The educator's responsibility as conceived by this philosophy is thus greater in every way than that of his colleague whose duty is to transmit information which the learners memorize. Such an educator can simply repeat what he has read, and often misunderstood, since education for him does not mean an act of knowing.

The first type of educator, on the contrary, is a knowing subject, face to face with other knowing subjects. He can never be a mere memorizer, but a person constantly readjusting his knowledge, who calls forth knowledge from his students. For him, education is a pedagogy of knowing. The educator whose approach is mere memorization is anti-dialogic; his act of transmitting knowledge is unalterable. In contrast, for the educator who experiences the act of knowing together with his students, dialogue is the seal of the act of knowing.

To be an act of knowing, then, the adult literacy process must engage the learners in the constant problematizing of their existential situations. This problematizing employs 'generative words' chosen by specialized educators in a preliminary investigation of what we call the 'minimal linguistic universe' of the future learners. The words are chosen firstly for their pragmatic value, that is, as linguistic signs which command a common understanding in a region or area of the same city or country (in the United States, for instance, the world *soul* has a special significance in black areas which it does not have among whites), and secondly for their phonetic difficulties which will gradually be presented to those learning to read and write. Finally, it is important that the first generative word be tri-syllabic. When it is divided into its syllables, each one constituting a syllabic family, the learners can experiment with various syllabic combinations even at first sight of the word.

Having chosen seventeen generative words,[8] the next step is to codify seventeen existential situations familiar to the learners. The generative words are then worked into the situations one by one in the order of their increasing phonetic difficulty. As we have already emphasized, these codifications are knowable objects which mediate between the knowing subjects, educator-learners, learner-educators. Their act of knowing is elaborated in the *circulo de cultura* (cultural discussion group) which functions as the theoretical context.

What is important is that the person learning words be concomitantly engaged in a critical analysis of the social framework in which men exist. For example, the word *favela* (slum) in Rio de Janeiro, Brazil, and the word *callampa* in Chile, represent, each with its own nuances, the same social, economic, and cultural reality of the vast numbers of slum dwellers in those countries. If *favela* and *callampa* are used as generative words for the people of Brazilian and Chilean slums, the codifications will have to represent slum situations.

There are many people who consider slum dwellers marginal, intrinsically wicked and inferior. To such people we recommend the profitable experience of discussing the slum situation with slum dwellers themselves. As some of these critics are often simply mistaken, it is possible that they may rectify their mythical clichés and assume a more scientific attitude. They may avoid saying that the illiteracy, alcoholism and crime of the slums, its sickness, infant mortality, learning deficiencies and poor hygiene reveal the 'inferior nature' of its inhabitants. They may even end up realizing that if intrinsic evil exists it is part of the structures, and that it is the structures which need to be transformed.

It should be pointed out that the Third World as a whole, and more in some parts than in others, suffers from the same misunderstanding from certain sectors of the so-called metropolitan societies. They see the Third World as the incarnation of evil, the primitive, the devil, sin and sloth — in sum, as historically unviable without the director societies. Such a manichean attitude is at the source of the impulse to 'save' the 'demon-possessed' Third World, 'educating' it and 'correcting its thinking' according to the director societies' own criteria.

The expansionist interests of the director societies are implicit in such notions. These societies can never relate to the Third World as partners, since partnership presupposes equals, no matter how different the equal parties may be, and can never be established between parties antagonistic to each other.

Thus, 'salvation' of the Third World by the director societies can only mean its domination, whereas in its legitimate aspiration to independence lies its utopian vision: to save the director societies in the very act of freeing itself.

In this sense the pedagogy which we defend, conceived in a significant area of the Third World, is itself a utopian pedagogy. By this very fact it is full of hope, for to be utopian is not to be merely idealistic or impractical but rather to engage in denunciation and annunciation. Our pedagogy cannot do without a vision of man and of the world. It formulates a scientific humanist conception which finds its expression in a dialogical praxis in which the teachers and learners together, in the act of analysing a dehumanizing reality, denounce it while announcing its transformation in the name of the liberation of man.

For this very reason, denunciation and annunciation in this utopian pedagogy are not meant to be empty words, but an historic commitment. Denunciation of a dehumanizing situation today increasingly demands precise scientific understanding of that situation. Likewise, the annunciation of its transformation increasingly requires a theory of transforming action. However, neither act by itself implies the transformation of the denounced reality or the establishment of that which is announced. Rather, as a moment in an historical process, the announced reality is already present in the act of denunciation and annunciation.

That is why the utopian character of our educational theory and practice is as permanent as education itself which, for us, is cultural action. Its thrust toward denunciation and annunciation cannot be exhausted when the reality denounced today cedes its place tomorrow to the reality previously announced in the denunciation. When education is no longer utopian, that is, when it no longer embodies the dramatic unity of denunciation and annunciation, it is either because the future has no more meaning for men, or because men are afraid to risk living the future as creative overcoming of the present, which has become old.

The more likely explanation is generally the latter. That is why some people today study all the possibilities which the future contains, in order to 'domesticate' it and keep it in line with the present, which is what they intend to maintain. If there is any anguish in director societies hidden beneath the cover of their cold technology, it springs from their desperate determination that their metropolitan status be preserved in the future. Among the things which the Third World may learn from the metropolitan societies this is fundamental: not to reproduce those societies when its current utopia becomes actual fact.

There is no annunciation without denunciation, just as every denunciation generates annunciation. Without the latter, hope is impossible. In an authentic utopian vision, however, hoping does not mean folding one's arms and waiting. Waiting is only possible when, filled, with hope, one seeks through reflective action to achieve that 'announced' future which is being born within the denunciation.

That is why there is no genuine hope in those who intend to make the future repeat their present nor in those who see the future as something predetermined. Both have a 'domesticated' notion of history: the former because they want to stop time; the latter because they are certain about a future they already 'know'. Utopian hope on the contrary, is engagement full of risk. That is why the dominators, who merely denounce those who denounce them, and who have nothing to announce but the preservation of the *status quo,* can never be utopian nor, for that matter, prophetic.

A utopian pedagogy of denunciation and annunciation such as ours will have to be an act of knowing the denounced reality at the level of alphabetization and post-alphabetization, which both constitute cultural action. That is why there is such emphasis on the continual problematization of the learners' existential situations as represented in the codified images. The longer the problematization proceeds, and the more the subjects enter into the 'essence' of the problematized object, the more they are able to unveil this 'essence'. The more they unveil it, the more their awakening consciousness deepens, thus leading to the 'conscientization' of the situation by the poor classes. Their critical self-insertion into reality, that is, their conscientization, makes the transformation of their state of apathy into the utopian state of denunciation and annunciation a viable project.

One must not think, however, that learning to read and write precedes 'conscientization', or vice-versa. Conscientization occurs simultaneously with the literacy or post-literacy process. It must be so. In our educational method, the word is not something static or disconnected from men's existential experience but a dimension of their thought-language about the world. That is why, when they participate critically in analysing the first generative words linked with their existential experience; when they focus on the syllabic families which result from that analysis; when they perceive the mechanism of the syllabic combinations of their language, the learners finally discover, in the various possibilities of combination, their own words. Little by little, as these possibilities multiply, the learners, through mastery of new generative words, expand both their vocabulary and their capacity for expression by the development of their creative imagination.

To undertake such a work, it is necessary to have faith in the people, solidarity with them. It is necessary to be utopian, in the sense in which we have used the word.

Notes

1. The author gratefully acknowledges the contributions of Loretta Slover, who translated this essay, and João da Veiga Coutinho and Robert Riordan, who assisted in the preparation of the manuscript.
2. The digestive concept of knowledge is suggested by 'controlled readings'; by classes which consist only in lectures; by the use of memorized dialogues in language learning; by bibliographical notes which indicate not only which chapter, but which lines and words are to be read; by the methods of evaluating the students' progress in learning.
3. The English here would be nonsensical, as is the Portuguese, the point being the emphasis on the consonant *d*. *(Editor.)*
4. The Portuguese word here translated as *marginal man* is *marginado*. This has a passive sense: he who has been made marginal, or sent outside society; as well as the sense of a state of existence on the fringe of society. *(Translator.)*

5. Codification refers alternatively to the imaging, or the image itself of some significant aspect of the learner's concrete reality (of a slum dwelling, for example). As such, it becomes both the object of the teacher–learner dialogue and the context for the introduction of the generative word. *(Editor.)*
6. Decodification refers to a process of description and interpretation, whether of printed words, pictures or other 'codifications'. As such, decodification and decodifying are distinct from the process of decoding, or word-recognition. *(Editor.)*.
7. Re the oppressed consciousness, see: Frantz Fanon's *The Wretched of the Earth*; Albert Memmi's *Colonizer and the Colonized*; and my *Pedagogy of the Oppressed.*
8. We observed in Brazil and Spanish America, especially Chile, that no more than seventeen words were necessary for teaching adults to read and write syllabic languages like Portuguese and Spanish.

Index

Language and Literacy in Social Practice

Language and Literacy in Social Context

This Reader is part of an Open University Course (E825) forming one module in the MA in Education Programme. The selection is related to other material available to students. Opinions expressed in individual articles are not necessarily those of the course team or of the University.

Other volumes published as part of this course by Multilingual Matters Ltd in association with The Open University:

Language, Literacy and Learning in Educational Practice
    BARRY STIERER and JANET MAYBIN (eds)
Media Texts: Authors and Readers
    DAVID GRADDOL and OLIVER BOYD-BARRETT (eds)
Researching Language and Literacy in Social Context
    DAVID GRADDOL, JANET MAYBIN and BARRY STIERER (eds)

Other books of related interest, published by Multilingual Matters Ltd:

Critical Theory and Classroom Talk
    ROBERT YOUNG
Language Policy Across the Curriculum
    DAVID CORSON
Language, Minority Education and Gender
    DAVID CORSON
School to Work Transition in Japan
    KAORI OKANO
Reading Acquisition Processes
    G. B. THOMPSON, W. E. TUNMER and T. NICHOLSON (eds)
Worlds of Literacy
    D. BARTON, M. HAMILTON and R. IVANIC (eds)

Please contact us for the latest book information:
Multilingual Matters Ltd,
Frankfurt Lodge, Clevedon Hall, Victoria Road,
Clevedon, Avon BS21 7SJ, England.